CENTENNIAL

PACIFIC

OCEAN

Cape Campbell
▲Tapuaenuku 2885m
Cape Farewell

Kaikoura

Bullet n
Lake Rotoroa

Waiau

Reefton

Westport
Cape Foulwind

Rangiora
Christchurch
Lyttelton
Banks Peninsula
Kaiapoi
Lake Ellesmere

Greymouth

Hokitika

Lake Brunner

Arthur's Pass

Lake Coleridge

Darfield
Methven
Canterbury
Plains Canterbury Bight
Ashburton

South Island

Abut Head

Southern Alps

Mt Tasman 3498m
Lake Tekapo

Geraldine
Temuka
Timaru

Franz Josef Glacier
Fox Glacier

Mt Cook 3764 m ▲
Mt Sefton 3157 m ▲

Lake Pukaki

Waimate

Jackson Bay

Haast Pass

Lake Ohau

Twizel

Waitaki R.

Oamaru

Jackson Head

Lake Hawea

Ranfurly

Otago Peninsula
Cape Saunders

Mt Aspiring 3027m ▲

Lake Wanaka

Wanaka

Cromwell

Alexandra

Dunedin

Port Chalmers
Mosgiel
Milton
Balclutha
Clutha R.
Nugget Point

Milford Sound

Mt Alexander 1323m ▲

Caswell Sound

Secretary Island
Doubtful Sound

Resolution
Island

Dusky Sound

Chalky Inlet
Puysegur Point

Lake Wakatipu

Queenstown

Lake Te Anau

Te Anau

Fiordland

Caroline Peak 1722m ▲

Lake Hauroko

Lake Manapouri

Lumsden

Gore
Mataura

Winton
Riverton
Invercargill
Bluff

Te Waewae Bay

Waipapa Point

Foveaux Strait

Halfmoon Bay

Stewart Island

Codfish Island
Mason Bay

Solander Island

NORTH

0   100   200 km

Palmerston North.

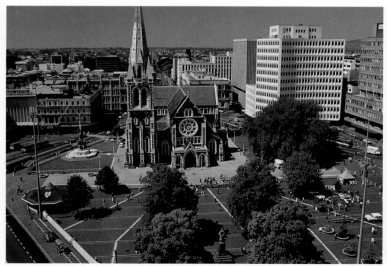

Christchurch.

Contents

New Zealand - Aotearoa

The Land of the Long White Cloud

The Maori name for New Zealand conjures up visions of high mountains piercing fluffy white clouds, of swirling mist and steam and boiling mud pools. When travelling, the ever-changing scenery passes before your eyes to reveal yet another wonder.

New Zealand is a compact land, a land of contrasts. There are sub-tropical rainforests and crystal clear lakes and rivers, thermal activity, and volcanoes (active, dormant and extinct) dotted around the islands. Green rolling hills covered with sheep, and seemingly endless forests, are quite often just an hour's drive from barren, rugged mountains and semi-desert areas. In the south, permanent snow covers many mountain tops and glaciers reach down into rainforests and wilderness areas. Magnificent fiords scratched into mountainous terrain contain thundering waterfalls and large peaceful lakes. The kaleidoscope is ever turning and presenting new patterns. Whatever your taste or mood, somewhere in New Zealand you are sure to find your "paradise on earth".

Location

New Zealand is a group of islands in the south-western Pacific Ocean approximately 1500km east of Australia, 10,600km west of South America, and 2300km north of Antarctica. The main islands lie between 34 and 48 degrees South, and 166 and 179 degrees East. For comparison: Sydney, Australia is 34 degrees South, and the southern-most point of Tasmania is 44 degrees South; in Europe, the southern-most tip of Spain is 34 degrees North, and the 48th parallel of latitude passes close to Brest, France, and Vienna, Austria; Los Angeles, USA is approximately 34 degrees North, and Vancouver, Canada, is approximately 48 degrees North.

New Zealand consists of three main islands: North Island, South Island, and the smaller, most southerly, Stewart Island.

Several small islands in the Pacific - Chatham Island, Bounty Island and Campbell Island - also form part of New Zealand.

Geography

The North Island has an area of 114,500 sq km; the South Island, 150,700 sq km; and Stewart Island, 1770 sq km. From north to south New Zealand is approximately 1700km long, and at its widest point measures 450km. It is similar in size to Great Britain, the State of Colorado in the USA, or Japan.

No part of New Zealand is more than 110km from the sea. It is **mountainous**, and less than 10% of the land is flat or undulating. Most of the country lies in an active volcanic region. Hot springs abound throughout the North and South Islands, and the centre of the North Island is dominated by three active **volcanoes** - Mt Ruapehu (2797m), Mt Ngauruhoe (2291m) and Mt Tongariro (1968m). The most unusual mountain of the North Island is the 2518m Taranaki (Mt Egmont). It is a dormant volcano with an almost perfect shape, and is often called New Zealand's Mt Fuji.

The South Island is effectively divided into the east and west coast regions by the **Southern Alps**, a mountain chain running from north to south. Sixteen peaks top the 3000m mark, and the highest peak in New Zealand at 3764m, Mt Cook, is found in the centre of the Alps.

There are seven small **glaciers** in the North Island, on the slopes of Mt Ruapehu, all of which are less than a mile long, but there are more than 360 that have been named in the South Island. The longest are found in the Mt Cook area: on the eastern side of the Alps are the Godley (10.5km), the Hooker (10.5km), the Mueller (13km), the Murchison (15km) and the Tasman (28km); on the western side of the Alps are the Franz Josef (10.5km) and the Fox (12km). The most spectacular of the glaciers in the South Island are the Fox and the Franz Josef because their termini are in the thick rain forests. The Tasman is notable because of its length.

In the south-western corner of New Zealand there are thirteen **fiords** whose beauty rivals those of Norway and Sweden. Milford Sound is the most famous and the one that is most often visited.

The geographical features of the west coast are truly spectacular, but the winds there can howl for days on end, and the rain storms are furious. The narrow plain along the central west coast receives over 2540mm of rain annually, and is covered with dense rain forest that reaches into the foothills of the Alps. The plains on the eastern side of the Alps are rolling grasslands.

Many of the **rivers** of New Zealand tend to be short and tempestuous, and offer many challenges for whitewater rafters. There are a few exceptions, though, for example the Waikato (345km), the Wanganui (225km) and the Clutha (338km). There are many **lakes** scattered throughout both the large islands, and they vary considerably in area from pond-size to Lake Taupo, which covers 616 sq km.

There is one small **desert area** in New Zealand, and it is found on the eastern side of the three active volcanoes, in the centre of the North Island.

Climate

The climate varies considerably from area to area, but generally speaking there is sharper contrast from west to east than from north to south because of the influence of the Southern Alps running south-west to north-east for 1300km. The climate is sub-tropical in the north of the North Island, and mostly marine-temperate elsewhere. There are areas in the South Island, east of the Alps near Cromwell and Alexandra, where the climate is distinctly continental in character even though the sea is less than 100km away.

Winds

On the west coast of the South Island, south of Dunedin, and in the North Island, the winds are usually south-westerly. In inland Otago and Canterbury they are usually north-westerly, and north-easterly on the Canterbury coast. Daytime coastal breezes usually extend inland for 35km during summer. The Cook and Foveaux Straits act as wind tunnels and the surrounding coasts are particularly windy.

Rainfall

Most of the country lies in the path of the Roaring Forties, but because of the barrier formed by the Southern Alps they lose most of their moisture on the western coast, resulting in an extremely high annual rainfall there of between 2000 and

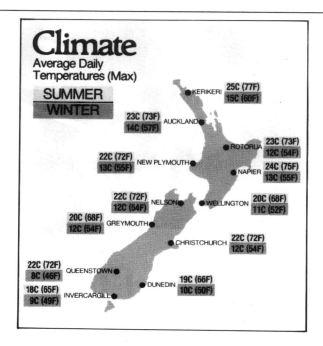

	Maximum Average Daily Temperature		Average Rainfall mm in.	Sunshine hrs.per year
Locality	Mid-summer deg.	Mid-winter deg.		
NORTH ISLAND				
Bay of Islands	25C (77F)	15C (60F)	1648 (65)	2020
Auckland	23C (73F)	14C (57F)	1268 (32)	2140
Rotorua	23C (73F)	12C (54F)	1511 (38)	1940
Napier	24C (75F)	13C (55F)	780 (19)	2270
Wellington	20C (68F)	11C (52F)	1271 (32)	2020
SOUTH ISLAND				
Nelson	22C (72F)	12C (54F)	999 (25)	2410
Christchurch	22C (72F)	12C (54F)	658 (16)	1990
Queenstown	22C (72F)	8C (46F)	849 (21)	1940
Dunedin	19C (66F)	10C (50F)	772 (19)	1700
Invercargill	18C (65F)	9C (49F)	1042 (26)	1630

7700mm. On the eastern slopes of the Alps it is much drier, receiving approximately 600-700mm annually. In the northern half of the North Island most of the rain falls in winter, but over the rest of the island the rainfall is generally spread evenly throughout the year. The Hawkes Bay area is usually very dry in late summer and early autumn.

The weather can be changeable with sunshine and showers alternating throughout the day. Even so, New Zealand is a land of sunshine with Wellington, Auckland, Rotorua, Napier, Nelson, Christchurch and Queenstown each receiving over 2000 hours of sunshine a year.

Frost and Snow

In winter, the North Island is free from frost except for the central plateau area. However, the South Island experiences frosts on clear nights from May to September. In the North Island the permanent snowline is at 2500m, but in winter snow rarely falls below 600m, and disappears quickly at that level. In the South Island the permanent snowline is at 2100m with snow falling down to sea level on one or two days each winter. On the west coast it doesn't lie at sea level, but may stay a day or two on the east coast. These snow falls are usually caused by southerly winds from the Antarctic.

Seasons

The seasons are the opposite to those in the Northern Hemisphere. Summer is from December to February, Autumn is from March to May, Winter from June to August and Spring from September to November. The table on page ??? illustrates the lack of temperature extremes in the larger cities and towns. Of course, temperatures are lower in the mountains, often dropping below freezing point in both summer and winter.

North of Auckland the temperature rarely goes below 10C and on Stewart Island the temperature is rarely more than 21C.

Flora

About one-quarter of the country is covered with forest. When the Maoris set foot on New Zealand soil, vast areas of the plains and foothills were covered with evergreen forests. Giant Kauri trees 50m tall with girths of 15m were fairly common. The arrival of Europeans saw most of the giants in the coastal areas felled by the early sailors and settlers. Today trees of this size are rare. Other giants of the forest are Rimu and Totara, which were used by the Maoris to make canoes.

In the last quarter of the 19th century, many of the forests were cleared and planted with pasture to graze sheep and cattle for the lucrative London meat market, accessible because of refrigerated shipping. However, in the wetter areas of the South Island there are still large forests of Antarctic beech trees. In the last two decades, many new forests of radiata pine have been planted to supply the building and wood-pulp industries, both at home and abroad.

Approximately three-quarters of New Zealand's native flora is unique. Ferns abound in the higher rainfall areas, and some reach heights of 15m. There are many beautiful flowering shrubs and trees. Two of the best known are the Kowhai, with its long yellow petals that hang down from a bell-shaped pod, and the Pohutukawa (NZ Christmas Tree) whose vivid flame-coloured flowers appear in December. The flora in the alpine regions differs vastly from alpine regions in other lands. In New Zealand, alpine plants are fascinating for their leaf forms. They are usually only white, cream or yellow, but their lack of bright colour is compensated by their profusion.

Fauna

The best known of all New Zealand wildlife is the Kiwi, and as a result New Zealand people are often referred to as 'Kiwis'. It is a flightless bird that stands about 30cm high and has a long tapering bill for picking up worms, grubs, insects and berries. Kiwis have powerful legs and strong toes and move through the bush at considerable speed. The female lays one or two enormous eggs, then lets the male do the hatching.

There are over 250 species of birds in New Zealand, and the majority are native. New Zealand does not have any snakes, and the only mammals are bats. The native Tuatara, a lizard, is the oldest reptile in the world, dating back to the pre-dinosaur age. The Maoris introduced rats and dogs to the islands, and Captain Cook gave pigs to the Maori chiefs. They are still known as Captain Cookers today. Other introduced animals include sheep, cows, goats and deer, as well as rabbits and opossums, which have been declared noxious.

Captain James Cook Memorial, Gisborne.

History

It is now generally agreed that the first inhabitants of New Zealand were Polynesians who arrived around 950AD. These people were peaceable and hunted the Moa, a large flightless bird that is now extinct, hence the name Maori. Most of the present-day Maoris can trace their genealogy back to one of the captains of the fleet canoes which, according to legend, arrived in New Zealand around 1350. The actual date of arrival has been disputed, and it has been suggested that the seven canoes may have arrived over a period of two hundred years.

There are many colourful Maori myths and legends of their forefathers' arrival. One popular legend is that a man named Kupe was fishing off Hawaii, his homeland, when he hooked a giant octopus which pulled him south for days until he came to a land which he called Aotearoa because of the long white clouds that were his first indication of land. According to the legend, he explored the island then returned home because he was lonely. Centuries later when the people were looking for a new homeland, they remember Kupe's story and set off to find Aotearoa.

Another popular legend is that a clever rascal called Maui hid in his brothers' canoe when they went fishing, because they had refused to take him with them. When they were out at sea he appeared, but they refused to share their bait with him. So he attached the jawbone of his grandmother to a line and caught the largest fish they had ever seen - the North Island of New Zealand.

A theory that has been put forward is *The Big Drift theory*. It supposes that the Maoris were the occupants of canoes that were overtaken by storms when sailing between islands and were carried south with the currents. The truth may be a combination of accidental drift and planned migration, but it is an indisputable fact that Maoris were living in New Zealand when the Dutchman, Abel Tasman, landed on the north-west coast of the South Island in 1642.

The next Europeans to set foot on New Zealand soil did not do so until 1769. They were with the French navigator Jean Francois Marie de Surville, who was sailing from India to Tahiti. When 54 of his crewmen died from scurvy, he decided to put into New Zealand for fresh fruit and vegetables. He landed at Doubtless Bay at the same time as Captain James Cook landed at Poverty Bay (near Gisborne). Cook had left England the previous year to sail around Cape Horn to Tahiti to view the transit of Venus, and then to sail south to Latitude 40 in search of Terra Australis Incognita. If he failed to find the great southern continent he was to examine New Zealand. Cook spent from October 7, 1769 to April 1, 1770 mapping and exploring New Zealand.

As early as the beginning of the 19th century, whalers and sealers came to New Zealand. Small settlements grew at Otago near Dunedin, Akaroa near Christchurch, and in the fiords of the south-west coast. The first permanent European settlement was founded at Kororareka, which is the present-day Russell. During this time much kauri was taken from the surrounding forest, and as it takes 800 years to mature, there is very little kauri to be found now. The first settlers were rough men accompanied by escaped or freed convicts from Australia, deserters and the like. These men did irreparable damage to Maori relations, both with the whites and the various tribes.

The first missionary to arrive was Samuel Marsden, in 1814, and he was quickly followed by others. Unfortunately, the Maoris were given muskets and gunpowder which they soon learnt to master, and warlike chiefs began attacking each other as well as the new settlers. The situation was untenable, and in 1840 Captain William Hobson, the first governor, arrived with orders to stop the bloodshed. He called over 40 Maori chiefs together to explain that Queen Victoria would protect their villages if they would live peacefully with the Europeans. After much negotiation the Treaty of Waitangi was signed by the chiefs.

Unfortunately, there were several disputes between Europeans and Maoris over land in the North Island, and several bloody wars, between both Maori chiefs and between Maoris and Europeans broke out in 1860 and continued for about ten years before peace was achieved.

The infant nation became a dominion of the British Empire in 1907, and obtained complete autonomy in 1947.

Government

New Zealand is a sovereign independent state with a parliamentary government and a constitutional monarchy.

Queen Elizabeth II is the Head of State and is represented in the country by a resident Governor-General. The parliament is modelled on the British system, but since 1950 it has only one chamber, the House of Representatives. The leader of the Parliament is called the Prime Minister, and there are two main political parties, National (Conservative) and Labour. Though now with the MMP system of election which New Zealand adopted in 1996 for the first time, many minor parties are now having a greater say in the political process. At the present time the National Party are in power with the support of a minor party, New Zealand First.

Maori Art and Culture

Centuries before the coming of the European, the Maoris developed their own culture and art, but unfortunately they had no written language and the only pre-European form of art to survive until the present are some rock drawings found in primitive shelters, mainly in the South Island. The range of subjects is rather limited - human figures, birds, fish and lizards. Very few of the wooden carvings from their houses have survived because when a man died his house became tapu, or untouchable, and was left to decay.

Maori life was tribal, and the most important building in the village was the *whare wakairo*, or meeting house. This served two functions - firstly, it was used as an assembly hall or council chamber of the tribe; secondly, it was a guest-house for honoured visitors. This building always had a rectangular shape with a high central ridge-pole running the length of the building, and an entrance porch formed by extending the roof and walls. The porch was richly carved, as was the interior, and the earthen floor was covered with straw and mats. Ceremonial rites accompanied its construction, and the preparation of the carvings was a sacred task in itself, always performed by a *tohunga*, or priest.

Maori carving is steeped in tradition, is highly stylised, and carvers abide by strict conventions. Human figures are generally distorted with out-thrust tongues, slanting or enormous eyes, and a three-fingered hand. The carvings represented the history of the tribe, a sort of pictorial genealogical table. Panels lining the walls of the porch and the interior were carved to represent great chiefs of the past. As

Maori group, Ohinemutu Meeting House, Rotorua.

well as ancestors, other creatures are featured. A curious being called a *manaia* is often depicted in profile with a single eye and a large bird-like beak. Its history is unknown. It could either be human in origin, or some mythical creature. Two other creatures often depicted are known as the *taniwha* and the *marakihau*. The *taniwha* was a man-eating monster, and the *marakihau* lived underwater waiting to trap passing canoes.

In the meeting house, two other art forms were also used: *tukutuku* work and rafter patterns. *Tukutuku* or *turapa* work is the woven latticework which adorns the interior of the house. It was used between the carved panels, and was done exclusively by the women of the tribe. In pre-European times there were about seven different patterns in use and the colours were always yellow and brown. New patterns have now evolved and several different colours are used. The basic pattern, though, is based on straight lines. The painted rafter patterns, on the other hand, are curved. They are very intricate but all stem from a single motif which is thought to represent the uncurling of a fern frond.

In post-European times, wall paintings have also appeared. These depict birds, canoes and sometimes tribal life, and break with tradition in that they often depict scenery. The tribal village was always built around a *marae,* or green. The tradition still survives today in most Maori settlements, even though the buildings around the green, with the exception of the meeting house, may be of European design.

People
The population of New Zealand is 3.6 million, mostly of British descent. Maoris form the largest minority group with 468,000 people (13%). Auckland is the most populous city with 952,600 residents.

Language
English is the main language of New Zealand. The Maori people have their own language and it is now widely taught in schools, although it is not in common usage.

New Zealanders use a few different words to British, Americans and Australians. Here are some you might come across:

dairy - the local shop
wee - small
bach - holiday house
section - a block of land
tramping - hiking, bushwalking or trekking
jandals - thongs

You will also hear people of European descent referred to as *Pakehas.* Kiwis also have an accent all their own, which is particularly noticeable when they pronounce 'i' as in six.

Public Holidays
The following are public holidays in the whole country:

New Year's Day - January 1
Waitangi Day - February 6
Good Friday and Easter Monday - March/April
Anzac Day - April 25
Queen's Birthday - first Monday in June
Labour Day - fourth Monday in October
Christmas Day - December 25
Boxing Day - December 26.

Entry Regulations

Visitors to New Zealand require a passport valid for at least six months beyond the date on which they are booked to leave New Zealand. In general, visas are not required for stays up to three months. You do need a return ticket or a visa for your next destination.

Duty Free Allowances

Visitors over 18 years of age are allowed the following concessions free of duty and tax:

Cigarettes, cigars, tobacco - 200 cigarettes or 250gm of tobacco or 50 cigars, or a mixture of all three not weighing more than 250gm.

Alcoholic liquor - 4.5l of wine and one 1125ml bottle of spirits or liqueur.

Goods up to a total combined value of NZ$700 are free of duty and tax, but goods in excess of this may attract both.

No vaccinations are required for entry into New Zealand.

Departure Tax

There is a departure tax of NZ$25 payable by everyone leaving from the international airports at Auckland, Wellington Christchurch, Dunedin, Hamilton and Palmerston North.

Embassies

The Embassies are in the capital, Wellington, and there are Consulates in Auckland.

Wellington

Australia: 72 Hobson Street, Thorndon, ph (04) 473 6411.
Canada: 61 Molesworth Street, ph (04) 473 9577.
Singapore: Kabul Street, Khandallah, ph (04) 479 2077.
UK: 2 The Terrace, ph (04) 472 6049.
USA: 29 Fitzherbert Terrace, Thorndon, ph (04) 472 2068.

Auckland

Australia: Union House, 32/38 Quay Street, ph (09) 303 2429.
Canada: 9th Fl., Jetset Centre, 48 Emily Place, ph (09) 309 3690.
UK: 151 Queen Street, ph (09) 303 2973.
USA: cnr Shortland & O'Connell Streets, ph 303 2724.

Money

The unit of currency is the New Zealand Dollar (NZ$) which equals 100 cents. Notes are in denominations of 5, 10, 20, 50 and 100 dollars, and coins are 5, 10, 20, and 50 cents and 1 and 2 dollars. Approximate exchange rates are:

A$1 =	NZ$1.15
Can$1 =	NZ$1.20
S$1 =	NZ$1.10
£1 =	NZ$3.00
US$1 =	NZ$2.00

Communications

Telephones

International Direct Dialling is available. The access code is 00.

Telecom International Directory Assistance, ph 0172, can provide information on country and area codes. The country code for New Zealand is 64. The Telecom International Operator can be reached by dialling 0170.

The easiest way to make a reverse charge (collect) call home is with the *Home Country Direct service*, which connects you with the operator in your country, and doesn't require you to have coins or a PhoneCard.

There are three types of PayPhones in New Zealand - CardPhones (green booth), Credit Card Phones (yellow booth) and CoinPhones (blue booth).

PhoneCards are available for $5, $10, $20 and $50 at shops and service stations displaying the PhoneCard signs. A local call from a public booth costs 20c a minute.

Standard credit cards can be used in the yellow phone booths, but there is a minimum charge of $2 per call.

There is no charge for local calls made from private telephones.

Time Zones

If you are intending to use the Home Country Direct service for a reverse charge call, it is a good idea to check what the time will be in the country you are calling.

People don't appreciate being woken in the middle of the

night to accept the charge for an international call.
When it is noon in New Zealand the following times apply:

Sydney, Australia -	10.00am
Perth, Australia -	8.00am
Canada -	8.30pm-3.00pm (previous day)
Singapore -	8.00am
UK -	midnight (previous day)
USA -	7.00pm-2pm (previous day)

New Zealand has daylight saving (Summer Time) from October to March, so remember to add an hour to the above.
Also remember to make allowances if your country has daylight saving.

Emergency Telephone Numbers

Police, Fire, Ambulance -	111	(country wide)
Emergency Medical	Wellington	472 2999
	Auckland	524 5943
Emergency Dental -	Wellington	472 7072
	Auckland	520 6609

Newspapers

Wellington has two daily newspapers, *The Dominion* in the morning and *The Evening Post*, Mon-Sat. The Sunday morning newspaper is the *Dominion Sunday Times*.
Auckland has one daily, *The New Zealand Herald*, and three *Sunday papers - Sunday Star*, *Sunday Times* and *Sunday News*.

Radio and Television

There are four national radio networks in New Zealand: non-commercial public service radio - National Programme (AM); non-commercial Concert Programme (Stereo FM); and a commercial pop AM and FM network. There are also many local pop FM stations. Deregulation has given rise to the opening of many small radio stations, including community, non-profit, and several Maori stations.

New Zealand has three national television networks, all commercial, screening a mixture of local, British and American programs. The SKY network is available in most hotels, and broadcasts the CNN news from the US daily.

Television and radio programs are published in the daily newspapers.

Mail

New Zealand's post offices are called "post shops", and they are open Mon-Fri, 9am-5pm.

The main post office in **Wellington** is at 43 Manners Street, ph (04) 473 5922, and it is open Mon-Fri 8am-5pm.

The main post office in **Auckland** is in Queen Elizabeth II Square, Downtown, ph (09) 792 200, and it is open Mon-Thurs 8am-5pm, Fri 8am-6pm.

The postage for aerograms and postcards is NZ$1.00 for any destination.

Miscellaneous

Business Hours

Banks are open Mon-Fri 9am-4.30pm.

Government Departments are open Mon-Fri 8.30am-4.30pm.

Shops are permitted to open seven days a week, 24 hours a day, but usual hours are Mon-Fri 9am-5.30pm (Thurs or Fri to 9.00pm), Sat 9am-noon, and Sun many shopping centres are open all day. It has made a great difference to the way people now spend their time, with supermarkets open until midnight and a flourishing cafe society dining out to all ours. Many of the cities especially on the north island enjoy a buzz with people in the streets in the evening and on the weekends.

Electricity

The standard current is 230 volts AC 50 hertz. Appliances designed for DC supply or different voltages will require a transformer.

Goods and Services Tax

This consumption tax was introduced on October 1, 1986, and is now applied at a universal rate of 12.5% to all goods and services, except for purchases at duty free shops.

Pests

New Zealand does not have any snakes or wild animals, but it does have a few pesky insects. Sandflies are common in the wetter areas and can deliver nasty bites, so insect repellents are a must in your luggage. Wasps have become prevalent in the beech forests in recent years, particularly in the central and northern parts of the South Island. It is wise to take medicated sprays, creams or antihistamines when travelling in these areas, particularly if you are prone to allergies.

Sunburn
New Zealand is under the influence of the southern "ozone holes", and this, coupled with the clear, unpolluted atmosphere, produces very strong sunlight. Wear a hat and a high number sunblock when outdoors for any length of time.

Tipping
Tipping is not really a way of life, although if you decide that the service you have received deserves it, go ahead and tip. On the other hand, no one will hassle you if you don't.

Water Supply
The tap water in all New Zealand cities and towns is fresh and safe to drink. However, it is not advisable to drink unboiled or untreated water from back-country rivers or lakes. Present in some of these is an internal microscopic parasite called Giardia, which can cause serious stomach illness.

Travel Information

How to Get There

By Air

This is the obvious way to visit New Zealand, but travellers from Europe or the United States have to be prepared for a long flight.

There is great competition between the various airlines that fly into the Land of the Long White Cloud, and it is worth taking the time to shop around and compare the various fares

> **Don't even consider limiting your trip to one island, because they are very different and both have a lot to offer.**

and accommodation packages available.

Following are examples of the availability of flights. These are not the only choices available, but will let you know that New Zealand is by no means inaccessible.

New Zealand has three international airports - Auckland (AKL), Wellington (WLG) and Christchurch (CHC).

Air New Zealand, the national carrier, has flights from:

Adelaide - to AKL and WLG - daily; CHC - Tues, Thurs & Sun.

Brisbane - to AKL - daily; to WLG - Mon, Wed & Fri; to CHC - Mon, Tues, Wed, Fri & Sun.

Chicago - to AKL daily.

Hong Kong - to AKL, WLG and CHC - Tues, Thurs & Sun.

London - to AKL - daily; to WLG and CHC - Mon, Thurs, Fri & Sun.

Los Angeles - to AKL, WLG and CHC - daily.

Melbourne - to AKL - daily; to WLG - Tues, Thurs; to CHC - Tues, Thurs & Sun.

San Francisco - to AKL - daily.

Singapore -   to AKL and WLG - Tues, Wed, Fri, Sat & Sun;
CHC - Sun.
Sydney -   to AKL, WLG and CHC - daily.
Toronto -   to AKL - Mon, Wed, Thurs, Fri & Sun.
Vancouver -   to AKL - daily, except Sat.

British Airways have flights from:
London -   to AKL - Wed, Fri, Sat & Sun.

Canadian Airlines have flights from:
Toronto -   Mon, Wed, Thurs, Fri $ Sun.
Vancouver -   Tues, Thurs, Fri & Sun.

Cathay Pacific has flights from Hong Kong to AKL - Tues, Thurs, Fri, Sat & Sun.

Qantas has flights from:
Adelaide -   to AKL and WLG - daily via Sydney
or Melbourne
Brisbane -   to AKL - daily;
to WLG - daily via Sydney;
to CHC - Tues, Thurs-Sat.
Cairns -   to AKL - Thurs, Sun;
to CHC - Thurs-Fri, via Brisbane;
to WLG - Mon, Thurs, Fri, Sun, via Sydney.
Hong Kong -   to AKL and WLG - daily, via Sydney.
Los Angeles -   to AKL - daily.
Melbourne -   to AKL - daily;
to WLG - daily;
to CHC - Mon, Fri & Sat.
Perth -   to AKL, CHC and WLG - daily, via Sydney
or Melbourne.
Sydney -   to AKL, WLG and CHC - daily.

Singapore Airlines have flights from:
Hong Kong -   to AKL daily; to CHC - Tues, Thurs, Sat & Sun.
London -   to AKL - daily.
Singapore -   to AKL - daily; to CHC - Thurs & Sun.

United Airlines have flights from:

Los Angeles -   to AKL - daily.

San Francisco -   to AKL - daily.

Toronto -   to AKL - daily.

Vancouver -   to AKL - daily.

By Sea

This is the only other way to travel to New Zealand, and many cruise liners call into Auckland for stays of a day or two. Before air travel became the be-all and end-all of getting from one place to another, there were many passenger ships that plied the Australia-New Zealand route, and it was a very leisurely three to four days on the ocean. Sadly, for those who like relaxed travelling, those days have gone.

Travel within New Zealand

New Zealand, compared with Australia or the United States, is small in area, making the distances between the various attractions relatively short. Therefore there is no need to fly around the country, unless your time is very limited. Many people hire a car or a motorhome, or even motor bikes. Others opt for organised bus tours with accommodation in their price range - from budget to international standard. If you decide to hire a car and drive yourself, it is a good idea to map out the route you are interested in and arrange all your accommodation before you leave home. This is particularly advantageous during school holidays when the local people are also touring, and accommodation may be at a premium. It could also work out cheaper.

Air

New Zealand has three main domestic carriers: Air New Zealand, Ansett New Zealand and Mount Cook Airlines. All have special fares and deals and your travel agent will have details of what is current when you are travelling.

Examples are:

Explore New Zealand Airpass, Air New Zealand, can only be purchased by residents of countries other than New Zealand, and is a discount voucher system (3 to 8 vouchers) for independent travellers, with a maximum of one stopover at any one city. Three sectors NZ$495 - 8 sectors NZ$1320. Must be purchased prior to departure.

Ansett New Zealand has several passes available:

New Zealand Airpass works on a coupon system and prices range from NZ$450 for 3 coupons to NZ$1140 for 8 coupons.

Scenic Standby Airpass offers unlimited travel, on a standby basis, for 14 days at NZ$699, and for 30 days at NZ$999.

Student/YHA Budget Airpass works on a points system, with 15 points costing NZ$99, and 30 points NZ$599.

Examples of the points are:

Auckland to Christchurch =   7 points

Auckland to Wellington =   4 points

Auckland to Queenstown =   10 points.

All these passes are only available outside New Zealand, and some conditions apply. The above prices are given as a guide only, and are subject to change.

Rail

Tranz Scenic (New Zealand's National Operator) has the following rail services:

Overlander Express - daily, daytime - Auckland-Hamilton - Taumarunui-Palmerston North - Wellington. Complimentary morning and afternoon teas, lunch and buffet and bar facilities. Seats have adjustable backrest and tray. No smoking.

Northerner - Sun-Fri, overnight - same route at Overlander. No snacks are provided but the buffet is available throughout the night with a light breakfast in the morning. A video is shown en-route. No smoking.

Bay Express - daily, daytime - Wellington- Palmerston North- Napier. On-train commentary is provided, and Devonshire teas, light meals and a full bar service are available.

Kaimai Express - daily, evening - Auckland-Hamilton-Tauranga. Complimentary refreshments are served at your seat and bar facilities are also offered. Bicycles cannot be carried on this service due to lack of space. No smoking.

Geyserland Express - twice daily, daytime - Auckland-Hamilton-Rotorua. Complimentary refreshments are served at your seat and bar facilities are also offered. Bicycles cannot be carried on this service due to lack of space. No smoking.

Coastal Pacific Express - daily, daytime - Christchurch-Kaikoura-Picton. Devonshire teas, light meals and full bar service are available. No smoking.

Tranz Alpine Express - daily, daytime - Christchurch-Arthurs Pass-Greymouth. Devonshire teas, light meals and full bar service are available. No smoking.

Southerner - Mon-Fri, daytime - Christchurch-Timaru-Dunedin-Invercargill. Buffet car has a good selection of snacks, ales and beverages. No smoking.

Discount Fares
Tranz Scenic has a limited number of early purchase discount fares on most train services, and they are only available at outlets in New Zealand.

Also available are the **Travelpasses**, which offer good value as well as the Sightpass book of discounts on popular sightseeing attractions.

The *3 in 1 Travelpass* allows unlimited travel on coaches, trains and the Interislander Ferry. Costs are:
5 days travel over 10 days -   adult NZ$350
8 days travel over 3 weeks -   adult NZ$470
15 days travel over 5 weeks -   adult NZ$590
22 days travel over 8 weeks -   adult NZ$690 ˙
Children aged 5-14 - 67% of adult fare.

The *4 in 1 Travelpass* has all the features of the 3 in 1 with the addition of one sector on Ansett New Zealand's airline network. Costs are:
5 days travel over 10 days -   NZ$580
8 days travel over 3 weeks -   NZ$700
15 days travel over 5 weeks -   NZ$820
22 days travel over 8 weeks -   NZ$920
Children aged 5-14 - 67% of adult fare.

Both passes are available from any Tranz Scenic ticketing agent, or at Tranz Rail travel ships in Auckland, Wellington or Christchurch.

Bus

Almost every city and town in New Zealand is connected to a network of coach services operated by either InterCity, Mount Cook or Newmans.

Mount Cook Landline's *New Zealand Explorer Pass* offers unlimited travel throughout the country on Mt Cook Landline and other selected operators, and includes crossing Cook Strait. It also comes with a Discount Booklet for a range of sightseeing venues.

Costs are:

7 days travel over 30 days -	NZ$335
10 days travel over 60 days -	NZ$400
15 days travel over 60 days -	NZ$464
25 days travel over 90 days -	NZ$544
33 days travel over 90 days -	NZ$699.

The pass can be purchased overseas through a travel agent, or in New Zealand at any Mount Cook Line Office.

Newman's *Stopover Pass* can be purchased in New Zealand, and offers travel from Auckland to Wellington, or from Wellington to Auckland, stopping off along the way. The Pass allows visitors 14 days to complete the trip, and travel can be on any route as long as it is in the one direction and doesn't backtrack. Each pass costs NZ$95, and includes a range of sightseeing discounts in Rotorua, Taupo, Turangi, Napier and Waitomo. For more information contact Newmans on (09) 309 9738 (Auckland), (04) 499 3261 (Wellington), or toll free (within New Zealand) on 0800 777 707.

Ferry

The Interislander has a daily service Wellington-Picton. This trip has been labelled as one of the roughest in the world, and takes 3 hours on the *Arahura*, and 3 hours 20 minutes on the *Aratika*. Sailing into Picton is extremely picturesque as the ferry makes its way through the Marlborough Sounds.

The ferries have cafeterias and carvery restaurants, and for entertainment there are video screenings, a movie theatre, televisions and bars. For children there are nurseries, toddlers' play areas and video games rooms.

Wellington to Picton	**Depart**	**Arrive**
Tues-Sat	1.30am	4.30am
Daily	9.30am	12.30pm
Daily	2.30pm	5.50pm
Daily	5.30pm	8.30pm
Daily	10.30pm	1.50am

Picton to Wellington	**Depart**	**Arrive**
Tues-Sat	5.30am	8.30am
Daily	10.30am	1.50pm
Daily	1.30pm	4.30pm
Daily	6.30pm	9.50pm
Daily	9.30pm	12.30am

The above timetable and fare structures are subject to change. Phone Freecall 0800 802 802 for enquiries and bookings.

Fares

Although Economy, Sailaway Saver and Super Saver exist, they have limited availability. The following are the standard rates:

Adult	NZ$44
Child (4-14 years)	NZ$22
Infant (under 4 years)	Free
Cars (up to 6m)	NZ$160
Excess per half metre over 6m	NZ$ 20
Motorcycles	NZ$ 44

Utilities, minibuses, vans, caravans or trailers (up to 2000kg gross laden weight)   NZ$160
Excess per half metre over 6m   NZ$ 20

Campervans, motor-homes (up to 2000kg gross laden weight)   NZ$190
Excess per half metre over 6m   NZ$ 40

Interislander Shuttle Buses

Wellington Service

A complimentary shuttle service runs between the Wellington Railway Station and the Interisland Terminal. The bus leaves platform 9 at the station 35 minutes before each ship's departure.

Picton Service
A complimentary service meets the 9.30am ferry from Wellington at 12.30pm and transfers passengers to the Picton Railway Station to connect with the 1.40pm departure of the Coastal Pacific. The bus also transfers northbound Coastal Pacific passengers to meet the 1.30pm ferry to Wellington.

Catamaran
The *Lynx* makes three return trips a day between Wellington and Picton, and the trip only takes 1.75 hours. Standard fares are: adult NZ$59.00; child (4-14 years) NZ$29.40; cars (up to 6m) NZ$190.00, excess per half metre NZ$20.00.

Other ferry services operate from Auckland to islands in the Hauraki Gulf, and from Bluff near Invercargill to Stewart Island.

Car
There are many car hire outlets in New Zealand, and we have listed them in the appropriate cities and towns.
   One-way hire is available between most company locations, but it is best to check first.
   Traffic drives on the left-hand side of the road, and most roads are two-way, so people accustomed to driving on the right have to be careful. Give way is to traffic on the right. The speed limit on the open road and motorways is 80km/h for cars towing trailers or caravans; 90km/h for heavy vehicles; and 100km/h for other vehicles. In towns and built-up areas the speed limit is 50km/h, or as sign-posted. New Zealand uses internationally recognised symbols for all road signs. Seat belts must be worn at all times by driver and passengers.
   International driving permits are recognised as are valid licences issued in Australia, Canada, United Kingdom, United States, Netherlands, Switzerland, Fiji, South Africa and the Federal Republic of Germany.

Accommodation
New Zealand has a wide range of accommodation, from backpacker hostels to 5-star hotels, and everything in between. In each chapter of this guide there are lists of accommodation in the main centres, with prices in NZ$ for a double room per

night, which should be used as a guide only. The prices stated
include GST.

Farmstays and homestays are very popular in the country
areas, and these can be arranged through New Zealand Farm &
Home Hosts in Auckland, ph (09) 810 9175, your local travel
agent, or the New Zealand Tourism Office in your home city.

Hotels and motels are usually of a high standard, are very
clean, and have tea and coffee making facilities. Motels that do
not have a restaurant can provide a cooked or continental
breakfast, delivered to units at a time chosen by the visitor
within a specified time range, eg between 6am and 8am.

Hiring a motorhome, and literally taking your
accommodation with you, is a good alternative especially if
you are travelling with children, or in a group.

Adventure Vans, PO Box 43 235 Mangere, Auckland, ph (09) 256
0255, fax (09) 275 3027, have many vans available for hire from
a 2-berth Pop-Top to a 6-berth Travelhome. Included in the
rental deals are bed linen, bath towels, crockery, cutlery,
cooking utensils, even clothes pegs. Peak season (November to
mid-April) prices range from A$96 per day for a 2-berth to
A$206 for the 6-berth. The company can also supply snow
chains, ski racks and baby seats.

Bookings can be made direct with the company, or through
the following:
Australia - Kirra Tours:
Adelaide - 6th floor, 118 King William Street, 5000, ph (08) 8212
7833, fax (08) 8231 2012. Brisbane - 3rd floor, 255 Adelaide
Street, 4000, ph (07) 3221 7288, fax (07) 3221 7305. Melbourne -
245 Charman Road, Cheltenham, 3192, ph (03) 9584 1177, fax
(03) 9584 2713. Sydney - 20th floor, 44 Market Street, 2000, ph
(02) 9299 7588, fax (02) 9299 7495. *Great Britain* - NZ Tourism
Board, New Zealand House, Haymarket, London, SW1 4TQ,
ph (083) 930 0900, fax 171 839 8929. *United States* - New Zealand
Tourism Board, 501 Santa Monica Boulevard #300, Santa
Monica, CA 90401, ph (310) 395 7480, fax (310) 395 5453.

Sunbeam Tours
This company includes motorhome hire amongst its range of
itineraries. The company's fleet ranges from a 2-berth van at
A$126 per day (Oct to mid-April) to a 6-berth at A$201 per day

(Oct to mid-April), plus NZ$13.50 per day for comprehensive insurance. Prices for the mid-April to September season range between A$64 to $103. There is also a refundable bond of NZ$845 that is required to be paid at the commencement of hire. Offices of Sunbeam are found at:

Australia: Brisbane - 4th floor, 231 George Street, ph (07) 3229 3800, fax (07) 3221 4569. Sydney - 11th floor, 89 York Street, ph (02) 9299 2355, fax (02) 9299 2372. Melbourne-Perth-Adelaide - Freecall 1800 502 355.

Great Britain - Sunbeam Tours (Internat.) Ltd, 1st floor, Russell House, 137-139 High Street, Guildford, Surrey, GU1 3AD, ph (1483) 452 392, fax (1483) 452 392.

United States - Sunbeam Tours (California) Ltd, 3150 Bristol Street, #150, Costa Mesa, CA 92626, ph (714) 434 1810, fax (714) 434 8009.

Your travel agent, or the New Zealand Tourism Office in your home city, will have details of other van companies and their offers. To drive a motorhome in New Zealand you only need an ordinary drivers' licence.

Food and Drink

Think of New Zealand cuisine and you conjure up thoughts of lamb, venison, trout and kiwi fruit. They are on the menus, of course, but there is much more to titillate your taste-buds in the Shaky Isles - seafood of every description, lovely fresh vegetables and fruit, and French-type cheeses that stand up well against the originals.

Then there are the New Zealand wines which are fast achieving an international reputation for excellence.

Kiwis claim their national desert is pavlova, made from meringue and lashings of fresh cream topped with different kinds of fruit. Most Aussies will argue it is Australian.

Restaurants may be either fully licensed to sell spirits and wine, may sell wine only, or are designated BYO, which means "bring your own wine". Some fully licensed restaurants may also allow customers to take their own wine if they wish, but not beer, spirits or soft drinks (soda).

Restaurant prices given in this guide are for a three course meal without wine or other drinks. Cafes and brasseries usually charge less than restaurants.

Entertainment

Auckland and Wellington have many late-night and 24-hour cafes and bar/restaurants, and some of the major hotel cafes stay open all night. Often these places have live entertainment.

Pubs are meeting places, and good for getting to meet the locals. Pub food is an experience, too, and is usually very reasonably priced.

Nightclubs are found in the cities and are usually open from 10pm to 3am or 5am, and cover charges can range from NZ$5 to NZ$20, with the odd one allowing free entry.

The cities are also where you will find the cultural offerings, theatres, concerts, etc, and cinemas, but smaller towns often have local productions that are worth checking out.

Details of what's on are published in the entertainment pages in local papers, usually the Thursday or Friday editions. You can also find out from the front desk of your hotel, or from the local visitor information office.

Shopping

Popular souvenirs include distinctive jewellery made from greenstone (New Zealand jade) and from the iridescent paua (abalone) shell. Carved greenstone tikis (Maori charms) are high on everyone's shopping list, as are Maori carvings in wood inlaid with shell. New Zealand woollen and sheep-skin goods are also much sought-after. The markets in the cities are great places for picking up hand-knits at reasonable prices.

Sport

New Zealand is a sporting nation and has produced many international champions. Rugby is in fact more like a religion than a sport, and the All Blacks, the national team, are everybody's heroes. Soccer and rugby league are also played in winter, as are basketball, netball and hockey. Summer sports are dominated by cricket, but include softball, tennis and motor racing. Thoroughbred horse breeding is an important industry, and all forms of horse racing attract crowds all year round.

Non-team sports include skiing, trout and salmon fishing, deep-sea fishing, diving, white water rafting, windsurfing, hunting, mountain and rock climbing, hiking, marathons, triathlons - there are facilities for every sport imaginable.

Ngamokaiaroko boiling mud pool,
Rotorua.

Detail of a carving in the Maori
Meeting House, Waitangi.

Rafting over rapids, North Island.

Northland

To describe Northland in one sentence you would have to say it is a "boaties' paradise". There are hundreds of boat ramps, moorings, jetties and marinas, and fishermen can be seen everywhere. Its sub-tropical climate enhances its natural beauty and makes this an extremely popular holiday destination for New Zealanders, as well as divers and big game fishermen from all over the world. Northland is the whole of the peninsula north of Auckland. This narrow strip of land stretches to Cape Reinga, 450km north of Auckland, and is indented with hundreds of tiny bays on the east coast, whilst the west coast has an almost unbroken strip of white sandy beaches, the longest of which is the Ninety Mile Beach, which is really only 64 miles (103km) but even so, it's a long beach.

The interior is covered with lush vegetation and it is here that the last of the giant kauris are found. There are marked walking trails and picnic areas in the Northland Forest Park, affording everyone the opportunity to see these giants. The Bay of Islands Maritime and Historic Park is a playground for the recreation lover, and if you only have limited time in Northland this is the place you should visit.

In all, there are fourteen beautiful harbours in Northland, including those of Whangarei, Tutakaka, Whangaroa, Mangonui, Houhora and Hokianga, so if you have more time you might like to visit a few of them.

The area is noted for its big game fishing, and the best months are January to May although the season officially ends on June 30.

A wide variety of fish are caught offshore, among them blue, black and striped marlin, the broadbill sword fish, mako, thresher and hammerhead sharks, yellowtail kingfish and tuna. The main big game bases are Bay of Islands, Tutukaka and Whangaroa. There are also several yachts available for charter in the area, and these can be either with a skipper or bareboat

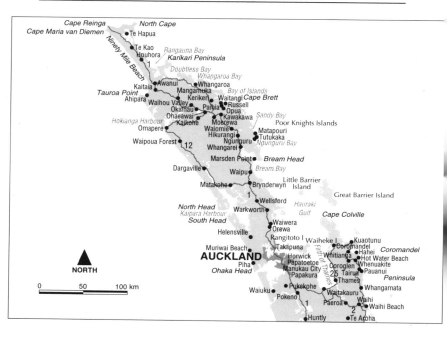

(no skipper). The line fisherman will also enjoy the area as snapper, blue cod and terakihi abound.

One of the world's five best sites for underwater photography, the **Poor Knight Islands**, attract thousands of divers to the area every year as well, but that doesn't mean that it's overcrowded as the coastline is full of small bays and it's easy to find some solitude.

The west coast beaches offer some exciting waves for surfers who don't seem to mind the colder waters of the Tasman Sea.

Climate

Sub-tropical - no frost or snow during winter. The East Auckland current flows along the east coast resulting in water temperatures of 20C in summer and 16C in winter.

How to get There

By Air

Air New Zealand (Eagle Airways) has flights daily from

Auckland to Kerikeri. Flights from Christchurch and Wellington connect at Auckland.

By Bus

InterCity has daily services from Auckland to Paihia and Whangarei.
Newmans has daily services from Auckland to Paihia and Whangarei.

By Car

Auckland-Kaitaia is 325km - approx 6 hours 45 minutes.
Auckland-Whangarei is 171km - approx 2 hours 40 minutes.

It takes 3½ hours to drive from Auckland to the Bay of Islands via the east coast, or 5 hours through the Waipoua Kauri Forest. If you have the time, the best way to see Northland is to make a round trip from Auckland taking the east coast road and returning along the west coast.

Suggested Self-drive Route

If you are driving from Auckland, cross the harbour bridge and take Highway 1, which passes through **Orewa, Waiwera** and **Warkworth.** There is a Marineland at Orewa which is open daily, and Waiwera is famous for its hot springs where the water temperature is about 37C all year round.

Near Warkworth is the satellite station which is linked to the Intelstat system. From here you can either follow the highway, or drive along the coast and rejoin Highway 1 at **Waipu.** This settlement was the last stage of a double migration by Reverend Norman McLeod and his followers, first from Scotland to Nova Scotia in 1819, and then after 32 years to Australia and New Zealand, where they were granted 47,600 acres in Waipu. The **House of Memories** in Waipu is a museum that commemorates the centennial of the pioneers' arrival in New Zealand.

Marsden Point is 60km further north, and its magnificent deep harbour is one of only twelve in the world which can accommodate oil tankers over 100,000 tons. The Marsden Point refinery supplies about three-quarters of New Zealand's petrol, diesel and by-products. Gas condensate from the Taranaki Fields is processed here.

Tourist Information

Bay of Islands - Marsden Road, Paihia, ph (09) 402 7345, open daily 8am-5pm. *Kaitaia* - Jaycee Park South Road, ph (09) 408 0879, open daily 9am-5pm. *Whangarei* - Tarewa Park, 92 Otaika Road, ph (09) 438 1079, open Mon-Fri 8.30am-5pm (daily 8.30am-6.30pm Dec 26-Mar 31). *Dargaville* - 65 Normanby Street, ph (09) 439 8360, open Mon-Fri 8.30am-5pm. *Waiuku* - 2 Queen Street, ph (09) 235 8924.

Whangarei

This industrial city was first settled by William Carruth in 1839 and attained city status in 1964. Whangarei is not your usual industrial city as it spreads along several valleys, and no matter in which part of town you find yourself, you will not be far from areas of bushland.

Accommodation

Following is a selection of accommodation with prices in NZ$ for a double room per night, which should be used as a guide only. The telephone area code is 09.

Hotels & Motels

Settlers Motor Hotel, 61-69 Hatea Drive, ph 438 2699, fax 438 0794 - 60 ensuite rooms, licensed restaurant, spa, swimming pool - $90-100.
Cherry Court Motor Lodge, 35 Otaika Road, ph 438 3128, fax 438 7972 - 15 units, spa, swimming pool, spa - $89-120.
Best Western Fountain Lodge Motel, 17 Tarewa Road, ph/fax 438 3532 - 12 units, swimming pool - $81-95.
Casa Blanca Motel, 397 Western Hills Drive, ph/fax 438 1759 - 20 units, swimming pool, spa - $72-78.
Aaron Court Motel, 22 Wolf Street, ph/fax 438 9139 - 10 units, swimming pool, barbecue - $68-79.
Regency Motel, 11 Cross Street, ph 438 3005, fax 438 9502 - 12 units, spa - $69.
Motel 6, 153 Bank Street, ph 438 9219, fax 438 7185 - 12 units, spa - $65-76.

Kensington Lodge Motel, 85-87 Kamo Road, ph/fax 437 0555 - 13 units, swimming pool, barbecue - $60-70.

Continental Motel, 67 Kamo Road, Kensington, ph/fax 437 6359 - 16 units, swimming pool, spa, games room - $60-90.

Otaika Motel, 136 Otaika Road, ph/fax 438 1459 - 8 units, swimming pool, spa, sauna, barbecue - $65.

Anchor in Marina Motel, 56-58 Riverside Drive (on Hatea River), ph/fax 438 7149 - 8 units, spa pool, barbecue - $56.

Motor Camps & Cabins

Alpha Caravan Park, 34 Tarewa Road, ph/fax 438 9867 - powered sites $9 adults, $4.50 children.

Blue Heron Holiday Park, Scott Road, off Heads Road, on Tamaterau Beach, ph 436 2293, fax 436 3013 - powered sites $8 adults, $5 children.

Otaika Motel Caravan Park, 136 Otaika Road, ph/fax 438 1459 - powered sites $8 adults, $4 children; tourist flats, sleep 2-4 - $45 x 2 adults, $8 children.

Tropicana Holiday Park, Whangarei Heads Road, ph/fax 436 0687 - powered sites $19.50 x 2 adults, $5 children; tourist flats, sleep 2-5 - $55-60 x 2 adults, $8 children; cabins, sleep 2-5 - $39 x 2 adults, $7 children; also smaller cabins and on-site vans.

William Jones Park, adjacent to Mair Park, ph 437 6856, fax 437 5897 - powered sites $8 adults, $4 children; cabins, sleep 2-6 - $30 x 2 adults, $6 children; also on-site vans.

Sightseeing

For the best view of the city, drive up Parahaki Memorial Drive to **Parahaki Hill**, 242m above sea level, and the whole of the city lies spread out before you.

There are a few interesting places to visit in Whangarei including the **Clapham Clock Museum** in Central Park where clocks and watches of all shapes, sizes and ages are displayed.

It is open daily 10am-4pm and guided tours are available, ph 438 3993.

Margie Maddren Fernery and Snow Conservatory is New Zealand's only all native fernery and features seventy varieties of ferns and several endangered species. The Conservatory is just over the bridge from Cafler Park and the Clock Museum, and is open daily 10am-4pm. There is no admission fee.

If you have some time to spare, the bushwalks through the

Mair and A.H. Reed Memorial Parks are worthwhile.

In the Boat Harbour you will usually see yachts from all over the world. The Whangarei Noumea Yacht Race starts from here. It is worth taking a cruise on the harbour.

Above Whangarei Heads stands the curiously shaped peak of Manaia (420m). According to Maori legend, this mount represents the chief Manaia, his three children and his unfaithful wife. Manaia is the human figure with the bird-like features found carved in bargeboards of Maori meeting houses.

From Whangarei you can either continue along Highway 1, or travel via the east coast.

Tutukaka and the East Coast Bays

Take the Ngunguru road and about 4km from town you will see a signpost to the **Whangarei Falls**. These falls have a fine bridal veil-like quality about them, and there is a walking track to the foot of the falls.

Only about an hour's drive away across the peninsula are the white sandy beaches around **Tutukaka**. The water in the harbour at Tutukaka is a vivid green, whereas the Pacific beyond is a deep blue.

The crystal clear water makes this area **ideal for scuba diving and snorkelling.** Boats leave here for Poor Knights Islands, one of the best and most accessible diving destinations in New Zealand. The fish life there is prolific and the drop-offs, caves and arches make them one of the most popular diving destinations in New Zealand. Visibility is usually 30-50m, but can be as much as 70m in summer.

If you are staying at the Youth Hostel, arrangements can be made through the hostel for diving. Otherwise you can contact one of the dive charter boats direct. The visitor information centres have lists of operators.

Tutukaka is popular with big game fishermen as the fishing areas are only a couple of kilometres off-shore. The coast road takes you past **Ngunguru, Tutukaka, Matapouri, Wolleys Bay** and **Sandy Bay** and back to Highway 1 at **Kawakawa**.

Just before you come to Kawakawa are the **Waiomio Caves**. These glow-worm and limestone caves are not worth the detour if you intend to visit the famous Waitomo Caves. From Kawakawa travel to Paihia on the shore of the Bay of Islands.

Bay of Islands

This beautiful bay, with approximately 144 islands, is the highlight of the trip to Northland. **The scenery here is superb, as is the fishing, boating and diving**. There are many hotels, motels, motor camps and holiday flats around the bay as it is a popular holiday destination for Kiwis as well as visitors. The main centres along its shores are **Russell, Paihia, Opua** and **Waitangi.**

Samuel Marsden founded the first European settlement in New Zealand at the Bay of Islands in 1814. In the 1830s and 1840s Russell had almost as many hotels and grog shops as residents, and was nicknamed the "Hell of the Pacific". Twice a year the whalers put in after chasing the migrating whales along the coast of New Zealand. In 1840 the Waitangi Treaty was signed by Captain Hobson, on behalf of Queen Victoria, and forty-five Maori Chiefs, thus bringing New Zealand into the British Empire.

Accommodation

The most accommodation is found at Paihia, and following is a selection with prices for a double room per night in NZ$. These should be used as a guide only. (The wide range of prices is due to seasonal fluctuations.) The telephone area code is 09.

Hotels

Quality Resort Waitangi, Tau Henare Drive (Waitangi National Trust Grounds), ph 402 7411, fax 402 8200 - 145 rooms (private facilities), swimming pool, tennis court - $166-195.

Beachcomber Resort Hotel, 1 Seaview Road, ph 402 7434, fax 402 7434 - 46 units, licensed restaurant, bar, private beach, swimming pool, sauna, tennis, squash, barbecue - $95-185.

Paihia Pacific Resort Hotel, 27 Kings Road, ph 402 8221, fax 402 8490 - 35 units, licensed restaurant, swimming pool - $118-153.

Paihia Holiday Motor Inn, Joyces Road (off Williams Road), ph 402 7911, fax 402 7729 - 65 units, licensed restaurant, bar, swimming pool, spa - $102.

Motels

Abel Tasman Lodge, Marsden Road (opposite beach), ph 402 7521, fax 402 7521 - 25 units, spa pool - $70-175.

Aloha Motel, Seaview Road, ph/fax 402 7540 - 15 units, swimming pool, spa, games room, barbecue - $75-135.

Bay View Motel, Marsden Road (waterfront), ph 402 7338, fax 402 7279 - 11 units, spa pool, barbecue - $75-165.

Marlin Court Motel, cnr Seaview & McMurray Roads, ph 402 7693, fax 4027910 - 12 units, swimming pool, spa, barbecue - $95-130.

Sands Motel, 136 Marsden Road (on waterfront), ph 402 7707, fax 402 6217 - 8 units - $70-110.

Bounty Inn, cnr Selwyn & Bayview Roads, ph 402 7088, fax 402 7081 - 29 units, licensed restaurant, spa, barbecue - $65-135.

Averill Court Motel, Seaview Road, ph 402 7716, fax 402 8512 - 18 units, swimming pool, spa, barbecue - $60-130.

Seaspray Motor Lodge, 138 Marsden Road (on waterfront), ph 402 7935, fax 402 8436 - 24 units - $75-135.

Aarangi Tui Motel, 16 Williams Road, ph/fax 402 7496 - 7 units, games room, barbecues - $60-180.

Ash Grove Motel, Ash Grove Circle, Haruru Falls, ph 402 7934, fax 402 6279 - 8 units, swimming pool, spa - $59-101.

Tradewinds Resort, Old Wharf Road, facing Haruru Falls, ph 402 7525, fax 402 7191 - 6 units, licensed restaurant, swimming pool, spa, barbecue - $70-195.

Bay of Islands Lodge, 54 School Road, ph 402 8558, fax 402 8280 - 16 units, swimming pool, gymnasium, barbecue - $60-120.

Hostels

Lodge Eleven, cnr Kings & McMurray Roads, ph/fax 402 7487 - $16-20.

Centabay Lodge, 27 Selwyn Rd, ph402 7466, fax402 8145 - dormitories $16 per person; twin rooms $39; studio units $50-80.

Motor Camps & Cabins

Bay of Islands Holiday Park Paihia, Lily Pond, Puketona Road, ph/fax 402 7646 - powered sites $9.50 adults, $4.50 children; cabins $37-80 x 2 adults, $6 children.

Smiths Holiday Camp, Cabins & Motels, Opua-Paihia Main Road, ph 402 7678, fax 402 6678 - powered sites $10 adults, $5 children; cabins $45; tourist flats $65; motel $85-100.

Waitangi Motor Camp, 21 Tahuna Road, ph 402 7866 - powered sites - $8.50-12 per person; cabins - $35-40; on-site caravans $26-30.

Sightseeing

Waitangi

This settlement is the birthplace of the nation. Historically speaking, the most important building in Waitangi is the *Treaty House* where the now-famous treaty was signed on February 6, 1840. The House is open daily 9am-5pm, and admission is $7 adults, $3 children.

The other building which shouldn't be missed is the *Maori Meeting House* which was opened on Waitangi Day 1940, and which contains carvings by Maori tribes from all over New Zealand, representing their particular tribal history. Nearby is the *Centennial Canoe*, 36m long and made from kauri from the Puketi Forest. Every year some one hundred Maori men train for the honour of being selected as one of the eighty paddlers who are needed to man it.

Just past the Treaty House is *Mount Bledsloe* from where magnificent photographs of the area can be taken.

Kelly Tarlton's *Museum of Shipwrecks* on the three-masted barque *Tui* moored near the Waitangi Bridge contains relics from local shipwrecks. It is open daily 10am-5pm, and admission is $6 adults, $2.50 children. The ship is also a licensed restaurant and is open in the evenings during the summer months. For more information, ph 402 7108.

Paihia

This holiday resort is a favourite for the boating fraternity, and deep sea fishing boats are available for charter. Divers are also catered for, and complete scuba and snorkel gear can be hired. There are actually four beaches, Te Haumi, Paihia, Horotutu and Te Ti. Minibus tours leave from here for the trip along the Ninety Mile Beach to Cape Reinga. The Haruru Falls on the Waitangi River are not very exciting but there is a good camping ground and motor lodge opposite the falls.

There are two ways to reach Russell, which is across the bay, either by ferry, jet boat or launch from Paihia, or by car ferry from Opua to Okiato and drive the last 8km.

Russell

Started out as a village and was first called *Kororareka*. By 1840 it was New Zealand's most important European settlement.
Although it was surrounded by mission stations, it seemed as if all the flotsam and jetsam of the Pacific ended up here. For nine months after the signing of the Waitangi Treaty it was the capital of New Zealand.

The first chief to sign the Treaty was Hone Heke Pokai who was to receive toll for every boat that entered the port of Russell. Unfortunately, when Customs Duty was imposed and the price of whale oil went down, his income was drastically reduced. He took his revenge by cutting down the flagpole on the hill. The Governor rescinded the Customs duties, and Hone Heke's income rose once more, so he rebuilt the pole. Unfortunately relations once again became strained and the chief cut it down again. The Government had it rebuilt only to find it cut down for the third time. The Governor then had a blockhouse built around it, but Hone Heke was not deterred. He managed to get in and cut it down for the fourth time and then proceeded to burn Russell to the ground.

One of the few buildings to be spared was the Anglican *Christ Church*, built in 1836. In the cemetery there are graves of Maori chiefs and settlers. The only other building to survive the razing of Kororareka was *Pompallier House* built by the Catholic Bishop. The original building was built in the French method with walls of rammed earth, clay and ashes and reinforced with stakes. It was allowed to fall into disrepair, then was restored and verandahs were added to help preserve the original walls. It is now open daily 10am-4.30pm, and admission is free.

Other buildings of interest in Russell are The Bungalow, built in 1853 by the first American Consul and later used as a school house; the Russell Police Station, built in 1870; and next door The Duke of Marlborough Hotel which was rebuilt for the fourth time in 1932 and boasts the first liquor licence every issued in New Zealand.

Russell, Bay of Islands.

The *Captain Cook Museum* houses a 6.7m replica of the *Endeavour* and is open daily 10am-4pm - admission $2.

Fullers Northland, ph 402 7421, operate a mini-bus tour of the town which visits the major attractions including Flagstaff Hill, which is not easily accessible on foot. If you are looking for a safe swimming beach, head for Long Beach, 1.6km out of town.

Recreation Activities

Cruises

No visit to the Bay of Islands would be complete without a cruise around the bay. It is a memorable experience as you visit the islands along with the daily deliveries of mail and supplies on *The Cream Trip* offered by Fullers Northland, ph 402 7421 (Paihia), 403 7866 (Russell) or 358 0259 (Auckland). The half-day, 65km cruise costs $65 adults, $33 children.

The *Hole in the Rock Cruise* to Cape Brett sails through the famous hole (9m long x 15m high x 12m wide). The cruise lasts 4.5 hours and for current prices, phone Fullers Northland on the numbers above.

Kings Tours & Cruises, ph 402 8288, fax 402 7915, has *See the Bay in A Day* which is two trips in one that follows the route of the Cream Trip, passes through the Hole in the Rock, and visits Cathedral Cave, with an island stopover.

Boat Hire and Fishing

If you prefer to do your own thing, you can hire boats of all sizes from dinghies up, and set off for a relaxing day on the water. Hand line fishing for snapper and terakhi is exciting, and some charter boats specialise in this type of fishing. Contact Kiwi Cruises, ph 402 7730.

Game Fishing

The game fishing enthusiast is also well catered for. A variety of fish are taken, eg tuna, yellowtail, sharks and blue, striped and black marlin, and at sunset a crowd gathers at the jetty to watch the weighing of the catch. Contact the tourist information centre for a complete list of charter boats. Contact Whangarei Deep Sea Anglers Club & Tutukaka Charters Ltd, Marina Road, Tutukaka, ph 434 3818, fax 434 3755, who will also arrange transport from all accommodation outlets in Whangarei to Tutukaka.

Snorkelling and Diving

These are extremely popular activities in the Bay of Islands too, as the waters are relatively sheltered from bad weather. There is good visibility most of the year except for the spring plankton bloom, but even though this reduces visibility, some of the deep water species move closer to the coast, and paper nautilus arrive at the Poor Knights and Bay of Islands. Contact Dive Charters Limited, Motel Road, Tutukaka, RD3, Whangarei, ph 434 3828.

Far North

Accommodation

Here is a selection of accommodation in the main centres of the Far North, with prices in NZ$ for a double room per night, which should be used as a guide only. The area code is 09.

Kaitaia

Orana Motor Inn, 238 Commerce Street, ph 408 1510, fax 408 1512 - 32 units, restaurant, bar, swimming pool - $60-75.

Best Western Wayfarer Motel, 231 Commerce Street, ph 408 2600, fax 408 2601 - 21 units, swimming pool, spa, games room - $66-78.

Sierra Court Motor Lodge, 65 North Road, ph 408 1461, 408 1436 - 16 units, swimming pool, spa, games room, barbecue - $70-90.

Motel Capri, 5 North Road, ph 408 0224 - 7 units - $50-75.

Kauri Lodge Motel, 15 South Road, ph/fax 408 1190 - 8 units, swimming pool, barbecue - $55-65.

Main Street Backpackers, 235 Commerce Street, ph 408 1275, fax 408 1100 - 9 rooms and 2 dormitories - $12-25 per person.

Pine Tree Lodge Motor Camp, Takahe Street, Ahipara, ph 409 4864 - powered sites $8 adults, $4 children; cabins, sleep 2-4, $12 adults, $6 children.

The Park Ninety Mile Beach, Waipapakauri Ramp, ph 406 7298, fax 406 7477 - licensed restaurant - powered sites $10 adults, $5 children; self-contained cabins $50-55; cabins $35-40.

Doubtless Bay

Acacia Lodge Motel, Mill Bay Road, Mangonui, ph/fax 406 0417 - 15 units - $75-139.

San Marino Motor Lodge, San Marino Drive, Coopers Beach, ph 406 0345, fax 406 0202 - 8 units, barbecue - $69-130.

Driftwood Lodge Motel, SH10 Cable Bay (on the beach), ph 406 0418, fax 406 0005 - 7 units, barbecue - $59-150.

Taipa Sands Motel, Adamson Road, Taipa (on the beach), ph/fax 406 0446 - 6 units, pool, games room, barbecue - $60-80.

Coopers Beach Motel, SH 10, Coopers Beach, ph 406 0271 - 9 units, barbecue - $75-120.

Old Oak Inn (Hostel), Beach Road, Mangonui, ph/fax 406 0665 - 7 rooms, licensed restaurant - $38-65.

Karikari Peninsula

Reef Lodge Motel, Rangiputa Beach, ph/fax 408 7100 - 8 units, spa - $65-175.

White Sands Motor Lodge, Rangiputa Beach, ph 408 7080 - 4 units, barbecue - $50-125.

Sightseeing

Kerikeri

About 20km north of Paihai is **Kerikeri** which is the centre of a large sub-tropical fruit growing area. It is also a major arts and crafts centre, as well as having the airport for the Bay of Islands. The town has the most selective shopping centre in the Far North, with a good selection of accommodation and restaurants.

It was here that Samuel Marsden set up his second mission station, and the Reverend John Butler, who arrived to run the mission in 1819, is thought to have planted the first English plants, vines, flowers and vegetables to be grown on New Zealand soil. The original missionary residence, *Kemp House*, was built in 1822 and is the oldest surviving building in New Zealand. It is open to the public daily 10am-2.30pm, 1.30-4.30pm and admission is $4.

Adjacent is the *Stone Store* built in 1833 and still used as a store. The building was erected by the Church Missionary Society and its top floor later housed the library of New Zealand's first Anglican bishop, George Augustus Selwyn.

Later still it was used as an ammunition store during conflicts with the Ngapuhi chief, Hone Heke Pokai. The store is open daily 9am-5pm, and has a small museum.

Rewa's Village lies across the river from the Stone Store and is a replica of an 18th century Maori village, built on the site of an authentic unfortified village or *ainga*, a temporary settlement. The village is open daily and admission is $2.

Spectacular views can be obtained from *Rainbow Falls* on the Kerikeri River, 5km from town. An interesting bush walk from the Stone Store leads to the Falls, or you can gain access to them from near the entrance to the Kerikeri Golf Course, one of New Zealand's best courses.

The *Orange Centre*, at the cross-roads on State Highway 10 heading north, has tours through a commercial citrus and sub-tropical orchard, and its Frazer-McKenzie Gallery has displays of wood-leather sculptures. The complex is open daily 9am-5pm.

Only 15km from town is the *Puketi Kauri Forest* where the forest giants can be seen beside the road and along a marked track through the forest. **You can then head north and rejoin Highway 10 just before Kaeo.**

Whangaroa Harbour

From there you can make another side trip to **Whangaroa Harbour** which is also a big fishing centre. A 2-hour cruise there will take you to the site of the wreck of the *Boyd* which was burnt by the Maoris. From Kaeo, Highway 10 passes Doubtless Bay and rejoins Highway 1 at Awanui which is the jumping off place for Cape Reinga.

A side trip off the road can be made to **Houhora Heads** and the *Wagener Museum and Homestead*, ph 409 8850. This is the original homestead built on this site in 1860-62, and it has stayed in the Subritzky-Wagener family since construction. The museum has the largest private collection of colonial furniture, machinery, household items, etc, in New Zealand and is open daily 8am-5pm. Admission is $5. The area is renowned for surf beaches and fishing, and has a very scenic 18 hole golf course. There are camping sites in the council-owned ground next to the homestead park.

Ninety-Mile Beach

The famous **Ninety-Mile Beach** is really only 103km long. This white sand beach has a wild desolate beauty of its own. Buses drive along the beach at low tide right up to, or down from Cape Reinga, depending upon the tide. If you wish to drive along the beach, it is best to follow the convoy of buses. Although this may rather spoil the atmosphere of this deserted stretch of sand it is, nevertheless, a wise precaution. The trip in itself is a memorable enough experience without getting bogged in the sand.

Te Reinga

Te Reinga is often considered to be the most northerly point of New Zealand, but that distinction actually belongs to the Surville Cliffs, a little to the east. The much-photographed 10m lighthouse stands 165m above the sea. The light flashes every 26 seconds and is visible for 50km. The sacred pohutukawa tree below the lighthouse is where (according to Maori legend) spirits depart this world for their journey to the spirit world. When you stand there and look at the waters of the Tasman and the Pacific foaming and swirling as they meet, and then out to the Three King Islands, which are just a faint smudge on the horizon, you can almost believe the legend.

The return journey south is via Kaitaia, 8km from Awanui where we joined Highway 1.

> **Most people going to Cape Reinga travel one way along the road, and the other way along the Ninety Mile Beach. The choice of route will depend upon the tide. The turn-off for the beach is at Waipapakauri a few kilometres north.**

Kaitaia

Kaitaia is the commercial centre of the Far North and has good accommodation and shopping facilities. The *Nocturnal Park*, where glow-worms and kiwis can be seen in their natural habitats, is worth a visit. It is open daily and the glow-worms can be seen indoors during the day and outdoors at night. Admission is $8 adults, $3 children.

The road south winds through the Mangamuka Gorge and the fertile Waihou Valley. Stay on Highway 1 to Ohaeawai, then take Highway 12 to the west coast and the heads of **Hokianga Harbour**. This large harbour stretches right into the forests.

From Hokianga the road winds through the Waipoua State Forest where paths lead to two of the forest monarchs, Tane Mahuta and Matua Ngahere, both around 1200 years old. Further south is the Trounson Kauri Park where kauris of all ages can be seen.

Dargaville

The next town you come to is **Dargaville** on the Wairoa River. It is a timber town, and attractions include the *Northern Wairoa Maori Maritime and Pioneer Museum* in Harding Park. It is open daily 9am-4pm and admission is $3 adults, 50c children.

The *Dargaville Maritime Museum* has relics of the Greenpeace sponsored *Rainbow Warrior*, including its fully rigged masts.

The Information Centre at 65 Normanby Street, ph 439 8360, has details of horse trekking on the Kauri Coast.

From Dargaville, Highway 12 continues south through farmland and kumara (sweet potato) plantations to **Matakohe** where there is a fine collection of kauri resin/gum in the museum. It is open daily 9am-5pm and admission is $6 adults, $3 children.

Highway 12 rejoins Highway 1 at the Brynderwyn junction and from there it is only a short run back to Auckland.

Auckland

(see Map inside back cover)

This beautiful city is situated on an isthmus of land with the Tasman Sea on one side and the Pacific Ocean on the other. The narrowest part of this isthmus is only a kilometre wide, but Auckland sprawls out along the shores of Waitemata and Manukau Harbours and along the Hauraki Gulf for many kilometres. No part of the city is far from the water so it is no wonder that there are literally thousands of boats with their brightly coloured sails on the harbours every weekend during the warmer months. It is therefore not surprising that Auckland is often called the "City of Sails".

Climate

Auckland has a temperate climate. The months with the most rainy days are June, July and August, and the months with the least rainy days are December, January, February and March. The average annual rainfall is 1204mm.

July is the coldest month, with an average maximum of 13C and a minimum of 8C; January and February are the hottest months with average maximums of 23C and minimums of 16C. The average annual hours of sunshine are 2100.

How to Get There

By Air

Travelling by air from overseas is covered in the Travel Information chapter. International Airlines phone numbers are: *Air New Zealand* (09) 379 3000; *British Airways* (09) 356 8690; *Canadian Airlines* (09) 309 0735; *Qantas* (09) 357 8900; *Singapore Airlines* (09) 303 2129; *United Airlines* (09) 379 3800.

Auckland Airport is about 35 minutes by road from the city centre, and has three separate terminals: the International Terminal and two Domestic Terminals - those of Air New Zealand and Ansett New Zealand.

A shuttle service operates between all three terminals for

which there is a small charge.

There are banking facilities at all terminals, as well as bars, restaurants, telephones, shops and left luggage facilities. At the international terminal arriving passengers emerge from a hallway into an amphitheatre with people waiting for friends and relatives seated in theatre style. Above the hallway is a large TV screen. So arriving passengers get the impression that they truly are the centre of attention. Off to the left are transfer facilities of the airlines, banks and phones.

Domestic Services

Air New Zealand and *Air New Zealand Link* (Air Nelson, Eagle Airways and Mount Cook Airline) have daily services from: Bay of Islands; Blenheim; Christchurch; Dunedin; Gisborne; Hamilton; Hokitika; Invercargill; Kaitaia; Mount Cook; Napier/Hastings; Nelson; New Plymouth; Palmerston North; Rotorua; Taupo; Tauranga; Timaru; Wanaka; Wanganui; Wellington; and Whangarei. There is also a service from Westport, daily except Saturday.

Mount Cook Airlines have daily services from: Kerikeri; Rotorua; Mt Cook and Queenstown.

Ansett New Zealand has daily services from:

Wellington; Christchurch; Dunedin; Blenheim; Invercargill; Nelson; Milford Sound; Queenstown; and Te Anau.

Transport from the Airport

AirBus coaches to the city leave from the Downtown Terminal every 20 minutes from 6.10am to 8.50pm daily, and from the Domestic Terminal every 20 minutes from 6.20am to 8.20pm daily. Fares are NZ$10 adults, NZ$3 children.

Super Shuttle, ph 307 5210, offers a door-to-door service between all parts of the city and suburbs and the airport. **Examples of fares are:** Airport to City - NZ$15 for 1, plus $5 for each extra person; Airport to Henderson - NZ$30 for 1, plus $7 for each extra person; Airport to Howick - NZ$30 for 1, plus $5 for each extra person; Airport to Takapuna - NZ$25 for 1, plus $7 for each extra person.

The taxi fare from the Airport to the City is around NZ$40.
This is expensive. The buses and shuttles are very efficient, and if you are hiring a car you can be met at the airport.

By Rail
Tranz Scenic **Overlander** and **Northerner** rail services travel to Auckland.

By Bus
InterCity coaches travel to Auckland on a daily basis from every town on their routes. *Newmans Coachlines* offer similar services.

By Car
Auckland-Wellington is 660km - approx 10 hours.
Auckland-Rotorua is 235km - approx 3 hours 30 minutes.
Auckland-New Plymouth is 368km- approx5 hours 40 minutes.
Auckland-Taupo is 279km - approx 4 hours 20 minutes.

Tourist Information

Airport Information Centres are found on the ground floor of the International Terminal (open for all inbound flights); and the ground floor of the Domestic Terminal (open daily, 8am to 9pm).

Downtown Visitors Centre, Aotea Square, 299 Queen Street, ph (09) 366 6888, is open Mon-Fri 8.30am-5pm, Sat-Sun and public holidays 9am-5pm.

Auckland West (Waitakere City) Visitor Information Centre, Scenic Drive, Centennial Memorial Park, Arataki,
ph (09) 817 7134.

Auckland South (Franklin District) Visitor Information Centre, Highway 1/Mill Road, Bombay, ph (09) 236 0670.

North Shore City Information Office, 49 Hurstmere Road, Takapuna, ph (09) 486 8670.

Throughout the area several Teletouch terminals have been installed. They are similar to 24-hour automatic teller machines and are easy to use, but give out information instead of money.

Money Exchange
Bank of New Zealand has outlets within the Auckland Airport complex and branches throughout Auckland, with the main one at 80 Queen Street, ph 375 1300. Open Mon-Fri, 9am-4pm.

During banking hours all banks will change currency and travellers cheques, but the following outlets are also open when the banks are closed:

Interforex, Endeans Building, 2 Queen Street, ph (09) 302 3031 - open Sat, Sun and public holidays 8am-7.30pm.
Interforex, Ferry Building, 99 Quay Street, ph (09) 302 3066 - open Sat-Sun and public holidays 8am-7.30pm.
Travelex, 32 Queen Street, ph (09) 358 9173 - open Sat 8am-8pm, Sun and public holidays 10am-8pm.
National Bank, 45 Queen Street, ph (09) 357 6417 - open Sat 10am-2pm, closed Sun and public holidays.
American Express, 101 Queen Street, ph (09) 379 8243 - open Sat 9.30am-12.30pm, closed Sun and public holidays.
Victoria Park Markets, Drake Street Office, ph (09) 309 6911 - open Sat-Sun and public holidays 9am-6pm.

Accommodation

Auckland has a wide range of accommodation with something to suit every lifestyle and every pocket. Here is a selection of accommodation, with prices in NZ$ for a double room per night, which should be used as a guide only. Discounts are sometimes available on weekends.

As with any large city, accommodation in the suburbs is usually cheaper, and you can check out what is available at the information office at the airport when you arrive, or make prior arrangements through your local NZ Tourism Board office. The telephone area code is 09.

Hotels

Sky City Hotel, cnr Victoria & Federal Streets, ph 912 6000, fax 912 6032 - 344 rooms (private facilities), 4 restaurants, bars, swimming pool, 24-hour casino, live theatre - opening mid-1997, prices on application.
The Stamford Plaza Auckland, cnr Albert & Swanston Streets, ph 309 8888, fax 303 0583 - 332 rooms (private facilities), restaurants, brasserie, cocktail bars - $355-433.
Carlton Hotel, Mayoral Drive, ph 366 3000 - 275 rooms (private facilities), 3 restaurants, bars - $195-265.
Novotel Auckland, 8 Customs Street East, ph 377 8920, fax 302 0993 - 188 rooms (private facilities), 2 restaurants, 4 bars - $167-270.
Hyatt Regency Auckland, cnr Princes Street & Waterloo Quadrant, ph 366 1234, fax 303 2932 - 275 rooms (private facilities), 2 restaurants, cocktail bar - $350.

First Imperial Hotel, 131-139 Hobson Street, ph 357 6770, fax 357 6793 - 61 rooms (private facilities), lic. restaurant, bar - $180.

Grafton Oaks Hotel, cnr Grafton Bridge and Grafton Rd, ph 309 0167, fax 377 5962 - 44 rooms, restaurant, cocktail bar - $145.

Park Towers Hotel, 3 Scotia Place, off Queen St, ph 309 2800, fax 302 1964 - 104 rooms (some with private facilities), restaurant, cocktail bar - $146 with private facilities, $74 without.

Abby's Tradewinds Hotel, cnr Wellesley & Albert Streets, ph 303 4799, fax 302 1451 - 70 rooms (private facilities), restaurant - $89-130.

Harbourcity Hotel, 96-100 Quay Street, ph 377 0349, fax 307 8159 - 188 units, licensed restaurant, sauna, gymnasium - $254.

Motels

Barrycourt Motor Inn, 10-20 Gladstone Road, Parnell, ph 303 3789, fax 377 3309 - 107 units, licensed restaurant, swimming pool, spa - $86-300.

Lincoln Court Motel, 58 Lincoln Road, Henderson, ph 836 0326, fax 837 0841 - 12 units, swimming pool, spa, barbecue - $80-100.

Dalma Court Motor Inn, 252 Great North Road, Henderson, ph 837 3370, fax 837 4282 - 30 units, licensed restaurant, swimming pool, barbecue - $80-140.

Eden Park Motor Inn, 697 New North Road, Mt Albert, ph 846 0086, fax 849 0086 - 33 units, licensed restaurant, swimming pool, spa, barbecue - $68-118.

Central Park Motor Lodge, 453 Great South Road, Penrose, ph 579 2450, fax 579 1128 - 8 units - $65-85.

Remuera Motor Lodge, 16 Minto Road, Remuera, ph 524 5126, fax 524 5639 - budget accommodation/motor camp - $69-95; camp sites $22-27.

Guest Houses

Ascot Parnell, 26 St Stephens Avenue, Parnell, ph 309 9012, fax 309 3729 - 9 rooms (private facilities) - B&B $117.

Chalet Chevron, 14 Brighton Road, Parnell, ph 309 0290, fax 373 5754 - 12 rooms (private facilities) - B&B $98-110.

Aachen House, 39 Market Road, Remuera, ph 520 2329, fax 524 2898 - 9 rooms (private facilities) - B&B $120-180.

Aspen Lodge B&B Hotel, 62 Emily Place, Auckland, ph 379 6698, fax 377 7625 - 26 rooms (no private facilities) - B&B $69.

Metropolitan YMCA of Auckland, Pitt Street, ph/fax 303 2068 - 119 rooms (no private facilities), restaurant - $35.

Hostels

City YHA Hostel, cnr City Road & Liverpool Street, ph 309 2802, fax 373 5083 - $19-22 per person (members).

Parnell Hostel, 2 Churton St, Parnell, ph 379 3731, fax 358 4143 - $17-20 per person (members).

Auckland Central Backpackers, 9 Fort Street, ph 358 4877, fax 358 4872 - bar, cafe, lounges - from $14 per person.

Auckland Mt Eden Backpackers Lodge, 5A Oaklands Road, Mt Eden, ph 638 6545 - $25-30 share twin.

Seafield Lodge, 49 Seafield View Road, Grafton, ph 302 4051 - $15-20 per person.

Local Transport

Bus

The main city bus terminal is between Commerce Street and Britomart Place, behind the Chief Post Office.

Airport and sightseeing buses depart from the Downtown Airline Terminal, Quay Street.

The *Yellow Bus Company*, ph 377 1990, is Auckland's largest public transport company. *Auckland Busabout Guide* is available from The Bus Place, cnr Hobson and Victoria Street West, and the Downtown Bus Terminal.

A Yellow Bus Company $8 "Busabout" Pass allows unlimited travel from 9am weekdays and at all times on weekends. The passes are available from the bus drivers.

United Airlines *Explorer* bus operates daily from the Ferry Building at the end of Queen Street. It departs on the hour from 10am till 4pm (from 9am Oct-April) and stops at Mission Bay, Underwater World, Auckland Museum, Parnell Village, Victoria Market and a bungee jumping venue. Tickets can be purchased from the Ferry Building at the commencement, or from the driver if you are joining at another stop. Prices are $15 adult, $7 child, and there is full commentary. A two day adult pass is also available for $25, ph (09) 571 3116.

Train

Suburban and long distance trains depart from Auckland Central Railway Station, Beach Road. Auckland does not have an underground city system.

Taxi

Taxis can be hired from stands throughout the city, or on-call by telephone. Some companies: Alert Taxis, ph 309 2000; Auckland Co-op Taxis, ph 300 3000; Citicabs, ph 379 9199; Kabs, ph 302 2213.

Taxis must be hired from a rank, or booked by phone (which attracts an extra charge). They cannot be hailed in the street. The charge for using a credit card is an extra $1 on the fare.

Car Hire

Ace Tourist Rentals (NZ) Ltd, ph 303 3112; *Action Rent-A-Car*, ph 267 5881; *Adventure Rental Cars*, ph 256 0255; *Affordable Rental Cars Ltd*, ph 630 1567; *Big Save Car Rentals*, ph 303 3928; *Budget Rent A Car*, ph 0800 652 227 (toll free); *Dollar Save Car Hire (NZ) Ltd*, ph 366 0646; *Henderson Rental Cars Ltd*, ph 838 8089; *McDonalds Rent A Car*, ph 276 8574; *Pegasus Rental Cars*, ph 275 3222; *Waiheke Rental Cars*, ph 372 8635.

Bicycle Hire

Active Leisure Cycle Express, ph 379 0779; *Pack 'N' Pedal*, ph 522 2161; *Adventure Cycles*, ph 309 5566.

Eating Out

Auckland has restaurants that cater for all occasions and pockets. There are licensed and many BYO (bring your own wine) restaurants with ethnic and New Zealand cuisine. All the five-star hotels have first class restaurants as well as a brasserie or the like.

Here is a selection of restaurants with approximate prices in NZ$ for a three course meal for one person, inclusive of GST, but without drinks.

Alhambra, 283 Ponsonby Road, Ponsonby, ph 376 2430 - **Licensed/BYO** - open Tues-Sun from 11.30am for lunch, 6pm for dinner - live jazz and blues - **$25-45** - credit cards accepted.

Bell House Restaurant, 75 Bells Road, Pakuranga, ph 576 4015 - **Licensed/BYO** - open Tues-Fri noon-2pm, Mon-Sat 6.30-10.30pm - in a NZ Historic Places Trust homestead - **over $45** - credit cards accepted.

Cin Cin on Quay, Ferry Building, 99 Quay Street, ph 307 6966 - Licensed - open daily 8am-3am - brasserie style - **$25-45** - credit cards accepted.

Harbourside Restaurant, 1st Floor, Ferry Building, 99 Quay Street, ph 307 0556 - **Licensed** - open daily 11.30am-midnight - balcony dining - **$25-45** - credit cards accepted.

Killarney Street Brasserie, 2 Killarney Street, Takapuna, ph 489 9409 - **Licensed** - informal brasserie - open Sun-Wed 11.30am-11pm, Thurs-Sat 11.30am-midnight - live jazz Sat and Sun lunch - **$25-45** - credit cards accepted.

Ponsonby Fire Station Chargrill & Seafood Bar, 1 Williamson Avenue, Ponsonby, ph 378 6499 - **Licensed/BYO** - open Tues-Fri noon-3pm, Mon-Sat 6-11pm - historic old building - **$25-45** - credit cards accepted.

Ramses Bar & Grill, cnr Crowhurst & Khyber Pass Road, Newmarket, ph 522 0619 - **Licensed** - casual, relaxed atmosphere - open daily noon-3pm, 6-11pm (happy hour in bar 5-7pm) - children's menu - **$25-45** - credit cards accepted.

O'Connell St Bistro, 3 O'Connell Street, City, ph 377 1884 - Licensed - casual, relaxed atmosphere, small- 9 tables open lunch and dinner - Monday to Friday, dinner only - Saturday - $30-$45 - credit cards accepted.

Chinese

Bamboo Village, 206 Jervois Road, Herne Bay, ph 376 7371 - **Licensed/BYO** - open nightly from 5pm - **under $25** - credit cards accepted.

Chinatown, 8 Lorne Street, ph 366 1642 - **BYO** - open daily 10.30am-5pm, 5-10.30pm - **under $25** - credit cards accepted.

Heng Kee Food Stall, 464 Queen Street, ph 302 0618 - **BYO** - open daily 11am-10.30pm - **under $25** - no credit cards.

Hong Kong Kitchen, 5-7 Albert Street, ph 302 1499 - **BYO** - open daily 11am-3pm, 5.30pm-late - **$25-45** - credit cards accepted.

Hong Kong Chinese Seafood, 164 Great South Road, Remuera, ph 524 4756 - **BYO** - open Mon-Sat noon-2.30pm, nightly 5-10pm - **under $25** - credit cards accepted.

Cosmopolitan

Cin Cin, 99 Quay Street, ph 307 6966 - **Licensed** - open Mon-Fri 11am-1am, Sat-Sun 8am-1am - outside tables available - **under $25** - credit cards accepted.

Copacabana, 178 Jervois Road, Herne Bay, ph 376 5367 - **Licensed/BYO** - open Tues-Sat 6pm-late - South American cuisine - **under $25** - credit cards accepted.

Java Jive, cnr Ponsonby Road and Pompalier Terrace, ph 376 5870 - **Licensed/BYO** - open nightly 6pm-3am - entertainment every night from 10pm - **$25-30** - credit cards accepted.

Italian
Prego, 226 Ponsonby Road, ph 376 3095 - **Licensed** - open daily noon-12.30am - **$25-45** - credit cards accepted.

Mexican
Mexican Cafe, 67 Victoria Street West, ph 373 2311 - **Licensed/BYO** - open Mon-Fri noon-2.30pm, Sun-Wed 5-11pm, Thurs-Sat 5pm-1am - **under $25** - credit cards accepted.
Senor Pepper, 100 Parnell Road, Parnell, ph 357 0000 - **Licensed/BYO** - entertainment Thurs, Fri and Sat - **$25-30** - credit cards accepted.

Entertainment
Following is a selection of entertainment venues. *The New Zealand Herald* has details of current attractions and shows.

Cinemas
Academy Cinema, cnr Lorne & Wellesley Sts, City, ph 373 2761.
   Berkeley Theatre, 85 Tamaki Drive, Mission Bay, ph 528 5296.
   Bridgeway Theatre, 122 Queen St, Northcote Point,ph418 3308.
   Civic Theatre, cnr Queen & Wellesley Sts, City, ph 303 3179.
   Classic Cinema, 321 Queen Street, City, ph 377 9382.
   Glenfield Mall Cinema, Glenfield Mall, Glenfield, ph 444 0100.
   Hoyts 6 Cinema Centre, Link Drive, Glenfield, ph 443 7755.
   Lido Theatre, 427 Manukau Road, Epsom, ph 630 0142.
   Mid-City Cinema Centre, 241-251 Queen St, City, ph 309 7445.
   Odeon Theatre, 310 Queen Street, City, ph 303 2364.
   Regent Theatre, 310 Queen Street, City, ph 303 2364.
   St James Cinema, 310 Queen Street, City, ph 303 2364.
   Tudor Cinema, 34 Anzac Street, Takapuna, ph 489 5562.
   Westend Theatre, 310 Queen Street, City, ph 303 2364.
   Village 6 Cinema Centre, Lakewood Court, Manukau City, ph 263 4415.

Theatres
ASB Theatre at Aotea Centre, Aotea Square, Queen St, City, ph 309 2677.

Auckland Town Hall Concert Chamber, 303 Queen Street, City, ph 307 7610.

Central Theatre, Lower Greys Avenue, City, ph 377 1755.

Dolphin Theatre, 12 Spring Street, Onehunga, ph 636 7322.

Maidment Theatre in the B/Side Theatre, cnr Princes & Alfred Streets, City, ph 308 2383.

The Pumphouse Theatre, Killarney Park, off Killarney Street, Takapuna, ph 486 2386.

Live Music Venues

Abby's, cnr Wellesley & Albert Streets, City, ph 303 4799.

Blues Barn, 510 Queen Street, City, ph 357 0965.

Cactus Jacks, 96 Albert Street, City, ph 302 0942.

Chelsea Park Hotel, Mokoia Road, Birkenhead, ph 418 3112.

Forester's Arms Tavern, Queen Street, Riverhead, ph 412 8902 live music Fri and Sat nights.

Java Jive, 308 Ponsonby Road, Ponsonby, ph 376 5870.

Park in the Bar, 4 Fort Street, City, ph 373 4742.

Powerstation, 33 Mt Eden Road, Mt Eden, ph 377 3488.

Rick's Blue Falcon, 27 Falcon Street, Parnell, 309 0854.

The Birdcage, 133 Frankyn Road, City, ph 378 9104.

The Gluepot, cnr Ponsonby & College Hill Road, Ponsonby, ph 376 5109.

Nightclubs

Alfie's Nightclub & Cabaret, 5 Century Arcade, Queen Street, City, ph 379 6096.

Cause Celebre, 35 High Street, City, ph 303 1336.

Club Polynz, 6-8 Commerce Street, City, ph 303 2591.

Custom House Nightclub, 22 Customs St, City, ph 358 2185.

Don't Tell Mama, 340 Karangahape Road, City, ph 379 03200.

Grapes Nightclub, 184 Victoria Street, City, ph 303 4633.

Metropolis Nightclub, cnr Wellesley & Albert Streets, City, ph 303 4799

Number 7, 7 Windsor Street, Parnell, ph 379 4341.

Staircase, 17 Albert Street, City, ph 377 0303.

Stanleys Nightclub, 192 Queen Street, City, ph 309 0201.

The Poedium, Northcote Road, Takapuna, ph 480 6109.

Vertigo Nightclub, 191 Queen Street, City, ph 307 0444.

Cabarets

Burgundys of Parnell, 289 Parnell Road, Parnell, ph 309 5112.

The Comedy Club, 2 Lower Albert Street, City, ph 303 0618.
NZI Convention Hall, Aotea Centre, Aotea Square, Queen Street, City, ph 309 2677.

Pubs and Taverns

De Bretts Hotel, cnr Shortland & High Streets, City, ph 303 2389.

Dog & Trumpet, 582 Karangahape Road, City, ph 378 1546 - open till 11pm daily.

Empire Tavern, cnr Nelson & Victoria Streets, City, ph 373 4389.

Esplanade Hotel, 1 Victoria Road, Devonport, ph 445 1291 - open Mon-Sat till 10.30pm.

Exchange Hotel, 99 Parnell Road, Parnell, ph 373 2531 - open daily till 1am.

Forester's Arms Tavern, Queen Street, Riverhead, ph 412 8902 - live music Fri & Sat nights.

King's Arms, 59 France Street, City, ph 373 3240 - open Mon-Sat till 10pm.

Kitty O'Brien's Pub, 2 Drake Street, City, ph 303 3936 - open Mon-Sat until 11.30pm, Sun 7.30pm.

Nag's Head Tavern, 117 St George's Bay Road, Parnell, ph 309 3586 - open nightly till 1am.

Occidental Pub, 6 Vulcan Lane, City, ph 373 4204 - open Mon-Sat till 10pm.

Queen's Head, 404 Queen Street, City, ph 302 0223 - open Mon-Thurs till 10pm, Fri-Sun 11pm.

Shakespeare Tavern & Brewery, 61 Albert Street, City, ph 373 5396 - open nightly till 1am.

Rugby Pub, 47 Fort Street, City, ph 377 0725 - open Mon-Thurs till 10pm, Fri-Sat 11pm.

The Sin Bin Bar, Northcote Road, Takapuna, ph 480 6109 - open Mon-Tues till 10.30pm, Wed-Sat 11.30pm, Sun 8pm.

Veranda Bar & Grill, 279 Parnell Road, Parnell, ph 309 6289 - open 7 days.

Windsor Castle, 144 Parnell Road, Parnell, ph 377 8071 - open Mon-Tues till 10pm, Wed 1am, Thurs midnight, Fri-Sat 1am.

Shopping

No matter where you where you shop, whether it is the rather busy Newmarket area on the road to Remuera with its old money homes or down town Queen Street you have a sensation that this is a small country with very interesting and innovative retail outlets. Wood styled shop fittings, retail structures in either wood, chrome or plastic mould seem to have a distinctly 'Kiwi' feel.

Ponsonby, Ponsonby Road

To the left of the city this yuppy styled area is replete with many small restaurants, shops selling locally produced designer clothes and other labels. Sadly only one small bookshop **Atticus** exits in the area on Jervois Road, but perhaps one of the best Children's bookshops this side of the equator is here - **Dorothy Butler's.**

Parnell Road, Parnell

Stacks of small shops all striving to appear classy and trendy with over priced gifts of all descriptions. This strip boasts some interesting galleries and pleasant if slightly pretentious restaurants. In the middle of all this opposite the oldest Catholic church in New Zealand is a superb little bookshop - **Parnell Books. Parnell** is only five minutes away from the major hotels and the waterfront. The shops and restaurants tend to be open seven days until well into the evening.

Downtown and Queen Street Strip

Downtown Shopping Centre, opposite Auckland Waterfront, Customs & Albert Streets, has seventy specialty stores under one roof. The centre is open Mon-Thurs 9am-5.30pm, Fri 9am-8pm, Sat 10am-2pm, and offers free parking Sat morning.

Along Queen Street from Customs Street to Wellesley Street is the main shopping area with all the internationally known specialty stores. Some streets that run parallel to Queen Street such as High Street and the short Elliot Street have some interesting arcades and shopping complexes - Centra among others.

Markets

Victoria Park Market has 200 carts offering souvenirs, leather wear, wood carvings, hand knits, designer men's and ladies' wear, fashion shoes, free entertainment, three licensed restaurants, vegetarian cafe, McDonald's, and much more. It is situated in Victoria Street West, ph 309 6911, and is open seven days.

China Oriental Markets, cnr Britomart and Quay Street on the waterfront, is also open seven days and has over 140 shops, live entertainment, cafes and restaurants. There is also a special flea market and craft bazaar every Sunday in the car park.

Market City, 67 Hurstmere Road, Takapuna, has a variety of stalls and food outlets. Open Mon-Fri 9.30am-5pm (Thurs to 8.30pm), Sat 9.30am-4pm.

Otara Fleamarket, Newbury Street off East Tamaki Road, in the heart of New Zealand's largest Polynesian community. Open Sat 6am-noon in the shopping centre car park and Te Puke Otara Community Hall.

Titirangi Village Market is held on the last Sun of the month 10am-2pm in the Titirangi War Memorial Hall, South Titirangi Road. It offers village crafts, home produce and entertainment.

West Auckland Sunday Market at the Ash Street entrance of Avondale Racecourse is open 7am-noon and has over 150 stalls.

Sightseeing

Auckland is New Zealand's largest city and main commercial and industrial centre. It is a cosmopolitan city with exciting modern architecture and many restaurants. It occupies the narrow isthmus which connects Northland to the rest of the North Island. The city has been built on top of and around some sixty extinct volcanoes. Originally, the sides of the volcanoes were smooth, but the Maoris built villages on some of them because they afforded protection from attack. The steep sloping sides were often terraced to accommodate their Pas and to grow food. **Mount Eden** is probably the best example of this as the broad terraces are unmistakable. It was quite a feat to have built such terraces as the only implements available were digging sticks and stone adzes.

One Tree Hill is the largest of the volcanoes and is an important archaeological site as all sides and slopes show evidence of being used by early man.

Mount Wellington also has evidence of Maori activity over many years. Carbon dating of stones from an ancient fireplace in the crater proved that Mt Wellington had been inhabited prior to the 15th century, and was probably abandoned by the 18th century. These three hills are worth a visit as not only are they of historical interest, they also afford panoramic views of the city.

The main commercial street of Auckland is **Queen Street**, which runs up the hill from Queen Elizabeth Square on Quay Street. The ferries to the north shore and islands in the gulf leave from the ferry wharf on Quay Street, opposite the bottom end of Queen Street. The **Downtown Bus Terminal** is to the right of Queen Street (when facing the harbour) in Galway Street, and the **Downtown Air Terminal** is to the left of Queen Street on Quay Street. If you walk up Queen Street from the harbour you will come to Victoria Street, which leads to Albert Park and its well kept gardens and floral clock. The **Art Gallery** is situated at the Wellesley Street end of this park, and further up Wellesley Street is **Auckland University**. Another block behind the University marks the beginning of the **Auckland Domain**. This park contains the War Memorial, the Winter Gardens and the Auckland Hospital.

The **Town Hall** is in Queen Street at the end of **Aotea Square**, where the information centre is located. A entertainment and convention complex (**Aotea Centre**) is next to the Town Hall.

Most of the sights in Auckland are obvious enough, but if you only have limited time you might like to join a walking tour, or take one of the city sightseeing tours.

Sightseeing by Foot
Brochures detailing city walks are available from the Auckland Visitors Information Centre. Listed below are the main attractions. They are grouped together under various headings, with directions on how to get there.

Museums
The *Auckland War Memorial Museum*, at the top of the Domain 3km from the centre, is open daily 10am-5pm and admission and guided tours are free, ph 309 0443. Here is housed the

world's largest collection of Maori artefacts, and a resident Maori concert party performs 11.15am and 1.30pm most days.

The second floor houses the World War One Hall of Memory and a developed exhibit of new Zealand's involvement in past conflicts, both world and local. Also a small exhibition of Colonial Auckland. Catch the 645 or 655 bus from Downtown Bus Terminal, or either of the Explorer buses. The *Winter Gardens* are also in the Domain, open daily 10am-4pm.

The *Museum of Transport and Technology*, Great North Road, Western Springs, ph 846 0199, has extensive indoor and outdoor displays covering aviation, photography, rail and road transport, with many hands-on exhibits. There are also tram rides and a pioneer village. The main site is open Mon-Fri 9am-5pm, Sat-Sun 10am-5pm. The *Aviation Museum* is open Mon-Fri 9am-4pm, Sat-Sun 10am-4.30pm. Admission is $8.50 adult. Take bus 045 from Customs Street East.

Parnell Village is only minutes from the city by bus - Meadowbank, St Johns and Glen Innes buses depart from Platform 3 at the Downtown Terminal behind the CPO, or take one of the Explorer buses. The village has cobbled walkways leading to picturesque courtyards surrounded by boutiques and restaurants. This area has been restored and there are many Victorian houses with wooden lace and wrought iron work. The Auckland Museum, Ewelme Cottage, Kinder House and the Holy Trinity Cathedral are nearby.

Rugby International Museum and Souvenir Shop, Unit 10, 39 Porana Road, Takapuna, ph 444 0914, is open Mon-Fri 9.30am-4.30pm, Sat 10am-1pm, and has one of the most extensive collections of international rugby jerseys in the world. In all there are 370 jerseys including 201 international, representing 97 of the 104 playing nations, all worn by famous players. There is a collection of 700 ties, old caps dating back to 1898, autographed balls of famous teams, rugby pins, original rugby paintings and a World Cup display. The shop has stocks of jerseys of just about every Rugby team you can think of, as well as many League jerseys and other football paraphernalia.

Historic Buildings

The *Town Hall*, Aotea Square, was built in 1911 and has a distinctive clocktower. *St Patrick's Catholic Cathedral* in Wyndham Street is built in the neo-gothic style. It could do with some sprucing up. Looking a bit tatty at the moment.

Ewelme Cottage, 14 Ayr Street, Parnell, ph 379 0202, was built in 1864 by the Reverend Vicesimus Lush so that his sons could attend the nearby Anglican Grammar School. The cottage remains virtually unchanged since then. It is open daily 10.30 am-4.30pm, and admission is $3.50 - take bus 635, 645 or 655.

Kinder House, 2 Ayr Street, Parnell, ph 379 4008, was the residence of a 19th century painter, photographer and educationalist. Open daily 10.30am-4pm, and Devonshire teas are available. Take bus 635, 645 or 655.

The Anglican Cathedral Church of St Mary, Parnell Road, Parnell, has one of New Zealand's finest old wooden churches incorporated in a modern building. It is still undergoing a refit.

The Old Custom house, 22 Custom Street West, was built in 1888 and is part of the grandeur of Auckland's historic past. Today it houses a cinema, restaurants and small shops.

Renall Street, just off Ponsonby Road, has been designated a conservation area as the buildings are of historical interest.

> **Even if you decide to "do the sights" on your own you might consider buying a Busabout ticket so that you can cover more ground in a day.**

There are excellent examples of 19th century wooden houses. **They are not open to the public.**

Alberton Historic House, 100 Mt Albert Road, Mt Albert, ph 846 7367, is a fully restored Victorian homestead built in 1862. It is open daily 10.30am-12.30pm, 1.30-4.30pm and admission is $3.50. Take bus 233 or 243 from Victoria Street West.

Highwic, 40 Gillies Avenue, Epsom, ph 524 5729, was built in 1862 and was the residence of prosperous stock and station agent Alfred Buckland. It is open daily 10.30am-12.30pm, 1.30-4.30pm and admission is $3.50. Take bus 297 or 298 from Civic Centre.

Howick Historical Village, Lloyd Elsmore Park, Bells Road, Pakuranga, ph 576 9506, is an authentic early colonial village depicting life over a hundred years ago. More than twenty buildings are surrounded by gardens. Open daily 10am-4pm and admission is $6.

Art Galleries

Auckland City Art Gallery, on the corner of Kitchener & Wellesley Streets, ph 307 7704, is New Zealand's premier art gallery. The gallery is open daily 10am-4.30pm, till 9pm on the last Thurs of every month. Guided tours are available Wed at noon and Sun at 2pm. General admission is free, but charges apply to all temporary loan exhibitions.

Peter Webb Gallery, cnr Wellesley & Elliott Streets, City, ph 373 4404.

John Leech Gallery, 367 Remuera Road, Remuera, ph 523 1325.

Rita Webster Galleries, 3 Scarborough Lane, Parnell, ph 309 0115.

Many fine galleries are also found in Ponsonby Road and Parnell Road.

Parks and Gardens

Albert Park, Wellesley Street East, was the site of Auckland barracks for British Imperial Troops until the 1860s. The garden is a five minute walk from Queen Street, City.

Auckland Domain, Park Road, Grafton, has 81ha of gardens, with tropical and subtropical plants in the Wintergardens, duckponds, scent garden for the blind, playing fields, tea kiosk and the War Memorial Museum. Take any 63, 64 or 65 bus from the Downtown Bus Terminal.

Botanic Gardens, Hill Road, Manurewa, alongside the Southern Motorway, have a good collection of native flora, and herb and rose gardens.

Cornwall Park in Epsom is home to Acacia Cottage, Auckland's oldest dwelling. There is also extensive parkland with playing fields, grazing sheep, tea kiosk and One Tree Hill, a dormant volcano that was once a Maori Fort. Take bus 302, 305 or 312 from Victoria Street East.

Eden Gardens, Omana Road, Epsom, ph 638 8395, are landscaped gardens established in an old quarry on the slopes of Mt Eden. Open daily 9am-4.30pm, admission is $2 adults, children free. Take bus 283 from Downtown or 297 from Wellesley Street outside the Civic Centre.

Ellerslie Racecourse, Greenlane Road, Greenlane, has excellent gardens and the grounds are open for viewing daily.

Parnell Rose Gardens, Sir Dove Myer Robinson Park, Gladstone Road, Parnell, has thousands of traditional roses which are a magnificent sight from November through to March.

Tahuna Torea Nature Park, at the end of West Tamaki Road, Glendowie, ph 575 6142, is a wilderness area with nearly sixty wild native and exotic bird species. Leaflets about the reserve can be picked up at shops in nearby Taniwha Street and Beverly Hills. Take bus 755, 756 or 765 from Downtown Bus Terminal Mon-Fri, Bus 715, 719 Sat-Sun.

Waitakere Ranges, 20km west of the city. The drive through the ranges offers excellent views of Auckland Harbour and the city, and to the south Manukau Harbour and the West Coast. There are number of excellent bush walks for all ages. For walking track information contact the Arataki Information Centre (5km from Titirangi), or ph 817 7134.

Auckland Zoological Park
Situated in Motions Road, Western Springs, the zoo is only five minutes from the city and has the largest collection of native and exotic animals in New Zealand. Free talks are given by various animal keepers on Sundays and public holidays. The zoo is open daily 9.30am-5.30pm, although the last admission is at 4.15pm, and entry is $11 adult, $6 child, $28.50 family, ph 360 3819. Busabout departs on the hour from the Downtown Terminal, or take Yellow Bus 045 (Pt Chevalier) from Customs Street East.

Auckland Observatory
The observatory is in One Tree Hill Domain, off Manukau Road, ph 624 1246, and weather permitting you can view the southern sky through a 50cm Zeiss telescope. The Stardome Show times are Tues-Sun 3pm and 4pm, Tues, Thurs-Sun 6.30pm, 7.30pm and 8.30pm, $9 adults, $4.50 children.

Telescope viewing is at 7.30pm on Tues, Thurs and Sat, and costs are $3 adults, $1.50 children.

Kelly Tarlton's Underwater World

The Underwater World is at Orakei Wharf, Tamaki Drive, ph 528 0603, and is open daily 9am-6pm (winter) 9am-9pm (summer). It is well worth a visit as a moving walkway runs through huge underwater tanks that contain a large variety of NZ fish as well as a bronze whaler shark. Admission is $18 adult, $9 child, and transport from the city is by bus 736, 756 or 766, or by either of the Explorer buses. There is a souvenir shop and continuous showing of a short movie about the adventures of the late Kelly Tarlton.

Expo Pavilion of New Zealand

The pavilion that was so popular with visitors to World Expo '88 in Brisbane is now set in parkland. Features include a giant waterfall, bush walk, the origins of the land, New Zealand's history in sport, technology, art and commerce, a restaurant, and shops offering 'Taste of New Zealand'. The complex is open daily from 9.30am-5pm, and there are shows on the hour. There is a 24 hour Infoline, 256 0111, or for details of current entry prices, ph 256 0192.

Rainbow's End Adventure Park

The park has 23 attractions including roller-coaster, pirate ship, human fly wall, mini golf, bumper boats and a video arcade. Situated on the corner of Great South and Wiri Stations Road, opposite the Manukau Shopping Centre, the park is open daily, 10am-8pm during summer holidays, 10am-5pm during winter. The Infoline is 262 2044, and admission prices are Minipass $15 (includes 3 rides); Superpass $30 adults, $20 children (unlimited rides), up to Familypass $124 (2 adults/4 children with unlimited rides).

Sheep World

Situated on Highway 1, 4km from Warkworth, 45 minutes drive north, is a 30 acre property which has sheep shearing and sheepdog demonstrations. Open daily 9am-5pm, ph 425 7444, $13.50 adults, $7.50 children.

Glenbrook Vintage Railway

The 70-years-old carriages depart from Glenbrook Station (7km east of Waiuku) on the hour from 11am-4pm, and travel 12km (return) of the old Waiuku branch line. Open every Sunday from the end of October to June, and each day of the Labour Weekend, Auckland Anniversary, Easter and over the Christmas period. Fares are $9 adult, $4 child, $22 family, and there are picnic and barbecue areas, refreshments, souvenirs and games for the whole family. For more information, ph 636 9361.

Harbour Cruises

The harbour and the bridge dominate the Auckland scenery and you will no doubt want to see them closer. The Harbour Bridge was opened to traffic in May 1959 after nearly a hundred years of proposals and rejections. It is 1020.5m long and its 244m navigation span rises 43m above the high-water

Auckland "City of Sails".

mark. When it was opened it had four traffic lanes but because it provided quicker access to the north shore, the area went ahead and soon the four lanes were inadequate. In 1969 another four lanes were added, two to the outside of each side of the bridge.

The best way to see the harbour and bridge is by taking a cruise.

Devonport Ferries, Ferry Building, Quay Street, City, ph 377 1771, have a catamaran Seabus service between Auckland and Devonport leaving every hour on the hour. They also have the historic ferry MV *Kestrel* which operates regular cruises with music, restaurant and bar on board.

Devonport Wharf has 26 specialty shops, Torpedo Bay Tavern and Grill, Port o' Call Seafood Restaurant and a Licensed Foodcourt, and they are all open seven days from 10am until late.

Fullers Cruise Centre, Ferry Building, Quay Street, City, ph 367 9111, offers luncheon cruises, coffee cruises, dinner cruises, and cruises to Rangitoto and Motuihe, Kawau Island, Great Barrier Island and Waiheke. They can arrange diving and fishing trips.

Quickcat to Waiheke, Ferry Building, Quay Street, City, ph 367 9111, operates seven days with six departures a day. The island's attractions include beaches, bush, scenic walks, arts, crafts, horse riding, and there are many restaurants.

The Pride of Auckland Company, Downtown Airline Terminal, cnr Quay & Albert Streets, ph 373 4557. They also have boats with the blue &white sails, and have luncheon and dinner cruises daily.

Subritzky Shipping Line, Half Moon Bay, Bucklands Beach, ph 534 5663, has a regular vehicular ferry service to/from Waiheke Island and Half Moon Bay.

Islands

The Hauraki Gulf Islands

The **Hauraki Gulf Islands** offer visitors a chance to get away from the rush of the city and relax without travelling too far. You can make it a day trip, or you can spend the night on some of the islands.

Waiheke

Waiheke is the largest island in the inner gulf and has a resident population of around 6000, which swells to over 30,000 during peak holiday time. According to legend the Maori canoe *Arawa* landed at Putiki Bay in the 13th century. The first European visitor was Samuel Marsden in 1820, and the first European settler was boat-builder Thomas Maxwell, who took up residence in 1825. The island is 19km from Auckland and the ferry trip takes 35 minutes. *The Helicopter Line* has flights from Auckland and they take 10 minutes, ph 377 4406.

Waiheke Rental Cars have an office at the ferry terminal at Matiatia, ph 372 8635, and they hire out cars, jeeps, motorcycles, scooters and push-bikes, and provide maps and information.

Guided rural, bush and beach treks are available from Shepherds Point Riding Centre, Onetangi Road, Waiheke Island, ph 372 8104, and bookings are essential. **This is a great place for a break away from the pressures of city life. Contact the Information Centre about how to rent a cottage for a couple of days.**

Rakino Island

Rakino Island can be reached by Sinclairs Ferry Division, ph 372 6892, leaving Auckland Fri at 6.30pm, Sat 9am and Sun 9am. The island has an area of 146ha, 10ha of which is owned by the Hauraki Gulf Park Board. Woody Bay is a popular beach.

Rangitoto Island

Rangitoto Island is a beautiful island formed by a volcanic eruption around 250 years ago. Fullers Cruises, ph 367 9111, have a service from Auckland that departs at 9.30am and 11.30am daily, and 2pm Sat-Sun. Make sure you wear good walking shoes so you can walk to the crater summit for spectacular views. The walk takes about an hour each way.

Great Barrier Island

Great Barrier Island is 88km off mainland New Zealand and is famous for its long white surf beaches and unspoiled bushland. It is also a very popular fishing spot. The Visitor Information

Office and Travel Centre, c/- Safari Tours, RD 1, Great Barrier Island, ph 429 0448, can provide information and arrange bookings for accommodation, fishing charters, tours, rental cars and mountain bikes.

The island can be reached by sea or air.

Great Barrier Airlines, ph 275 9120, have regular flights to the island and the trip takes 30 minutes. They were suspended in 1998 from operating for 2 weeks because of 'irregularities'. Maybe go by ferry!

Fullers Cruise Centre, ph 367 9111, have a ferry service, and *Gulf Trans*, Wynyard Wharf, Auckland, ph 373 4036, offer transport on their motorised barges MV *Tasman* and MV *Sealink*. The sea trip takes around two hours. Accommodation on the island ranges from camping grounds to motels and holiday lodges, and there are plenty of restaurants.

Kawau Island

Kawau Island is off the east coast, 60km north of Auckland. It was once the home of an early governor, Sir George Grey, and his Mansion House has been restored and opened to the public. The island offers plenty of bush walks and picnic spots. **Ferry services** are offered by: *Matata Cruises*, ph 425 6169, from Sandspit (Warkworth); *Warkworth Taxi and Charter Service*, ph 425 9081 from Warkworth Information Centre, on request..

Motuihe and **Motutapu** can be reached by *Fullers Gulf Ferries*, ph 367 9102, and are great places to get away from it all.

Beaches

The **city beaches** are along Tamaki Drive and in the suburb of Herne Bay, and are easily accessible by public transport. Judges Bay, Okahu Bay, Mission Bay, Kohimarama, St Heliers, Lady's Bay, Gentleman's Bay and Karaka Bay all have white sand and are good for sailing, boating, fishing, water skiing and swimming. Skiers must stay 200m off shore.

There are numerous boat ramps along Tamaki Drive, and most beaches have picnic spots, play areas, public toilets and changing sheds.

The **eastern beaches** are on the coastline facing the Tamaki Strait, south-east of the city. Bucklands, Eastern Mellons Bay,

Howick, Cockle Bay, Omana, Maraetai, Umupula, Kawakawa Bay and Orere Point are all sheltered by the offshore islands of Waiheke and Ponui, and have either white sand or shingle. Most have good swimming areas, and Eastern Creek has marked lanes for water skiers.

Waikowhai Bay, Blockhouse Bay, Wood Bay, French Bay, Titirangi Beach, Laingholm, Mill Bay, Cornwallis, Kaitarakihi and Huia are on the south facing coast of **Manukau Harbour**. Most have sandy beaches and grassed picnic areas, and offer good swimming for children.

North Shore beaches include Devonport, Cheltenham, Takapuna, Milford, Campbells Bay, Mairangi Bay, Rothesay Bay, Browns Bay and Long Bay, and are accessible by bus and ferry. Most have sheltered sandy coastlines, grassed picnic areas and change rooms. Browns Bay and Upper Harbour have marked lanes for water skiing.

The best-known of the **west coast** beaches are Cornwallis, Huia, Whatipu, Karekare, Piha, Bethells and Muriwai. Cornwallis and Huia are on the coast of Manukau Harbour and are sheltered, the others are ocean beaches, with black sand and crashing waves. Several are patrolled by life savers, and it is wise to swim between the flags as there are strong rips that are very dangerous. Muriwai is one of Auckland's regional parks and has New Zealand's northernmost mainland gannet colony.

The Wine Trail

West Auckland is one of the country's major grape growing areas, and the historic trail of vineyards follows a route along Lincoln Road and Henderson Valley to Taipaki. Most wineries have tasting rooms and some have restaurants or picnic areas. Auckland Adventures, ph 528 3036, have bus and minibus tours to the vineyards, and offer a pick-up service from city centre hotels.

Sport and Recreation

Abseiling
Abseil New Zealand can arrange trips for experienced and

inexperienced individuals and groups, ph 473 6631.

Bungy Jumping
Bungy Bats, Freemans Bay, Halsey Street, City, ph 303 0030 - open daily 11am-6pm.

Golf
Chamberlain Park Municipal Golf Course, Western Springs, ph 846 6758 - 18-hole course - club and buggy hire - bus 045 from Victoria Street West.
Takapuna Golf Course, Northcote Road, ph 443 5002 - 18-hole course - club and buggy hire - driving range - bus 922 (Mon-Sat), 927 (Sun) from Victoria Street West.

Horse Riding
Paradise Valley Ranch, Goudie Road, off Rimmers Road, Helensville, ph 420 7269.
Fruitfields Riding Centre, Highway 18, Coatesville, ph 415 8487.

Ice Skating
Paradice Rink, Lansford Crescent, Avondale, ph 828 8286.

Indoor Bowls
Target Bowls, Royal Oak Bowling Centre, 685 Mt Albert Road, ph 624 3569.

Roller Skating
Skatelands, Mountain Road, Panmure, ph 570 4811.

Scuba Diving
Day trips available for all levels of experience, ph Rex Gilbest 833 9886.

Snooker
Pot Black Snooker Centre, 119 Lincoln Road, Henderson, ph 837 1611 - open Mon-Fri noon-11pm, Sat-Sun 11am-11pm.
Royal Oak Entertainment Centre, 685 Mt Albert Road, ph 624 3569 - open daily 8.30am-11pm.

Squash
Auckland Squash Centre, cnr Karaka & France Streets, City, ph 379 4115 - open Mon-Fri 9am-10.30pm, Sat 9am-6pm, Sun 9am-8pm.

Swimming Pools

Aquatic Park, Parakai Domain, 45km north of Auckland, ph 420 8998 - open daily 10am-10pm.

Takapuna Aquatic Centre, 37 Killarney Street, Takapuna, ph 486 3286 - open Mon, Wed, Fri 7am-8.30pm, Tues, Thurs 7am-6pm, Sat-Sun 10am-6pm.

Tepid Baths, 22 Customs Street West, ph 379 4794 - open Mon-Fri 6am-10pm, Sat-Sun 7am-8pm.

Walwera, 35km north of Auckland, ph 426 5369 - open Mon-Fri 9.30am-10pm, Sat-Sun 9.30am-11pm.

West Auckland Swimming Complex, Alderman Drive, Henderson, ph 837 5505 - open Sun-Fri 6am-7pm, Sat 6am-9pm.

Tennis

ASB Tennis Centre, 48 Stanley Street, City, ph 373 3623 - open Mon-Fri 7am-11pm, Sat-Sun 8am-11pm. Equipment can also be hired.

Windsurfing

Lessons and hire of equipment are available from the Tamaki Yacht Club at Tamaki Beach, and at Mission Bay.

Spectator Sports

Auckland's most famous sporting venue is probably Eden Park, off Sandringham Road, as it is home to international **Rugby** and **Cricket** matches.

Greyhound Racing

Auckland Greyhound Racing Club Inc, Orlando Drive, Manukau City, ph 263 7077 has meetings every month with full totalisator facilities. Admission is $2 per person.

Horse Racing

Ellerslie Racecourse, Greenlane Road, Greenlane, ph 524 4069, is the premier racecourse in the country. The grounds are immaculately landscaped and there is also a racing museum.

Avondale Racecourse, Ash Street, Avondale, ph 828 3309, also has regular meetings.

Alexandra Park Raceway, Greenlane Road, Epsom, ph 630 5660 is the main trotting venue, and home to the Trotting Hall of Fame.

Bay of Plenty

Holiday makers from all over the country head for the Bay of Plenty for its surfing, swimming, boating and deep-sea fishing. The Bay is also the home of the famous kiwi fruit, with many orchards around Te Puke devoted to this export-dollar fruit.

To get to this region take the motorway south to Pokeno, approximately 50km from Auckland, then turn off onto Highway 2.

Coromandel Peninsula

The attractions of the Coromandel Peninsula are many. It is largely covered by forest through which wind many bush walks. Gem fossicking is popular in the area and there are many historical mining relics in the bush dating back to the gold mining era. As well, there are wonderful sweeping ocean beaches where you can swim, surf, fish, dive or collect shellfish. The economic activities of the region range from forestry and farming to commercial fishing, horticulture and wine making, to cottage industry arts and crafts. Visitors like to come to the area for its unspoiled environment and peace and quiet. For further information contact the Visitor Information Office in Thames.

How to Get There

By Air
Air Coromandel has a twice daily service between Auckland and Whitianga Airport, ph (09) 275 9120. The company also services Pauanui, Matarangi, Tauranga, Whangarei, Great Barrier Island and Coromandel township.

By Bus
InterCity have a regular service to Thames from Auckland, Hamilton and Tauranga.

By Car

From Pokeno, travel along Highway 2 until you reach Waitakaruru. Just after this town there is a turn-off to Thames, the largest town on the peninsula. Thames is 115km from Auckland.

Tourist Information

Thames Visitor Information Office, 405 Queen Street, ph(07)868 7284.

Sightseeing

Thames

Thames is the service town for the region. It has good accommodation, a hostel, craft shops, gallery, wharf, boat ramp, an historical museum (cnr Cochrane and Pollen Streets, open 1-4pm, entry $2.50 adults, $1 children), a mineralogical museum (cnr Brown and Cochrane Streets, open Tues-Sun 11am-3pm, entry $2.50 adults, $1 children), a gold mine and stamper battery (Main Road, north end of town, check with the Information Office for hours, entry $4 adults, $2 children) and an airfield. Tours of the mine are available and can be arranged at most times through the Information Office. In the summer time there is usually someone available at the mine.

Thames is an excellent starting point and provides good access to all of the Coromandel Peninsula - boating, fishing, etc.

From Thames you can drive 54km north along Highway 25, which follows the west coast of the peninsula to **Coromandel**. It was here in 1852 that gold was first found in New Zealand, and it is still a popular rockhounding (fossicking) area. Coromandel is a favourite holiday resort offering boating, fishing, swimming, and bush and coast walks.

From here Highway 25 crosses the peninsula to Kuaotunu, and then heads along the east coast to Whitanga. Continue on this road past Coroglen and there is a turn-off to Hahei Beach and Hot Water Beach. Hahei Beach is popular with divers as the sand is coloured pink from crushed sea shells. There are two blowholes nearby, as well as two Pa sites. An easy two hour walk will take you to an underwater grotto. From Hahei

Beach you have to backtrack to get to Hot Water Beach where hot water springs bubble up in the sand. It is best seen at low tide.

Back on Highway 25 you pass through Whennakite and then Tairua, which has ocean and estuary beaches and is a great place for surfing, wind surfing, fishing, canoeing, sailing, etc. Across the estuary from Tairua is **Pauanui**, a particularly attractive resort, well planned and built amongst pine trees. Pauanui has a beautiful ocean beach.

From Tairua you could head back to Thames and Auckland, or keep heading south along the coast to Whangamata, another popular holiday resort. Highway 25 rejoins Highway 2 at Waihi. Gold was discovered at Waihi in 1878, but it wasn't until 1892 that the Martha Mine brought prosperity to the town. At the beginning of this century Waihi had three times the population of Hamilton. The Martha Mine closed in 1952 after hundreds of kilograms of gold and silver had been won from it. There is a mining museum in the town that has photos of gold mining sites and also explains details of the Martha Mine. **From Waihi continue along Highway 2 to Tauranga.**

Tauranga/Mount Maunganui

Tauranga is called the sunshine city of the Kiwi Fruit Coast and is surrounded by orchards and pine forests. A wide variety of fruit (including tamarillos and citrus) is grown in the district but, of course, kiwi fruit predominate. It is a rich dairying area as well, and Tauranga is New Zealand's largest export port. It began as a missionary station and was the scene of one of the bloodiest battles of the Maori Wars.

Across the harbour is Mount Maunganui (or as the Kiwis affectionately call it The Mount). The ocean beach there is New Zealand's most popular surfing beach.

The whole of the Bay of Plenty area has an extremely mild climate and receives about 10% more sunshine than Auckland. The average temperature is usually, one degree celsius warmer than Auckland.

How to Get There

By Rail
The daily *Kaimai Express* travels between Auckland and Tauranga, via Hamilton.

By Bus
InterCity has three daily Auckland-Tauranga services leaving at 7.45am, 1.30pm and 6pm, arriving at 11.15am, 5.15pm and 9.40pm respectively.

Newmans Auckland-Tauranga leaves at 2.50pm and arrives at 6.55pm, Sun-Fri.

Inter-City has a daily Rotorua-Tauranga service leaving at noon and arriving at 1.05pm.

Newmans daily Rotorua- Tauranga service leaves at 5.40pm and arrives at 6.05pm.

Tourist Information
Tauranga Visitor Information Office, The Strand, ph (07) 578 8103.

Accommodation
There is no shortage of accommodation in Tauranga, but booking ahead is still a wise move. Following is a selection with prices for a double room per night in NZ$, which should be used as a guide only. The telephone area code is 07.

Hotels
Bennett's Tauranga Motor Inn, cnr 15 Avenue & Turrett Street, ph/fax 578 5041 - 22 units, licensed restaurant, swimming pool, spa, mineral pools - $80-99.

Bureta Park Motor Inn, Vale Street, ph 576 2221, fax 576 1226 - 19 units, licensed restaurant, swimming pool - $88.

Motels
Macy's Motor Inn, cnr 11th Avenue & Edgecumbe Road, ph 577 9764, fax 578 9279 - 18 units, BYO restaurant (Mon-Thurs), swimming pool, spa - $95-110.

Aaron Court Motel, 151 Waihi Road, ph 578 0135, fax 578 2701 - 14 units, private indoor spa, swimming pool - $80-96.

Summit Motor Lodge, 213 Waihi Road, ph 578 1181, fax 578 1354 - 24 units - swimming pool, spa, games room - $80-110.

Bay City Motel, 166 Waihi Road, ph 578 0588, fax 578 9335 - 14 units, swimming pool - $82-95.

Birchwood Motel, 249 Waihi Road, ph 578 4461,fax 578 6604 - 7 units, private spa, swimming pool - $79.

Eighteenth Avenue Motel, 50 Eighteenth Avenue, ph 578 3179, fax 578 3178 - 21 units, swimming pool, indoor mineral pool, sauna - $70-88.

Cobblestone Court Motel, 86 Chapel Street, Otumoetai, ph 576 9028, fax 576 1397 - 12 units, swimming pool, spa - $70-88.

Boulevard Spa Motel, 261 Waihi Road, ph 578 3268, fax 578 3298 - 12 units, private spa pool, swimming pool - $70-82.

Bridgeway Motor Lodge, 93 Turret Road, ph 578 9186, fax 571 8655 - 8 units, swimming pool, private spa pool - $70-82.

Tauranga Motel, 1 Second Avenue, ph 578 7079, fax 578 0812 - 26 units, private beach access - $69-125 per room.

Hostels

Bell Lodge, 39 Bell Street, ph 578 6344, 578 6342 - communal kitchen, dining room, lounge, laundry, barbecue - 4 double cabins (en suite) $36; 4 cabins sleep 4 (en suite) $42 pp; 2 bunkrooms $15 pp; tent site $8 pp.

Waireinga Hostel, 171 Elizabeth Street, ph/fax 578 5064, - YHA hostel, full day facilities and several family rooms - $15 pp.

Motor Camps and Cabins

Bayshore Leisure Park, Highway 29, Bayshore, ph/fax 544 0700 - communal kitchen, showers, toilets, laundry, store, hot mineral pools, bbq - camping $8 pp; powered sites $9 adults, $5 children; 4 cabins sleep 2-6 with kitchen facilities $30 x 2.

Omokoroa Tourist Park, 165 Omokoroa Road, RD2, ph/fax 548 0857 - communal kitchen, toilets, showers, laundry, TV room, games room, 3 hot mineral pools, store - camping $9 pp; powered sites $11 pp; 8 tourist flats, kitchen facilities $55-59 x 2; 7 cabins, kitchen facilities $30-39 x 2.

Mount Maunganui has a smaller selection of accommodation, and following are some samples.

Hotels & Motels

Bayfair Motor Inn, 21 Girven Road, Mt Maunganui, ph 575 5089, fax 575 9768 - 42 rooms (private facilities), licensed restaurant, bar, swimming pool - $95-105.

Fawlty Towers Waterfront Motel, 28 The Mall, ph/fax 575 5883 - 4 units - $75.

Ocean Waves Motel, 74 Marine Park, ph/fax 575 4594 - 7 units - $90-145.

Outrigger Beach Motel, 48 Marine Parade, ph 575 4445, fax 575 8024 - 18 units, barbecue - $85-150.

Wainui Thermal Motel, 35 Maunganui Road, ph 575 3526, fax 575 3556 - 5 units, thermal pool and spa - $70-110.

Motor Camps & Caravan Parks

Cosy Corner, 40 Ocean Beach Rd, Omanu, ph 575 5899, fax 575 5670 - pool, barbecue - powered sites $11 adults, $5.50 children; tourist flats (sleep 4) $50 x 2; on-site caravans $38 x 2.

Golden Grove Motor Park, 73 Girven Road, ph/fax 575 5821, games room, private spa pool, shop - powered sites $10 adults, $5 children; tourist flats (sleep 2-6) $55 x 2; cabin (sleep 2-4) $35-40 x 2.

Local Transport

Taxis

Tauranga Taxi Society, The Strand, ph 578 6086.

Car Hire

Avis, ph 578 4204; Budget, ph 578 5156; Hertz, ph 578 9143.

Eating Out

Chateau du Raisin, 404 Pollen Street, Thames, ph 868 9838 - Licensed - open daily 11am-late - wide choice menu, but the attraction is the wine list with over 200 to choose from - under $25 - credit cards accepted.

Harbourside Brasserie & Bar, Old Yacht Club, Strand Extension, ph 571 0520 - Licensed - open daily 11.30am-late - regional winner in *Cheap Eats* - over $25 - credit cards accepted.

Baywatch, cnr The Strand & Wharf Street, Tauranga, ph 578 8322 - Licensed - open daily 11.30am-2.30pm, 5pm-late - overlooks the harbour and has outdoor settings - over $25 - credit cards accepted.

Bella Mia, 73A Devonport Road, Tauranga, ph 578 4996 - BYO - open Tues-Sun noon-2pm, 5pm-late - pastas and pizzas with checked tablecloths - under $25 - no credit cards.

Circus Bar & Grill, cnr First Avenue & Devonport Rd, Tauranga, ph 578 1930 - Licensed - open Mon-Fri 11.30am-late, Sat 5pm-late, Sun 10.30am-late - under $25 - credit cards accepted.

Sightseeing

The **Strand Gardens** along the harbour are a pleasant contrast to the hustle and bustle of the main shopping centre on the other side of the street. The **Maori War Canoe** (Te Awanui) is on the downtown foreshore. It is used on special occasions and was carved by Mr Tuti Tukaokao in the traditional manner of the great war canoes.

The Coronation Pier and the Tauranga-Mount ferry terminal are found behind the Herries Gardens on The Strand.

Tauranga Historic Village, 155 17th Avenue, is a must. Allow plenty of time as it features a recreation of a typical Bay of Plenty village of the 19th century, with changing displays. Regular "live days" are a feature, so check with Visitor Information as it's worth visiting when the machinery and vehicles are working, or during a craft market. Concerts are also held here. The museum traces the development of Maori culture as well as that of the town. Open daily 10am-4pm and admission is $10 adult.

Monmouth Redoubt is all that remains of the town fortifications that were built in the 1860s during the Maori Wars. The gory Battle of Gate Pa, in which the British suffered heavy losses, was fought in Tauranga in 1864. The site of the Gate Pa battle is in Cameron Road and is now occupied by the Parish Church of St George. Inside the church there is a map of the battle. Robbins Park is adjacent to the Redoubt. This beautifully maintained park overlooks the port and features formal rose gardens and a begonia house.

The **Military Cemetery** in Cliff Road stands on the site of a Maori Pa. A walk through here tells the story of Tauranga's history as it is the resting place of many who were killed in the Maori Wars, both Pakeha and Maori.

The Elms in Mission Street, off Cliff Road, was the original mission house, built in 1838. The garden is amongst the oldest in the country. The two tall norfolk pines in the grounds were used by early sailors as navigational markers.

Tauranga's Marina is found on the eastern head of the harbour. The whole of the reclaimed area surrounding it has been developed as a recreation park. There is a boat launching ramp, and the Yacht & Power Boat Club has its headquarters there. Deep sea fishing charters can be arranged through them, or through the Information Office.

Mount Maunganui has three main attractions:
The Mount which is 220m high and was once a Maori Fortress. The view from the summit is spectacular, and on a clear day you can see White Island, 80km away. There are several walking tracks around the lower portion of The Mount, in addition to the one to the summit.

The Ocean Beach, which is 13km long, and is a mecca for thousands of holiday makers in the summer. There are also natural hot salt water pools in Adams Avenue, Mt Maunganui, ph 577 7201 - open daily 8am-10pm, and admission is charged.

The Port of Tauranga, New Zealand's largest export trading port. A great variety of cargoes are handled here.

Sport
Canoes, surfboards, windsurfers and catamarans can be hired on the harbourside.

Tauranga Aero Club operates scenic tours daily.

There are three golf courses and a racecourse, and the Bay Park Raceway at Mt Maunganui.

Festivals
The Jazz Festival is held at Easter; The Festival of Tauranga is February/March.

Outlying Attractions

Katikati Bird Gardens, Walkers Road East, Katikati, is a bird sanctuary and botanical gardens. Open daily 9am-4pm, and admission is $6.

Fernland Spa, a little over a kilometre along Cambridge Road, off Waihi Road, Tauranga, has hot pools and barbecue areas. Open daily 10am-10pm.

New Zealand's World of Horses, 14km north of Tauranga off Highway 2 at Station Road, ph 548 0404, is a refreshingly original equestrian theme park. You can visit the working stables and meet the stable companions, explore the curios and graphic displays, browse through the arts and crafts and souvenir shops, or go trekking or trail riding. There's even Shetland Ponies for the littlies. Also in the complex is Stables Coffee Lounge and a Courtyard Tea Garden.

Kiwifruit Country is 6km from Te Puke (the kiwi fruit capital of the world) on the main Tauranga-Rotorua Highway, ph 573 6340.

You can take a ride on the tractor train (shaped to look like kiwi fruit of course), see the NZ-shaped lake with its amazing tap fountain, and visit the Palace of Magic Mirrors. It has a licensed restaurant, an audio-visual theatre, information and souvenir centre, and you can sample kiwi fruit wine and other exotic fruits. Phone the complex for hours and admission fees.

Next door is **Te Puke Vintage Auto Barn**,with 70 vintage and classic vehicles.

Rafting on the Wairoa River (only minutes from Tauranga) is an exhilarating experience for all from teenagers to grandparents. The Wairoa is one of New Zealand's most accessible rivers, and a great place to try rafting. The season is limited due to hydro-electric development on the river. *Woodrow Raft Tours*, ph 576 2628, can answer queries.

White Island, 80km out to sea, is an active volcano from which steam rises continually. The locals say that this is the safety valve for the whole of the thermal region. Trips to the island can be arranged by boat or by air from Tauranga - contact the Information Office to book. From Tauranga you can either travel along the Bay of Plenty to Whakatane on Highway 2 and then along Highway 30 to Rotorua, OR take the more direct route to Rotorua along Highway 33. The road between Tauranga and Whakatane follows the coast for quite a distance, past sandy beaches and sandstone cliffs.

On the outskirts of **Whakatane** is the New Zealand Forest Products Board Mill, a large paper mill that is open for inspection. On The Strand in the centre of Whakatane is a wooden arch where Maoris were ritually tattooed. It is now a war memorial. At Whakatane Heads, 2km from town, a plaque commemorates the arrival of the legendary Mataatua canoe. High on the heads if a statue of Wairara, the daughter of the canoe's captain. According to legend this woman saved the women and the canoe from destruction. As the men slept on the beach the canoe started to drift away from the beach with the women on board. Wairara awoke and realised their plight and called out "I'm acting as a man" as she grabbed the oars which were considered taboo to the women. The other women followed suit and that is how the town got its name. Whakatane means 'to act like a man'.

White Island Scenic Flights, ph 308 4188, have helicopter flights from Whakatane that land on White Island where you can walk across the moonscape, and sense the imposing volcanic power. They depart from Silverhill Deer Farm.

From Whakatane, Highway 30 goes to Rotorua. This road crosses the Rangitaiki Plains, and winds through the fern-clad Rotoma Hills and past Lakes Rotoma, Rotoehu and Rotoiti before reaching Lake Rotorua.

Waikato

The Waikato region lies in a broad basin surrounded by hills, and is south of Auckland, west of Rotorua and north of Taupo. The region takes its name from the Waikato River, the longest river in New Zealand, which begins its 425km journey from Lake Taupo and empties into the sea at Port Waikato.

The Waikato farmlands are renowned for their butter, cheese and lamb. The Te Rapa milk powder factory is the largest plant of its kind in existence. Milk from the surrounding area is brought daily to the factory by stainless steel tankers for processing. The main city in the region is Hamilton.

Hamilton

Hamilton is the third largest city (population 156,000) in the North Island. It is a university town as well as a manufacturing town, and the service centre for the Waikato region.

The area was inhabited by the Tainui Maori people for two to three centuries before the arrival of the first Europeans in the 1830s. The first settlers to venture inland to the river came across a village named Kirikirioa on the west bank. It was the smallest of three Maori villages in the area, but today it is the largest inland city in New Zealand.

The first European settlement began on August 24, 1864, when a party of soldier-settlers established a camp near the present Memorial Park. The town was named after Captain John Fane Charles Hamilton, an officer of the Royal Navy, who was killed at the Battle of Gate Pa, near Tauranga, in 1864.

How to Get There

By Air
International
Freedom Air, owned by Air New Zealand operates flights to and from Hamilton to the Australian cities of Coolangatta, Sydney and Brisbane. This is a budget airline owned and operated by

Air New Zealand that was set up in competition to *Kiwi Air* which subsequently closed down. Many people blame the competition created by this Air New Zealand subsidary.

Sydney to Hamilton -   Monday, Friday
Coolangatta to Hamiton   Saturday
Brisbane to Hamilton   Thursday, Sunday
Cost is between A$419-$569.

Domestic

Air New Zealand Link has daily flights to Hamilton from: Auckland, Blenheim, Christchurch, Dunedin, Gisborne, Hokitika, Invercargill, Napier/Hastings, Nelson, New Plymouth, Palmerston North, Timaru, Wanganui, Wellington and Whangarei.

There are less frequent services from:
Kaitaia - daily except Sat
Westport - daily except Sat

Airport Shuttle, PO Box 9106, Hamilton, provides a service for travel from the airport to the city terminal at the corner of Ward & Anglesea Streets, ph (07) 847 5618. The fares are $7 adults, $2 children. A door to door service is also available.

By Rail

The daily day-time *Overlander* between Auckland and *Wellington* stops at Hamilton, as does the Mon-Sat *Northerner* night service.

By Bus

InterCity and *Newmans* have services to Hamilton from all major towns in New Zealand.

By Car

Hamilton-Auckland is 130km - approx 1 hour 40 minutes.
Hamilton-Wellington is 521km - approx 8 hours.
Hamilton-Rotorua is 109km - approx 1 hour 45 minutes.
Hamilton-Waitomo Caves is 72km - approx 1 hour.
Hamilton-Taupo is 153km - approx 2 hours 30 minutes.

Tourist Information

Tourism Waikato is in the Municipal Buildings, Garden Place, ph (07) 839 3580. They can book accommodation, transport and sightseeing as well as handling all enquiries.

Accommodation

As would be expected in a city of its size, Hamilton has a wide range of accommodation. Here is a selection with prices in NZ$ for a double room per night, which should be used as a guide only. The telephone area code is 07.

Hotels

Hotel Alcamo, 290 Ulster Street, ph 839 0200, fax 838 3240 - 56 suites, licensed restaurant, bar, swimming pool, spa - $120-350.

Hillcrest Lodge, 334 Cobham Drive, Hillcrest, ph 856 7075, fax 856 7073 - 24 units, restaurant, swimming pool, spa, barbecue area - $79-95.

Glenview International Hotel, Ohaupo Road, Melville, ph 843 6049, fax 843 3324 - 35 rooms, licensed restaurant, swimming pool - $87-145.

Aaron Court Motor Inn, 86 Ulster Street, ph 838 2599, fax 838 2594 - 44 units, licensed restaurant, bar, swimming pool, spa - $90-110.

Ambassador Motor Inn, 86 Ulster Street, ph 839 5111, fax 839 5104 - 53 units, licensed restaurant, swimming pool - $80-150.

Motels

Fountain City Motor Inn, 305 Ulster Street, ph 839 3107, fax 839 3108 - 35 units, swimming pool, spa, barbecue - $110.

Camelot Motor Inn, 231 Ulster Street, ph 834 2122, fax 834 2199 - 31 units, swimming pool, spa - $105-150.

AA Host Tudor Motor Lodge, 24 Thackeray Street, ph 838 2244, fax 838 2243 - 24 units, licensed restaurant next door, swimming pool, spa - $75-110.

Chloes Motor Inn, 181-185 Ulster Street, ph 839 3410, fax 839 3427 - 14 units, meals available, swimming pool - $96-135.

Boundary Court Motor Inn, 36 Boundary Road, ph 855 9082, fax 855 0077 - 20 units, swimming pool, spa - $88-105.

Manor Inn, 199-209 Grey Street, Hamilton East, ph 856 9029, fax 856 9028 - 24 units, sauna, spa - $80-110.

Sherwood Motel, 240-242 Ulster Street, ph 839 5380, fax 839 5389 - 10 units, swimming pool, spa - $75.

Abbotsford Court Motel, 18 Abbotsford Street, ph 839 0661, fax 838 9335 - 10 units - $62-82.

Abbey Travel Lodge Motel, 12 Lorne Street, Melville, ph/fax 843

4368 - 10 units, spa - $70.
Manhattan Lodge, 218 Grey Street, Hamilton East, ph/fax 856
3785 - 9 units, spa - $72-76.

Motor Camps

Hamilton East Tourist Camp, 61 Cameron Road, Hamilton East,
ph 856 6220/fax - powered sites $16 x 2, children $4; tourist
flats $45 x 2; cabins (sleep 2-7) $35 x 2.
Municipal Motor Camp, 14 Ruakura Road, Claudelands, ph 855
8255, fax 855 3865 - powered sites $17 x 2, tent sites $15 x 2;
accommodation $24-45.

Youth Hostel

Helen Heywood Hostel, 1190 Victoria Street, ph 838 0009, fax 838
0837 - $15 per person.

Local Transport

Bus

Hamilton has an efficient bus service, and a timetable of all
routes is readily available for 50c. The bus terminal and ticket
office is on the corner of Ward and Anglesea Sts, ph 834 3457.

Taxi

Hamilton Taxis, ph 847 7477, have a seven day 24-hour taxi
service, and can also arrange sightseeing tours.

Car Hire

Budget, 404 Anglesea Street, ph 8383585; Hertz, 8 Milton Street,
ph 839 4824; Avis, 413 Anglesea Street, ph 839 4915; Thrifty, 532
Anglesea Street, ph 838 0350.

Eating Out

Hamilton has a good selection of restaurants to satisfy every
taste and budget.
Here is a selection for you to try.
Valentine's Restaurant & Bar, cnr Clarence & Anglesea Streets,
ph 839 1990 - **Licensed** - open daily for lunch and dinner,
Fri-Sun breakfast - **$30-45** - credit cards accepted.
MV Waipa Delta, Memorial Park, ph 854 9419 - **Licensed** - lunch
noon-2pm, afternoon tea 3-4.30pm, dinner 7-11pm -

paddlesteamer floating restaurant - **lunch less than $25, dinner $30-45** - credit cards accepted.

Hungry Horse Bar & Restaurant, southern end of Victoria Street (in the historic Hamilton Hotel building), ph 839 2515 - **Licensed** - open Tues-Sun 11.45am-2pm, nightly from 5pm - steak/seafood and largest salad bar in Hamilton - special children's menu & video room for kids while mums and dads enjoy the bar - **around $25** - credit cards accepted.

Tosca's Restaurant, 931 Victoria St, ph 834 3045 - **Licensed** - open Mon-Sat for lunch and dinner - **$25-30** - credit cards accepted.

Gerards, 252 Ulster Street, ph 839 5949 - **Licensed/BYO (wine)** - open Mon-Sat for lunch and dinner - **$25-30** - credit cards accepted.

Restaurant Charise, 86 Ulster Street, ph 839 5111 - **Licensed/BYO** - open daily for lunch and dinner - **$25-30** - credit cards accepted.

McDonalds **have three outlets** in Hamilton - cnr Victoria Street & Claudelands Road, ph 838 0247; Greenwood Street, Frankton, ph 847 2780; Chartwell Square Shopping Centre, ph 854 8325.

Pizza Hut **has two** - Ulster Street, ph 839 5050; 124 Grey Street, East Hamilton, ph 856 2966.

KFC **can be found at**: cnr Grey & Wellington Streets, East Hamilton, ph 856 4687; Ulster Street, ph 839 5228; and 111 Greenwood Street, Frankton, ph 847 5888.

Entertainment

Theatres

Andersons Restaurant & Theatre, 106 London Street, ph 839 5957, is open Tues-Fri from noon, Tues-Sun from 6pm, and has live shows and cabaret.

Founders Memorial Theatre, Tristram Street, ph 838 6600.

Hamilton Operatic Society, Trustbank Community Theatre, Clarence Street, ph 839 3082.

Left Bank Theatre, Marlborough Place, ph 839 2162.

Riverlea Telecom Arts Centre, Riverlea Road, ph 856 5450.

Cinemas

Village 5 Cinema Complex, Centreplace Shopping Centre, ph 839 5816.

Bars

Down Under Bar, Basement, Post Office Mall, Victoria St, ph 838 0233 - open Mon-Wed 11am-10pm, Thurs-Sat 11am-late - popular bar/bistro, a place to meet the locals - credit cards accepted.

Victoria's Tavern, 851 Victoria Street, ph 839 2314 - open Mon-Sat 11.30am-11.30pm, dance bands Thurs-Sat - dining room with blackboard menu - credit cards accepted.

Fox & Hounds, Ground Floor, Village 5 Cinema Complex, Ward Street, ph 834 1333 - open Mon-Sat 11am-11pm - English-type pub complete with ploughman's lunches, etc. - cash only.

Shopping

Victoria Street is Hamilton City's main street and shopping drag. The street is often called the "Golden Mile" from claims that the road foundations were made from quartz rock brought from the Karangahake Gorge Coalmines near Waihi.

All shops are open Mon-Fri 9am-5pm, and Sat 9am-noon. Late night shopping, until 9pm, is either on Thurs or Fri. Some shops stay open until 4pm on Sat, and some open on Sun.

Centreplace Shopping Centre, ph 839 5816, is in the "Heart of the City", bounded by Victoria, Bryce and Ward Streets. It is a one-stop shopping experience with dozens of specialty shops, as well as the Fox and Hounds English Pub and the Village 5 Cinema complex. This centre is open until 4pm on Sat, 10am-4pm Sun, and light night shopping is on Thurs.

Chartwell Square, cnr Comnes & Hukanui Roads, ph 855 6153, has over eighty shops, including McDonalds.

Collingwood Court, cnr Collingwood & Alexandra Streets.

Nawton Shopping Centre, cnr Grandview Rd & Hyde Ave is open until 4pm on Saturday, with late night shopping Thursday.

Farmers Department Store is diagonally opposite Collingwood Court.

Sightseeing

Hamilton is situated on the Waikato River, the longest river in New Zealand. Originally a military outpost, the river was the main means of transport for the early pioneers. There are several large hydro-electric power stations on the river as it flows from Mt Ruapehu down to Lake Taupo, through it, and

River Cruises

The old paddlewheel steamer, the Mv *Waipa Delta* was launched in 1877 to transport people and goods on the river. It now has luncheon and dinner cruises and for information on sail times and menus phone 854 9415.

Cruises depart from the jetty in Memorial Park on Memorial Drive.

on to the Tasman Sea. The Waikato meanders its way through Hamilton, and a cruise is one way to see the town.

Hamilton Gardens are set on the banks of the river, and are one of the newest gardens in the country, with new developments continually underway. It's a great place for a picnic and has plenty of parking. Entrances to the gardens are on Hungerford Terrace and Grey Street.

Lake Rotoroa (Hamilton Lake) is surrounded by well-established parks and is a wildlife sanctuary. The Lake is bounded by Ruakiwi Road, Domain Drive and Lake Crescent. The **Waikato University** is one of Hamilton's boasts. Its campus is one of the better ones in the country.

At night the **Mormon Temple** in Tuhikaramea Road is flood-lit and dominates the skyline. It is 8km south-west of the city centre and is open daily 9am-9pm. Guided tours are available.

Waikato Museum of Art and History, cnr Victoria & Grantham Streets, has a collection of Maori artifacts which includes a 140-year-old canoe which was a gift from Queen Dame Te Atairangikaahu. The museum is open daily 10am-4.30pm, and admission is $2 adults, 50c children.

Expressions, the shop at the museum, has a good selection of work by New Zealand's finest craftspeople, including bone carving, jewellery, jade, glass, silk, pottery, and hand-painted and souvenir T-shirts.

Hamilton Zoo is in Brymer Road, ph 838 6720, and is open daily 9am-5pm. Admission is $7 adults, $3.50 children.
Waterworld Centennial Pools, Garnett Avenue, Te Rapa, has four indoor heated pools, including championship, diving and toddlers', outdoor lido pool, spa pools, hydroslide, mini golf,

and picnic and barbecue facilities. The complex is open Mon-Fri 6am-9pm, Sat-Sun 9am-9pm, ph 849 4389, and admission is $3 adults, $1.50 children, $1 spectators.

Top Nut Chocolate Factory, on the road to Gordonton, ph 824 3622, has tours available but bookings are essential. The factory is open daily 9am-5pm, and admission is $5 adults, $2.50 children.

Outlying Attractions

National Agricultural Heritage, Mystery Creek, ph 843 7990, has agricultural displays and wagon rides. It is open Sun-Thurs and admission is $5 adults, $2.50 children.

Te Awamutu is south of Hamilton on Highway 3 and is known as the Rose Town of New Zealand. It public gardens have over 80 varieties of this beautiful flower.

Te Awamutu Museum in Roche Street, contains many Maori treasures and is open daily 10am-4pm, with no admission fee.

The town of **Matamata** is east of Hamilton, and is home to the *Firth Tower Museum*, which was built as a lookout but now contains a collection of local artifacts. Near here are the *Opal Hot Springs*, and the town offers easy access to the Waihou River and the Kaimai Ranges.

Huntly Power Station is north of Hamilton, and is the country's largest electricity generating station. It is operated by Electricorp, ph 828 9590, and is open for inspection 10am-3pm, and admission is free. The Huntly Mining & Cultural Museum in Harlock Place has exhibits on the mining history of the area. It is open daily 10am-3pm and there is no admission charge.
North of Hamilton is Ngaruawahia, an important Maori settlement. The Turangawaewae Marae here is the home of the Maori Queen, Te Arikinui, Dame Te Atairangikaahu.

Waingaro Hot Springs are 23km south-east of Ngaruawahia, and attractions include 3 thermal mineral pools, the longest open hot water slide in New Zealand, bumper boats, a deerpark, and barbecue and picnic facilities. The Springs are open daily 9am-10pm, and there is an entry fee. The complex also has a motel and a caravan park, ph (07) 825 4761.

Agricultural Tours to local farms, orchards and nurseries can be arranged through Agritour, ph 839 1652.

Sport & Recreation

Hamilton has all the sporting facilities you would expect of a city of its size, and the Visitor Information Office can supply you with details.

Tramping

There are a variety of interesting walkways in the Waikato region. The Pirongia Mountain, Maungakawa, Hakarimata, Karamu, Te Aroha Mountain, Raglan, Kakepuku, Mt Maungatautari and Waitomo Walks all incorporate beautiful native bush and scenery.

Maps are available from the Waikato Visitor Information Office of the Department of Lands and Survey.

Fishing

There is good fishing at Raglan and Kawhia, with good trout fishing in the southern Waikato region.

Surfing
Raglan is one of the better surfing beaches in New Zealand.

Golf
Hamilton Golf Club, St Andrews Terrace, ph 849 2069.
Horsham Downs Golf Club, River Road North, ph 829 4709.
Park International Country Club (Westlands), Whatawhata Road, Main Raglan Highway, ph 847 4374.

Ten Pin Bowling
Garnett Avenue, ph 849 7195.

Ice Skating
Hamilton Ice Arena, 4 Kells Place, ph 846 7376.

Horse Riding
Bobundra Riding Academy, opposite Cambridge Golf Course, SH 1, Cambridge, ph 827 7235.
Mikado Horse Riding, SH 1 Hamilton, ph 849 1132.
Waikato Equestrian Centre, Pukete Road, RD 8, Frankton, ph 849 6756.

Spectator Sports
Rugby Park is bounded by Seddon Road, Mill Street, Tristram Street and Willoughby Park.
Te Rapa Race Course is on Te Rapa Road, and details of race meetings will be found in the newspaper.

Waitomo

Among the best known attractions in New Zealand are the glow worm caves at Waitomo (population 234), 75km south of Hamilton.

How to Get There

By Bus
InterCity has a daily service from Hamilton to Waitomo.

By Car

From Hamilton take Highway 3 south to Hangatiki, where there is the turn-off to the Caves.

Tourist Information

Waitomo Caves Visitor Information Office is in Main Street, ph (07) 878 7640.

Accommodation

There is limited accommodation in Waitomo, and many people prefer to stay at either Otorohanga or Te Kuiti. Here is a selection of places available, with prices for a double room per night in NZ$, which should be used as a guide only.

The telephone area code is 07.

Caves Motor Inn, 70m south of Waitomo Caves turn-off, 11km from Te Kuiti, ph/fax 873 8109 - 20 units, licensed restaurant - $65-75. Backpackers' accommodation available - $20-32.

Glow Worm Motel, Waitomo Caves turn-off, Hangatiki, ph 873 8882, fax 873 8856 - 9 units, swimming pool, spa - $69-73.

Waitomo Colonial Motel, 58 Main Road North, Otorohanga, 16km from Caves, ph/fax 873 8289 - 12 units, swimming pool, spa - $75-85.

Panorama Motor Inn, 59 Awakino Road, Te Kuiti, ph 878 8051, fax 878 6782 - 12 units, licensed restaurant, swimming pool - $70-75.

THC Waitomo Caves Hostel, ph 878 8227 - 40 rooms, 2 restaurants, 2 bars - $17 per person.

Otorohanga Kiwi Town Caravan Park and Motor Camp, Domain Drive, Otorohanga, 16km north of Caves, ph/fax 873 8214 - powered sites $15 for 2, tent sites $13 for 2, and on-site caravans $27 per night.

Cavelands Waitomo Ltd, Main Road Waitomo Village, ph 878 7639, fax 878 8895 - powered sites $9 per person; cabins $35 x 2.

Sightseeing

The Caves

The caves are the main attraction and the reason why over 150,000 people visit the area every year. They were known to the early Maoris, but were first rediscovered by Fred Mace in 1887. They have been developed over the years and the Museum of Caves at the Visitor Information Centre has some great displays and an audio-visual show telling you everything there is to know. The Centre is open daily 8.30am-5pm, admission to the museum is $3.50.

Ruakuri Cave
There are three caves, with **Ruakuri** being the largest and most dramatic. **Two Black Water Rafting expeditions, organised by the Museum of Caves, are available in this cave.** Strictly speaking, they are not really rafting trips as transport is by tyre inner tubes, but the thrill of rafting is still there. The first trip takes about three hours and costs $65. The second is, as the brochures say, "bigger, bolder and more mysterious than #1", and bookings have to be made as there is no set timetable. This trip costs $125.

Then there are a couple of **Lost World Adventures**, also organised by the Museum of Caves. The Lost World lies 100m down in the *Mapunga cave system*. Access is by abseiling, then the journeys involve walking, wading and swimming. No previous experience in abseiling is needed as instruction is given on the spot, but these trips are obviously not for the faint-hearted.

Much tamer, but still fascinating, tours of the **Aranui** Cave depart daily at 10am, 11am, 1pm, 2pm and 3pm. They cost $17.50 adults, $9.25 children, and family packages are available.

A trip through the **Glow Worm Grotto** is not to be missed. Transport is by boat on the underground river, and as you drift through, the caves are lit up like fairyland. These tours run every half-hour from 9am-5pm. Costs are $17.50 adults, $9.25 children, and family packages are available.

Above Ground
Meanwhile, above ground there are a few interesting places to visit. The **Ohaki Maori Village** at Waitomo was closed during the winter of 1997, but is expected to re-open for the summer. It has displays of traditional Maori lifestyle and culture, and the

Information Office will be able to tell you the present situation.

The **Waitomo Walkway** is a 3 hour return walk beginning at the Merrowvale Tearooms. It goes through native forest and karst country, with a view of Ruakuri Natural Bridge.

The Shearing Shed (formerly Rabbit World), in Waitomo village, ph 878 8371, has a large herd of the largest fibre producing rabbits, as well as angora garments and products. Admission is free and rabbit shearing exhibitions are given at 1pm daily.

About 1½km from the village is **Woodlyn Park**, which offers pioneer farm shows with lots of audience participation. Show times are 1.30pm and 3pm and admission is $9.50 adults, $4.50 children, with family packages available, ph 878 6666.

If horse-riding through the Waitomo Wilderness sounds attractive to you, enquire at the Information Office about horse trekking. Costs are $25 for 1 hour; $35 for two hours; $60 for a half-day; $100 for a full day, and no experience is necessary.

Another interesting trip is provided by Mano Off-roaders. It involves a 14km round trip through the area native bushland, and costs are $45 per person. Again the Information Office has all the details.

From Waitomo, you can drive to Te Kuiti and turn off onto Highway 30, passing through Kopaki and the Pureora State Forest Park and along the shores of Lake Whakamaru.

Leave Highway 30 and continue onto Atiamuri, then follow the signs to Wairakei and Taupo. OR, you can stay on Highway 30 and go directly to Rotorua.

Central North Island

The centre of the North Island contains a few of New Zealand's most famous attractions - Rotorua, Lake Taupo and Tongariro National Park, home of Mounts Ruapehu, Tongariro and Ngauruhoe.

Rotorua

Rotorua is situated on the fault line right in the centre of the North Island's active thermal region, which stretches from White Island down to the Tongariro National Park. This whole area is unique, and you could spend many weeks here and not really see it all. One thing that is impossible to overlook is the sulphur smell in the air as you near Rotorua. This rotten-egg smell is really offensive when you first arrive, but after a few hours you get used to it.

How to Get There

By Air
Mount Cook Airlines have daily services between Auckland and Rotorua with a flight time of 40 minutes. They also have daily flights from Christchurch, Queenstown and Wellington, and Mon-Sat from Bay of Islands.
Air New Zealand fly daily to Rotorua from Auckland, Christchurch and Wellington.
Ansett New Zealand have daily flights to Rotorua from Christchurch, Queenstown and Wellington.

By Rail
The Geyserland Express travels twice daily between Auckland and Rotorua.

By Bus
InterCity has daily services to Rotorua from:

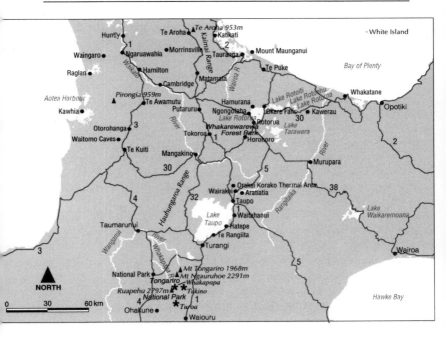

Auckland, Hastings, Napier, Paihia, Palmerston North, Taupo, Tauranga and Wellington; and from Hamilton Thurs-Sun.
Newmans have daily services to Rotorua from:
Auckland, Hamilton, Palmerston North, Taupo, Tauranga and Wellington.

By Car
Auckland-Rotorua is 269km - approx 3 hours 30 minutes.
Wellington-Rotorua is 462km - approx 6 hours 40 minutes.
Taupo-Rotorua is 82km - approx 1 hour 20 minutes.
Waitomo Caves-Rotorua is 166km - approx 2 hours 40 minutes.

Tourist Information
Rotorua Visitor Information Office, 67 Fenton Street,
ph (07) 348 5179.

Accommodation
Rotorua has extremely good accommodation in all price ranges
and because of the competition, offers good value for money.

Most establishments also have a hot mineral pool for the use of guests. Here is a selection, with prices in NZ$ for a double room per night, which should be used as a guide only. The telephone area code is 07.

Hotels

Royal Lakeside Novotel Rotorua, 9-11 Tutanekai Street, ph 346 3888, fax 347 1888 - 230 rooms, restaurants, bars, Maori concert and feast, spa, sauna - $167-260.

Regal Geyserland Hotel, Fenton Street (overlooking Whakarewarewa Thermal Reserve), ph 348 2039, fax 348 2033 - 67 rooms (private facilities), restaurants, bars, thermal pools - $140-158.

The Heritage, 349 Fenton Street, ph 347 7686, fax 346 3347 - restaurant, bar, swimming pool, spa, tennis court, barbecue - $110-190

Rotorua International Plaza Hotel, Froude Street (overlooking Whakarewarewa), ph 348 1189, fax 347 1620 - 124 rooms (private facilities), restaurants, bars, Maori concert and feast nightly, swimming pools, spas - $100-150.

Motels

Gwendoline Court, cnr Fenton & Gwendoline Streets, ph 347 8630 - 16 units, private spa pools - $120-140.

Coachman Motor Inn, 335 Fenton Street, ph 349 0960, fax 349 2207 - 19 units, private spa pools - $100-140.

Ashleigh Court Motel, 337 Fenton Street, ph/fax 348 7456 - 13 units, private spas - $107-129.

Golden Glow Motel, 253-255 Fenton Street, ph 348 6183, fax 348 9037 - 18 units, private spas - $75-99.

Best Western Thermal Gardens, 88 Ranolf Street, ph 347 9499, fax 347 9498 - 12 units, private thermal pools - $65-110.

Gibson Court, Gibson Street, ph 346 2822, fax 348 9481 - 10 units, private mineral pools - $82-105.

Ambassador Thermal Motel, 1 Hinemaru Street, ph 347 9581, fax 348 5281 - 19 units, swimming pool, mineral pools - $88.

Havana Motor Lodge, 12 Whakaue Street, ph 348 8134, fax 348 8132 - 22 units, private mineral pools, outdoor swimming pool - $75.

Cleveland Motel, 113-119 Lake Road, ph 348 2041, fax 347 8059 - 30 units, swimming pool, spa - $68-88.

Pineland Motor Lodge, 245 Fenton Street, ph 348 6601, fax 347

1952 - 10 units, private mineral and spa pool - $65.
Kiwi Paka, 60 Tarewa Road, ph 347 0931, fax 346 3167 - 22 chalets, licensed cafe and bar, thermal pool - $44-48.

Hostels & Cabins

Colonial Inn YHA Hostel, cnr Eruera & Hinemaru Streets, ph 347 6810, fax 349 1426 - thermally heated and has its own thermal pool. Daily tours to the thermal areas and tickets to the Maori Concert available from the hostel - $17 pp.
Cactus Jack Downtown Backpackers, 54 Haupapa Street, ph/fax 348 3121 - swimming pool, barbecue - $13-25.

Caravan Parks & Motor Camps

All Seasons Motor Park, 50-60 Lee Road, Hannahs Bay, ph 345 6240/fax - communal facilities include: kitchen, laundry, toilet, showers, lounge, games room; private hot spa pool, swimming pool, sporting facilities, camp store, boat ramp - powered caravan sites $18 x 2; tourist Flats, 1 or 2 bed rooms or studio, with kitchen, fridge - 1 or 2 bedroom $45-55.
Blue Lake Holiday Park, Tarawera Road, ph 362 8120, fax 362 8600 - communal kitchens, toilets, showers, laundries, lounge, recreation hall, plus store, canoes for hire - camp sites $18 x 2; tourist flats - 8 units sleep 5-6, kitchen, showers - $56-62 x 2; standard cabins - $28-34; tourist cabins $38-45 x 2.

Local Transport

Bus

Local buses are operated by Intercity. Contact Tourism Rotorua for timetables, or ph 349 0590.

Car Rental

Avis, ph 345 6055; Budget, ph 348 5767; Hertz, ph 348 4081.

Bike Rental

Bikes can be rented from Rotorua Cycle Centre, Hinemoa Street, ph 348 6588.

Sightseeing Tours

Carey's Sightseeing, ph 347 9917 have tours to all of Rotorua's sights.

Scenic Flights

Volcanic Air Safaris, Downtown Lakefront, ph 348 9984, have volcanic fault-line scenic flights by helicopter, float-plane and fixed wing craft.

Eating Out

Rotorua has a wide variety of restaurants. They have a McDonalds, a Kentucky Fried Chicken, Smacker Jacks and Pizza Hut, as well as plenty of takeaways and coffee shops. Here is a selection of restaurants with prices for a three course meal, without drinks.

Aorangi Peak Restaurant, Mountain Road, Mt Ngongotaha, ph 347 0046 - Licensed - open daily noon-2pm, 6pm-late - award winning restaurant with NZ cuisine - great views - $35-60 - credit cards accepted.

Caravel, Sheraton Rotorua Hotel, Fenton Street, ph 348 7139 - Licensed - open for dinner 6-10.30pm - award winning restaurant specialising in seafood - $25-45 - credit cards accepted.

Lewishams Restaurant, 115 Tutanekei Street, ph 349 1786 - BYO - open Mon, Wed-Fri 11.45am-2pm (summer), Wed-Mon 6-10pm (all year) - NZ cuisine - $25-45 - credit cards accepted.

Incas, cnr Fenton & Pukaki Streets, ph 348 3831 - Licensed/BYO - open Wed-Fri 11.30am-2.30pm, nightly 5.30pm-1am - Mexican/Italian cuisine - around $25 - credit cards accepted.

Latakia, 284 Tutanekai Street, ph 346 2970 - no BYO licence - open Mon-Fri 10am-late, Sat 10am-6pm - Middle Eastern cuisine - backpackers' heaven - around $15.

La Pizza Fiorno, 31 Pukuatua Street, ph 347 9854 - BYO - open Mon-Thurs 11.30am-8.30pm, Fri-Sat 11.30am-late, Sun noon-8.30pm - pasta and pizza with home deliveries for orders over $25 - $14 the dearest medium pizza - cash only.

Passage to India, 44 Hinemoa St, ph 346 3766 - Licensed/BYO - open daily from 11am - vegetarian dishes range between $9 and $12, but non-vegetarian more expensive, around $30 for three courses - credit cards accepted.

Steak House, Tutanekai Street, ph 347 9270 - Licensed/BYO - open daily 11am-10pm - select your steak and pay by the weight - around $25 for three courses - credit cards accepted.

Sightseeing

You will need about three days to see Rotorua and the surrounding attractions.

The major sight in Rotorua itself is **Whakarewarewa Thermal Reserve** at the end of Fenton Street, 3km from the centre of town. If you are fit you might like to walk as it is really not that far, but bear in mind that you will be walking all around the reserve, so you might prefer to catch the local bus back to town. It runs about every hour Mon-Fri, but the service is poor on the weekends.

The reserve is known as *Whaka* for short, as most tourists have trouble pronouncing the full name. There are Maori guides at the reserve, and often Maori boys will dive off the bridge for coins which people throw into the water below. The guides will show you how they use the boiling water to cook, and will explain about the reserve.

There are well-defined paths through the hissing steam and past the boiling mud pools, and if you are lucky you will see the two geysers playing.

If the smaller *Prince of Wales Feathers* starts to play, *Pohutu* will follow shooting hot water and steam about 20m into the air. It is certainly an impressive sight and can be seen from most places in Rotorua. The display usually lasts about twenty minutes. Further along the path are the boiling mud pools which are fascinating to watch as an endless variety of shapes

are formed when the mud bubbles and then bursts. Also in the reserve is a reconstructed Pa enclosed with palisades and a magnificent carved gateway (a great place to take photos).

Through the gateway is the **Maori Arts & Crafts Institute** where young students are trained in ancient hand crafts by tribal elders. It is open to the public and you can see weavers and wood carvers at work. The complex is open daily 8.30am-4.30am and admission is $11 adult.

While you are in Rotorua you shouldn't miss seeing a **Maori Concert** as they are great fun as well giving you an insight into Maori culture. There are nightly concerts at Ohinemutu Meeting House at 8pm ($13).

When combined with a Maori Hangi or feast, the concerts are even more memorable, and these are held nightly at the following venues:
Lake Plaza Hotel, ph 348 1174, at 7pm - $43, concert only $18.
Sheraton Hotel, ph 349 5200, at 7pm - $49, concert only $22.
Quality Inn, ph 348 0199, at 6.45pm - $41, concert only $17.

The **Government Gardens** are in the city centre and stretch down to the lake. They have beautiful trees and lovely flowers in spring. At the entrance to the gardens are the Government Baths which have two natural thermal pools. Also in the gardens is Tudor Towers which houses the Museum and the Art Gallery.

On the lakefront is **Ohinemutu Village**. The Tamatekapua Meeting House and St Faith's Church are both definitely worth visiting. St Faith's has elaborate Maori carvings and wonderful stained glass windows, one of which depicts Christ dressed in a Maori Chief's robe, and the figure appears to be walking on the water of the lake.

While you are on the lakeshore you might like to take a cruise, hire a boat or yacht, go trout fishing, or take a scenic flight on a floatplane. The *Lakeland Queen*, which is a replica paddle steamer with a fully licensed restaurant on board, cruises on Rotorua Lake, ph 348 6634.

If you have the time, then you shouldn't miss out on the trip from Rotorua to **Te Wairoa**, the Buried Village, Lake Tarawera and the Blue and Green Lakes.

This is the thermal area where the famous Pink and White Terraces stood before the eruption of Mt Tarawera in 1886. Carey's Sightseeing, ph 347 9917, offer a full-day tour that includes the volcanic valley, a cruise on the crater lake, a visit to the buried village and lunch for $140 adult. Shorter tours are also available.

If you have your own transport, drive south on Highway 5 (Rotorua-Taupo) to the Waimangu turn-off. From there it is five minutes to the coffee shop and entrance to the valley. From the shop there is a safe walking track, suitable for people of all ages, which leads to the Emerald Pool, the Waimangu Cauldron which is 50C, Ruaumokos Throat and Warbrick Terrace, which is orange, brown, black and green. Admission to the Buried Village is $9.50 and it is open daily 8.30am-5pm. If you must leave Rotorua after seeing Waimangu, you can head back to the main road and continue south to Taupo.

Just past the Waimangu turn-off is **Waiotapu Thermal Area**. This area is famous for its extraordinary colours. One of the terraces is called Artists Palette, and at the foot of it are the Bridal Veil Falls. Other attractions include the Champagne Basin which bubbles when the sand is disturbed, and the Lady Knox Geyser, which plays daily at 10.15am.

On Fairy Springs Road, 5km from Rotorua is **Rainbow Springs** which has interesting native bush walks, walk through native bird aviary, a nocturnal Kiwi House, and tuataras, wild pigs and deer. There is also an international shopping complex and a licensed restaurant. Rainbow Springs is open daily 8am-5pm and admission is $10, ph 347 9301.

On the opposite side of the road is **Rainbow Farm Show** which features sheep dogs, sheep shearing demonstrations, milking cows, bull handling, all with plenty of audience participation. The shows are daily at 10.30am, 11.45am, 1pm and 2.30pm. The complex is open daily 8am-5pm and admission is $9.50, ph 347 8104. There is a 10% discount on entry to both the springs and the farm.

The **Agrodome** on Riverdale Park Western Road, Ngongotaha, offers a glimpse of New Zealand agriculture, including the renowned ram display, which shows that maybe these animals can actually think. Added attractions are the licensed Farm View Café, helicopter flights, 4 wheel farm bike tours, horse back tours and clay bird shooting. The dome is open daily and shows times are 9.30am, 11am and 2.30pm, ph 357 4350. Admission is $10.

On Valley Road is **Paradise Valley Springs**, a wildlife park with rainbow trout, native animals and birdlife, and a lion pride that often has a few cubs of pattable size. The park is open every day, and the lion feeding is at 2.30pm. There is also a cafe and gift shop, ph 348 9667, and admission is $10.

Taniwha Springs, on the Hamurana Road 12km from Rotorua, is on the site of an old Pa. It has over a hundred springs, trout pools and picnic grounds.

At **Hamurana** there is a golf course and restaurant, and you can hire dinghies and feed the ducks, geese and swans.

At the Ohau Channel, where Lake Rotorua and Lake Rotoiti meet, there is a secondary road to Tauranga (86km) and along it are the **Okere Falls**. From the top stairs lead to the foot of the falls. Afterwards you will need to turn back to the Ohau Channel and continue around Lake Rotorua. A few kilometres further on, Highway 30 branches off to Whakatane. This road has some really spectacular scenery as it winds through the trees and around Lakes Rotoiti, Rotoehu and Rotoma. Only a few kilometres past the turn-off is another thermal area, **Hell's Gate**. This reserve covers 10ha and has a hot thermal waterfall, boiling mud and unusual sulphur covered terraces of pumice.

Sport & Recreation

Walking Trails
Redwood Grove, Longmite Drive off Tarawere Road, quite close to town, has colour-coded walks which last from 10 minutes to 6 hours and take you through the forest. There are also walkways at Okataina, Blue Lake, Hongi's Track, Mt Tarawera, Rainbow Mountain - contact the Information Office for details.

Whitewater Rafting
Raftabout Wilderness Expeditions, ph 345 4652, offer rafting down the Rangitaiki or Wairoa rivers with lunch included for $79.
White Water Excitement, ph 345 7182, offer half or full day rafting on the Kaituna and Rangitaiki rivers from $38-79.

Jet Boating

Longridge Park, Highway 33, 12km south of Te Puke, ph 533 1515, have jet boating on Kaituna River.

Kiwi Jet Tours, ph 307 0663, have several exciting jet boat tours.

Helicopter Flights

Kiwi Copters, ph 347 7575; *Marine Helicopters Ltd*, 357 2512; *Tarawera Helicopters*, ph 348 1223.

Horse Riding

Foxwood Park, ph 345 7003, are open daily and offer treks over 340ha of unspoiled bush and cater for both experienced and inexperienced riders.

Paradise Valley Horse Riding, ph 348 8195, offer trekking in the countryside and forests.

Golf

There are seven golf courses in Rotorua. The most central is the one in Government Gardens in the city centre.

Hot Pools & Swimming Pools

Aquatic Centre, Tarewa Road, has a heated 50m pool; *Polynesian Pools*, Hinemoa Street, have private and public hot mineral pools; *Waikite Pools* are 8km off Highway 5 to Taupo and have an outdoor hot mineral pool.

Trout Fishing

There are eleven fishable lakes in the areas, as well as rivers and streams. A licence is required, but can be purchased from sporting stores, shops and some service stations. The season is all year round on Lake Rotorua, but most other lakes are closed July-September. Guides and equipment are available through the Information Office.

Taupo

Taupo is at the northern end of Lake Taupo, which is the largest of the New Zealand lakes. It has an area of 616 sq km, is 48km long, 357m above sea level, and lies in a series of craters produced by many years of volcanic activity. During clear weather you can see the mountains of Tongariro National Park in the distance. Taupo is famous for its trout fishing and the season on the lake lasts all through the year.

Because of its size, this lake is subject to wind squalls and can turn quite rough very quickly, so care should be taken if you hire a rowing boat and head out to the middle. Don't let this stop you enjoying the lake though, as there is nothing more pleasant and relaxing than a cruise to some of the quieter beaches. You will pass over the control gates that regulate the level of Lake Taupo as you drive into the town. Taupo is a very popular resort and during peak periods it is best to book your accommodation.

Climate

Taupo has a temperate climate. The summers are a little warmer and winters a little colder than most of the North Island. The continuous mountain ranges to the east and south-east leave the lake open to prevailing westerlies. The average rainfall is 1200mm, but snow is rare.

How to Get There

By Air
Air New Zealand has daily flights to Taupo from Auckland and Wellington.
Mount Cook Airlines has daily flights from Rotorua to Taupo.

By Bus
InterCity and *Newmans* have daily services from Auckland, Napier and Rotorua.

By Car
Auckland-Taupo is 280km - approx 4 hours.
Wellington-Taupo is 380km - approx 5 hours 15 minutes.
Napier-Taupo is 143km - approx 3 hours.

Rotorua-Taupo is 80km along Highway 5. If you drive straight through it only takes approx 1 hour 20 minutes, but Waimangu and Waiotapu Thermal Areas are off this road, so you may want to visit them on the way. The turn-off to Orakei Korako Thermal Area is 70km from Rotorua on Highway 5. It is a bit off the beaten track (25km from Highway 5), but it is one of the best. **The Aratiatia Rapids** and **Wairakei Power Station** are also along Highway 5, but as they are only a few kilometres from Taupo they can easily be visited from there (see Taupo Outlying Attractions for details of these attractions).

Tourist Information

The Information Office, 13 Tongariro Street, ph (07) 378 9000.

Accommodation

There is a wide variety of accommodation to suit all pockets. Here is a selection, with prices in NZ$ for a double room per night, which should be used as a guide only. Note that prices may increase substantially during school holiday periods. The telephone area code is 07.

Hotels

Oasis-Manuels Resort Hotel, 241 Lake Terrace, ph 378 9339, fax 378 9325 - 22 units, restaurants, bars, swimming pool, sauna, tennis court - $85-134.
Suncourt Motor Hotel, 14 Northcroft Street, ph 378 8265, fax 378 0809 - 48 units, restaurant, bar, swimming pool, spa - $90-125.
Tui Oaks Motor Inn/Lake Terrace Motel, 88 Lake Terrace, ph 378 8305, 378 8335 - 37 units, restaurant, bar, swimming pool, spa - $85-120.
Cutters Lakeview Motor Inn, 60 Lake Terrace, ph/fax 378 6015 - 24 units, restaurant, bar, spa - $55-75.

Motels

Cottage Mews Motel, 22 Lake Terrace, ph 378 3004, fax 378 3005 - 11 units, private whirlpools - $85-125.

Cedar Park Motor Lodge, Two Mile Bay, ph 378 6325, fax 377 0641 - 24 units, swimming pool, spa pools - $88-105.

Anchorage Resort Motel, Lake Terrace, Two Mile Bay, ph 378 5542, fax 378 7287 - 15 units, swimming pool, private mineral spas, sauna - $90-120.

Adelphi Motel, cnr Kaimanawa & Heuheu Streets, ph 378 7594, fax 378 5374 - 10 units, hot spa pools - $55-80.

Barcelona Motel, 21 Taniwha Street, ph 378 8915, fax 378 8900 - 14 units, heated spa - $75-95.

Acapulco Motor Inn, 19 Rifle Range Road, ph 378 7174, fax 378 7555 - 19 units, private spa pools - $68-88.

Continental Motel, 9 Scannell Street, ph/fax 378 5836 - 9 units, private spa pool - $70.

Shoreline Motel, Highway 1, Waitahanui, ph/fax 378 6912 - 6 units, private beach - $55-75.

Hostels

Rainbow Lodge Backpackers Hostel, 99 Titiraupenga Street, ph 378 5754, fax 377 1568 - 5 double or twin rooms, 4 bunk rooms, communal kitchen/dining, showers, etc, pool table, sauna - $34 x 2 (rooms); $14 per person (bunkrooms).

Sunset Lodge Backpackers, 5 Tremaine Avenue, ph 378 5962 - 10 rooms, single and double beds and bunks, communal kitchen, showers, etc, TV lounge - $13-16 per person.

Taupo Cabins, 50 Tonga St, ph/fax 378 4346 - 11 standard cabins $15 per person; 16 tourist cabins $40 x 2; tourist flats$50 x2.

Motor Camps and Caravan Parks

De Bretts Thermal Resort, Highway 5, 1km from lake, ph 378 8559, fax 377 2181 - communal kitchen, dining room, toilets, showers, laundry, common room, 2 mineral swimming pools, 12 private indoor thermal pools, one fresh water pool, store - powered sites - $20 x 2; cabins $40-60; lodges $72-85.

Taupo Motor Camp, 15 Redoubt Street, ph/fax 377 3080 - communal kitchens, toilets, showers, laundry, TV rooms - tent sites $9 per person; cabins/on-site caravans $30-35.

Eating Out

There is a good selection of licensed and BYO restaurants in Taupo. Here are a few.

Cafe Renoir, 77 Spa Road, ph 378 0777 - **Licensed/BYO** - open Mon-Sat 6.30pm-midnight - 3 dining rooms and an exhibition of work by NZ artists - award winning family restaurant - **$25-45** - credit cards accepted.

Edgewater Restaurant, Manuels Motor Inn, Lake Terrace, ph 378 5110 - **Licensed** - open daily 6.30-10pm - rated as one of NZ's best restaurants - NZ cuisine - **over $45** - credit cards accepted.

Hudders Licensed Restaurant, 22 Tuwharetoa Street, ph 378 5919 - **Licensed** - open daily noon-10pm - a movie theme with great music and food and friendly staff - **under $25**, credit cards accepted.

Truffles Restaurant, 116 Lake Terrace, ph 378 7856 - **Licensed/BYO** - open noon-2pm (December-January), Tues-Sun 6.30-11pm - great mountain views from Terrace Bar - specialises in NZ cuisine - **$25-45** - credit cards accepted.

Echo Cliff, 5 Tongariro Street, ph 378 8539 - **Licensed/BYO** - open Mon-Fri noon-2pm, nightly from 5.30pm - family restaurant with varied menu - **around $25** - credit cards accepted.

Hare & Trout, 703 Acacia Bay Road, ph 378 8886 - **Licensed** - open Mon-Fri 5pm-midnight, Sat-Sun midday-midnight - choose from the bar meals or the more expensive general menu - **the latter around $30** - credit cards accepted.

Margarita's, 63 Heu Heu Street, ph 378 9909 - **Licensed** - open nightly 4pm-2am - Mexican/American cuisine - live music, and music and sports videos - happy hours 5-7pm and 9-10pm - **around $30** - credit cards accepted.

Peppers, Manuals Motor Inn, Lake Terrace, ph 378 5110 - **Licensed** - open daily 7.30-10am, 6.30-9.30pm - the casual restaurant at this Motor Inn (see Edgewater Room above) - varied menu - **around $20** - credit cards accepted.

Sightseeing

The main attraction is the lake, of course, and a trip on it is a "must". You can take a cruise on the *Ernest Kemp*, or hire a boat and fish and swim for as long as you like. While here you should see Orakei Korako (if you haven't already visited it), the Aratiatia Rapids, the Wairakei Power Station, and the Huka Falls. Apart from that, you should have a swim in one of the many thermal pools. Also listed are other places to visit.

Lake Taupo, North Island

The **District Museum of Art and History**, Story Place, near the post office, ph 378 4167, is open Mon-Sat 10am-4.30pm and has a large collection of Maori and European artefacts from the area. Admission is free.

Cherry Island, on the Waikato River between Taupo and the Huka Falls, has animals and birds, underwater viewing of rainbow trout. Open daily, admission is $7.50 adults, $3.50 children. The Cherry Island Cafe & Bar is open for breakfast, morning and afternoon teas, cafe meals or barbecue lunches and dinners. Open Mon-Thurs 9am-5pm, Fri-Sun 9am-9pm (summer); daily 9am-5pm (winter).

Trainsville, upstairs at 35a Heu Heu Street, has New Zealand's biggest model railway display with over 200m of track and ten trains operating. Open Mon-Fri 9.30am-5pm, Sat 9.30am-1.30pm, and admission is $3 adults, $1.50 children.

Lake Cruises are available on the *Ernest Kemp*, a replica of a steam ferry of bygone days. They last two hours, depart at 10am and 2pm, and tickets are available at the wharf, or from the Information Office. There are also two and half hour cruises on sailing boats, and a two hour cruise on the historic river boat *Waireka*.

Outlying Attractions

Orakei Korako Thermal Area is off the beaten track and lies between the Taupo-Hamilton Highway and the Taupo-Rotorua Highway. It is 40km from Taupo and 70km from Rotorua; 23km from Highway 5 and 15km from Highway 1. You have to take a jet boat across Lake Ohakuri, which was formed as part of a hydro-electric scheme, to get to the area.

Unfortunately, about three-quarters of the area was submerged beneath the lake, but what remains is still worth seeing. The main attractions are: *Aladdin's Cave*, which is lined with mosses and climbing plants; the *Diamond Geyser*: the *Golden Fleece*, a silica terrace; and many smaller geysers and hot springs.

I feel that this area is one which is most often overlooked, and it is one of the best. It is open daily 8.30am-4.30pm, and admission is $12.50 adults, $5 children.

Aratiatia Rapids are 11km from Taupo along Highway 5, just past the junction with the Auckland-Hamilton Highway which is on the outskirts of Wairakei. The rapids should be visited at 10am or 2.30pm when the flood gates are opened allowing water through the rapids for ninety minutes. The rest of the day the water is diverted through the power station.

Wairakei is famous for its Geothermal Power Station where natural steam is used to produce electricity. There is an Information Centre near the road which provides details of the bore-field and powerhouse. It is open daily 9am-noon, 1.00-4.30pm, and arrangements can be made there to visit the power station. On the opposite side of the highway is the remains of Geyser Valley which may still be inspected but is not really worth bothering about after seeing the others.

   Wairakei Tourist Park is open daily and attractions include a NZ Woodcraft shop and Honey Village.

The **Craters of the Moon** thermal area is on Karapiti Road, Wairakei, and is open daily. Admission is free.

Huka Falls are just off the highway between Taupo and Wairakei. They are only 24m high, but a great volume of water rushes over them as the Waikato is the only river out of Lake Taupo whereas forty rivers feed in. A bridge across the river leads to other vantage points and the start of the Taupo walkway to the Aratiatia Rapids.

Sport & Recreation

White Water Rafting
Rapid Descents Rafting Co, ph 377 0419, and *River Rats*, ph 378-7667, have trips daily.

Jet Boating
Huka Jet Ltd, ph 374 8572, have trips to Huka Falls and Aratiatia Dam.

Bungy Jumping
Taupo Bungy, 202 Spa Road, ph 377 1135, have all the necessary equipment for 46m jumps out over the Waikato River.

Sky Diving

Taupo Tandem Skydiving, ph (mobile) 025 428 688, operate at Taupo Airport. No experience is necessary, and a courtesy shuttle bus will take you out there.

Swimming

De Bretts Thermal Resort, on the Taupo-Napier Highway, ph 378 8559, has indoor and outdoor hot pools, set in beautifully kept grounds. It is rather a long way out of town, but is open daily 8am-9.30pm.

AC Thermal Baths, AC Baths Avenue, off Spa Road, ph 378 7321, have a large heated swimming pool, private mineral pools, sauna, roller coaster and water slide. Open daily and admission is $4.

From Taupo you should visit the Tongariro National Park, just past the end of Lake Taupo, as it is a fascinating area. It has three active volcanoes and many hot springs.

Highway 5 to Napier branches off at Taupo for the Hawke's Bay Area, but you shouldn't miss out on the Tongariro National Park even if you have to backtrack later. From Taupo take Highway 1 to Turangi.

The town of **Turangi** has grown around the hydro-electric station. The Information Centre in Ngawaka Place, ph 386 8999, is open daily 9am-5pm, and has a large display on forestry, fishing and the hydro-electric scheme.

There are several motels in the town as well as lodges and motor camps. Fishing, tramping and hunting guides can be hired through the Information Centre. Also in town is a trout hatchery. Several hunting and fishing lodges are scattered throughout the area and there are plenty of walks for keen trampers.

Tongariro National Park

This is one of the most spectacular areas in the North Island and you will probably want to spend a day or two here. In winter and spring when the mountains are covered in snow, it is particularly beautiful as the white snow contrasts starkly with the dark rocks, though really the scenery is fantastic whatever the season.

How to Get There

By Bus

InterCity buses stop at National Park, 16km from The Chateau on their Auckland/Wellington services, and taxis are available to take you to The Chateau.

By Train

The *Overlander* and the *Northerner* stop at National Park.

By Car

From Turangi take Highway 1 to Rangipo, 11km from Turangi, then turn off onto Highway 48 which skirts around the National Park. Stay on Highway 48 until you come to the turn-off to **The Chateau** and you will be at the foot of Mt Ruapehu (2797m). Mt Ruapehu is the highest of the three volcanoes in the park.

The volcanoes are grouped together, but are really quite different: **Ruapehu** had a permanent snow cover and a steaming crater lake until August 1996 when it erupted in an awesome sound and light show that completely ruined the ski season; **Ngauruhoe** is the most impressive of the three, being cone-shaped and belching smoke most of the time; and **Tongariro** has three peaks and in comparison, seems rather nondescript, but it does have several lakes and both hot and cold springs.

There are several well-defined walking tracks in the park and if you enjoy tramping you will really be in your element here.

Skiing

There are two ski-fields on Mt Ruapehu: **Whakapapa behind The Grand Chateau; and Turoa 17km from Ohakune.** These fields have exciting terrain with lava cliffs and gullies which extend even the best skiers, as well as gentler slopes for learners.

The ski season usually lasts well into November on the southern slopes of the mountain. Accommodation is available in the nearby towns of Ohakune, Raetihi, National Park, Turangi and at The Chateau. The Grand Chateau is expensive, but there are cabins and a motel just up the road from Park Headquarters that are more reasonably priced.

The ski-fields are about 5km from The Chateau and shuttle buses from the nearby towns are available in winter, but in summer you have to walk. There are many privately owned ski club huts around the base of the chairlift. In winter it is easy to get to the top of the mountain, you can take a helicopter or a snowmobile. In summer you have to climb up following the poles to the Alpine Club Hut and then climb up the Whakapapa Glacier. The view from the crater edge is fantastic, with neighbouring Ngauruhoe and Tongariro, and in the background Lake Taupo stretching off into the distance. On a clear day you can also see Taranaki (Mt Egmont), 120km away. (For information on the skifields, see page ???.)

Driving Advice

If you are travelling by car and want to go to Auckland or Napier, you might like to drive around the park. If you do, turn left when you reach Highway 48 and go to National Park. From there take the road to Ohakune and Waiouru, then drive along the Desert Road, through an interesting area between Waiouru and Rangipo. As the name implies, very little grows along this road and the landscape is dominated by the three volcanoes.

If you are heading for Wellington or New Plymouth, drive to National Park then take Highway 4 to Wanganui. If you want to visit the Waitomo Caves you should take Highway 4 in the opposite direction.

East Coast

The East Coast has wilderness areas and beaches, forests and neat farmland, and an easy-going lifestyle. It can be reached from the Bay of Plenty area in the north, from Taupo in the centre, or from Wellington in the south. The three main towns are Gisborne in the Eastland Province, and Napier and Hastings in the Hawke's Bay Province. The beaches in the Hawke's Bay Province tend to have pebbles or darker sand, while the beaches in Eastland have light sand like the beaches of the Bay of Plenty.

How to Get There

By Air
Air New Zealand fly to Gisborne and Napier from Auckland and Wellington daily. They also have daily direct flights from Auckland and Wellington to Palmerston North.

By Rail
The *Overland Express* and the *Northerner* stop at Palmerston North.

By Bus
InterCity and *Newmans* have daily services from Auckland and Wellington to Gisborne, Napier and Palmerston North.

By Car
Tauranga-Gisborne is 293km - approx 4 hours.
Taupo-Napier is 147km - approx 3 hours.
Palmerston North-Napier is 176km - approx 2 hours 40 minutes.
Napier-Gisborne is 215km - approx 3 hours 30 minutes.
Wellington-Napier is 319km - approx 4 hours 40 minutes.
Wellington-Gisborne is 534km - approx 8 hours 10 minutes.

Guide to Touring by Car
If you are driving from the Bay of Plenty area you will first

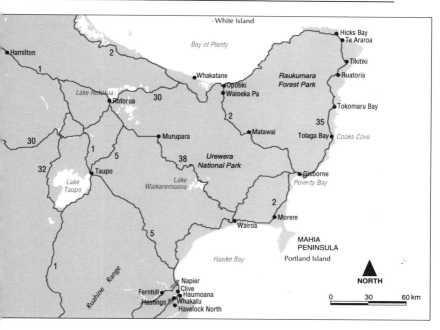

come to **Opotiki**, the northern gateway to the East Coast. The St Stephen the Martyr Church at Opotiki is worth seeing. Raft and jet boat trips on the Motu River can be arranged through the Information Office, cnr St John & Elliott Streets, Opotiki, ph (07) 315 8484.

From Opotiki you can follow Highway 35 around the coast to Hicks Bay and then down to Gisborne (345km) **or** you can take Highway 2, the inland route, through the Waioeka Gorge, direct to Gisborne (148km), via Matawai.

The road from Opotiki to Hicks Bay takes you along one of New Zealand's most scenic coastal drives.

There are several walkways from Hicks Bay and a glow-worm grotto. The road from Hicks Bay winds it way through several seaside and pastoral townships. The largest Pohutukawa tree in New Zealand can be seen at Te Araroa. It is believed to be 600 years old, and has twenty-two trunks and a girth of 20m.

From Te Araroa you can drive to East Cape, the most easterly point of New Zealand. The International Date Line passes close to here, so this area is the first to greet each new day. There is a magnificently carved Maori church at Tikitiki and a museum at Ruatoria.

Continuing south to Gisborne, the road passes Tokomaru Bay, an art centre, and Tolaga Bay, a growing resort. From here is the start of the two hour return walk to Cooks Cove.

Gisborne

This city is called the "First City of the Sun" because of its proximity to the International Date Line. It was the site of the first landing on New Zealand soil by Captain Cook. Gisborne is situated on three rivers and has some superb beaches.

Tourist Information

The Visitor Information Office is at 209 Grey Street, ph (06) 868 6139.

Accommodation

Gisborne offers a fair range of accommodation from hotels, motels and guest houses to a youth hostel. Here is a selection with prices for a double room per night in NZ$, which should be used as a guide only. The telephone area code is 06.

Hotels

Gisborne Hotel, cnr Huxley & Tyndall Roads, Kaiti, ph 868 4109, fax 867 8344 - 27 rooms (private facilities), restaurant and cocktail bars, swimming pool - $90-125.

Pacific Reef Resort, 62 Moana Road, Wainui Beach, SH 35, ph 867 008, fax 867 8348 - 12 units, restaurant, swimming pool, spa, barbecue - $79-98.

Motels

Pacific Harbour Motor Inn, 24 Reads Quay, ph 867 8847, fax 867 4586 - 22 units, spa - $105-160.

Champers Motor Lodge, cnr Gladstone & Campion Roads, ph 863 1515, fax 863 1520 - 14 units, swimming pool, spa - $85-140.

Teal Motor Lodge, 479 Gladstone Road, ph 868 4019, fax 867 7157

- 20 units, swimming pool - $90-113.

Whispering Sands Motel, 22 Salisbury Road, (on Waikanae Beach frontage), ph 867 1319, fax 867 6747 - 14 units, barbecue - $85-135.

Beachcomber Motel, 71-73 Salisbury Road, Waikanae Beach, ph 868 9349, fax 868 6974 - 14 units, spa, barbecue - $80-90.

Eastland Motor Lodge, 798 Gladstone Road, ph 868 4115, fax 867 3604 - 17 units, swimming pool, spa, barbecue - $85.

Wainui Beach Motel, 34 Wairere Road, Wainui Beach, ph 868 5882, fax 868 8482 - 9 units, swimming pool, spa, barbecue - $75-90.

Endeavour Lodge, 525 Gladstone Road, ph 868 6075, fax 868 6074 - 9 units, swimming pool, barbecue - $70-80.

Motor Camps & Cabins

Showgrounds Park Motor Camp, 20 Main Road, Makaraka, ph 867 5299 (closed 4 days in October for show) - powered sites $12.50 x 2, children $4; tent sites $10.50 x 2, children $4; cabins (sleep 2-6) $15-20 x 2, $4 children; on-site caravans $25.

Waikanae Beach Holiday Park, Grey Street, ph 867 5634, fax 867 9765 - tent sites $14 x 2; powered sites $16 x 2; tourist flats $48 x 2; cabins $22 x 2.

Hostel

Gisborne Hostel, 32 Harris Street, ph 867 3269 - $14 per person.

Eating Out

A walk along Gladstone Road will present many outlets to tempt your taste buds. A popular budget restaurant is *Scotty's Bar & Grill*, at no 23, ph 867 8173 - open Mon-Sat 11am-late - live music and very busy, but the food is secondary to the atmosphere. At no 55 is *Steakout*, ph 868 9646, which is open for lunch and dinner Tues-Sat. *Burger Wisconsin* is at no 26, ph 867 6442, and you can phone orders ahead, then eat in or take away. *Dago's Famous Pizzeria* is on the corner of Gladstone Road and Cobden Street, ph 867 0543, and you can have 'da best pizza in town' home delivered, or dine in, or takeaway. If you have a hankering for seafood, head for the *Regent Restaurant* at no 61, ph 867 7457, but remember that it is BYO.

Another street to try is Peel Street, which is home to *The Irish Rover* (no 69, ph 867 1112) - pub meals and live entertainment; *China Palace Restaurant* (no 55-61, ph 867 5037) - fully licensed, open 7 days, with an excellent smorgasbord Fri-Sun 6-9pm for $16.80 per adult, children under 12 half price; *Mega Bite* (no 22, ph 867 5787) - opens 6am for great hearty breakfasts and stays open to take care of lunch.

Sightseeing

A panoramic view of the river and beaches can be obtained from **Kaiti Hill** on Queens Drive. Other sights worth seeing are the **Poho O Rawiri** Meeting House, which is not far from Kaiti Hill; the **Museum & Art Centre**, 18-22 Stout Street, open Mon-Fri 10am-4pm, Sat-Sun 1.30-4pm admission free, includes **Wylie Cottage**, the oldest house in Gisborne containing period furniture; the **Museum of Transport & Technology**, Main Road, Makaraka, open daily 9.30am-4.30pm, admission $2 adults, children 50c; and the **Eastwoodhill Arboretum** near Ngatapa, open daily, admission $5 adults, children free.

You also might like to tour the **Poverty Bay Wineries** - contact the Information Office for details. They will also provide you with information on the Historic Turanga tours of the city and Maori meeting houses and maraes.

From Gisborne you can either take the narrow, winding inland route (Highway 36) or the coastal road (Highway 2) to Wairoa, which is just over 90km away by either route.

At **Morere** on the coastal route to Wairoa, you will pass through an area dotted with hot mineral pools. The Lands & Survey Department has trapped these waters to form an extensive pool that is great for all ages.

Wairoa is the Eastern Gateway to the Urewera National Park, which is about an hour's drive along Highway 38 towards Rotorua. The park is renowned for its deer, wild pig, goat and opossum hunting as well as for trout fishing. Wairoa is unusual in that it has a lighthouse in its main street on the banks of the river. Originally this lighthouse was located on offshore Portland Island, but it was shifted to the town in 1961. The Takitimu Marae Meeting House in Wairoa is also worth seeing. Between Wairoa and Napier you will see the Mohaka railway viaduct which is the highest in the southern hemisphere. South of Wairoa (130km), on the other side of Hawke's Bay, is Napier.

Napier

In 1931 Napier and nearby Hastings were virtually destroyed by an earthquake and fires in which 250 people died. The present day Marine Parade was formed from the rubble of Napier's buildings.

Tourist Information

The Napier Visitor Information Office is in Marine Parade, ph (06) 834 1911.

The Hastings Visitor Information Office is in Russell Street North, ph (06) 878 0510.

Accommodation

As this is a summer resort, there is an excellent range of reasonably priced accommodation from luxury hotels to a huge youth hostel. Here is a selection with prices for a double room per night in NZ$, which should be used as a guide only. The telephone area code is 06.

Hotels

Tennyson Motor Inn, cnr Tennyson Street & Clive Square, ph 835 3373, fax 835 8500 - 42 units, restaurant - $98-145.

Napier Travel Inn, 311 Marine Parade, ph 835 3237, fax 835 6602 - 59 units, restaurant, swimming pool - $130.

Ormlie Lodge, Omarunui Road, Waiohiki, ph 844 5774 - 4 suites, restaurant in 90-year-old mansion - $130-150.

Westshore Hotel, Main Road north, Westshore, ph 835 9879 - 6 hotel rooms, 7 motel units, licensed restaurant - $40 hotel, $30 motel.

Motels

Marineland Motel, 20 Meeanee Quay, Westshore, ph 835 2147, fax 835 7710 - 23 units, restaurant, swimming pool, spa - $75-150.

Fountain Court Motel, 409-411 Hastings Street, ph 835 7387, fax 835 0323 - 19 units, restaurant, swimming pool, barbecue - $94-124.

Edgewater Motor Lodge, 359 Marine Parade, ph 835 1148,

Marine Parade, Napier.

fax 835 6600 - 20 units, spa - $90-170.

Ace High Motor Inn, 399 Kennedy Road, ph 843 3109, fax 843 4189 - 16 units, swimming pool, spa - $78.

Snowgoose Lodge Motel, 376 Kennedy Road, ph 843 6083, fax 843 6107 - 18 units, swimming pool, spas, games room - $85-120.

McLean Park Lodge, 177 Wellesley Road, ph 835 4422, fax 835 4081 - 13 units, spa - $70-90.

Lisa Rose Motel, 377 Kennedy Road, ph 843 4400, fax 843 2164 - 13 units, swimming pool, spa - $70-85.

Colonial Lodge Motel, 164 Gloucester Street, Taradale, ph/fax 844 7788 - 17 units, swimming pool, spa, games room, barbecue - $65-170.

Blue Lagoon Motel, 27 Meeanee Quay, Westshore, ph/fax 835 9626 - 8 units, swimming pool, spa, barbecue - $55-150.

Motor Camps & Cabins

Kennedy Park Holiday Complex, Storkey Street, ph 843 9126, fax 843 6113 - powered sites $20 x 2; tourist flats $70; cabins $25-40; motel units $68-78.

Westshore Holiday Camp, Main Road, Westshore, ph/fax 835 9456 - powered sites $8 adults, $4 children; tourist flats (sleep 2-6) $40-70 x 2, $9 children; cabins (sleep 4) $28 x 2; cabins (sleep 2-4) $30 x 2.

Eating Out

Bayswater Restaurant, Hardinge Road, ph 835 8517 - **Licensed** - open daily (summer), Wed-Sat (winter) 11.30am-2pm, 6pm-1am - waterfront restaurant with outdoor tables - NZ cuisine - **$25-45** - credit cards accepted.

Alfresco's Cafe and Bar, 65 Emerson Street, ph 835 1181 - **Licensed** - open Mon-Sat noon-2pm, 6pm-late - popular casual eatery - **around $25** - credit cards accepted.

Blues Bar & Grill, 189 Marine Parade, ph 835 0068 - **Licensed** - open daily noon-2pm, 6pm-late - carries the American blues theme from the decor to the names of the dishes - good music - **around $25** - credit cards accepted.

Alsops, 15 Hastings Street, ph 835 8053 - **Licensed/BYO** - open Mon-Wed 3pm-midnight, Thurs-Sat 3pm-late - set in an old grocer's shop, a very popular venue with good music - **under $25** - credit cards accepted.

Harston's 17 Hastings Street, ph 835 0478 (next door to Alsops) -

BYO - open Tues-Fri noon-1.30pm, nightly 6pm-late - 2 dining areas, one much quieter than the other - **under $25** - credit cards accepted.

Singapore, Hastings Street, ph 835 1836 - **Licensed/BYO** - open nightly from 6pm - mixture of cuisines from Singapore and Hong Kong - **$25** - credit cards accepted.

Sightseeing

The main attractions on the beachfront are **Marineland**, **Hawke's Bay Aquarium** and the **Kiwi House**, all on Marine Parade. Marineland has performing dolphins, sea lions, sea leopards and other marine animals. It is open daily 10am-4.30pm with shows at 10.30am and 2pm, and admission is $8. The Aquarium houses fresh water fish from all over the world, is the largest in the southern hemisphere, and is open daily 9am-5pm with shows every half-hour on the half-hour. Admission is $7. The Kiwi House is open daily 11am-3pm with shows at 1pm, and admission is $3. (Incidentally this may by your only chance to see a kiwi that is not tucked away in its nocturnal habitat). There is a superpass that allows entry to all three attractions for $15.

Also on Marine Parade are the **Stables Museum & Waxworks**, open daily 9am-5pm, admission $6, which has an audio-visual presentation of the 1931 earthquake; Napier Skating Club's roller skating rink; a Putt Putt golf course; the Sound Shell; and at its end the **"Spirit of Napier"**, a statue of a girl that symbolises the rise of Napier from the chaos of the earthquake.

Napier is renowned for its unique architecture. Almost completely rebuilt during the Depression, it has the most concentrated collection of buildings in Art Deco and associated styles popular in the early 1930s.

Art Deco Walks leave the Museum every Sunday and Wednesday at 2pm, or you can buy a walk guide from the Museum or the Information Office and walk it on your own.

The **Cape Kidnappers Gannet Reserve** in Hawke's Bay has the largest, most accessible mainland gannet colony in the world. The Gannet is a member of the Booby family, and is related to the families of shags, pelicans and frigate-birds. Adult

Sunset over Pahurehure Inlet, Manukau Harbour, Auckland.

Australasian gannets have a wing span of up to 2m and an average weight of 2kg. Whilst ungainly on land, these birds are designed for graceful flying, and for diving from great heights into the sea to catch fish. Although not a migratory bird as such, the first trip for the new chicks is across the Tasman to Australia where they stay for two-and-a-half to three-and-a-half years before they return to New Zealand to live. This exhausting journey has a high mortality rate.

Gannet Beach Adventures, ph/fax 875 0898, run guided tours to Cape Kidnappers from the end of October to Easter. The tours last 4 hours and cost around $18. You can walk to the colony along the beach, but you have to check on the tides or you might get stranded. Independent walking is permitted from the end of October to July. It takes about two hours each way.

Hawke's Bay Wine Trail

Hawke's Bay is one of the largest wine growing areas in New Zealand and the wine produced here has a distinctive taste. There are sixteen wineries in the area and they welcome visitors. *Bay Tours*, ph 843 6953, fax 843 2046, have guided wine tours and general sightseeing for $25-35.

A booklet called *Tread the Wine Trail* has been published by the Hawke's Bay Vintners, and is available from the Information Centre. It contains a map showing the location of the wineries and information about each vineyard.

Heading south, continue along Highway 2 and you will come to Hastings, which is only 20km from Napier. It has an exceptional climate with a minimum number of rainy days, a maximum of sunshine hours and only occasional frosts in winter, making it an ideal area for fruit growing. Although Hastings is surrounded by orchards and vineyards, it has around 200 industries as well. It has a few nice parks and gardens, and Oak Avenue is lined for 2km with oaks raised from acorns imported from England many years ago. Fantasyland Adventure Park is worth a visit if you have children with you.

From Hastings it is about 160km to Palmerston North. To get there drive along Highway 2 to Woodville and then turn off to Palmerston North.

Palmerston North

Palmerston North is a city situated in the midst of a thriving agricultural community, and is a prosperous industrial and commercial centre as well as a centre of learning and research.

How to Get There

By Air
Air New Zealand has several daily flights to/from Auckland, Christchurch and Wellington.

Ansett New Zealand has daily flights to/from Auckland, Christchurch and Wellington.

By Rail
The *Overlander Express*, the *Northerner* and the *Bay Express* stop at Palmerston North.

By Bus
Newmans and *InterCity* connect Palmerston North with all major towns in the North Island.

Tourist Information
The Information Office is in the Civic Centre, The Square, ph (06) 358 5003. It is open Mon-Fri 8.30am-5pm, Sat-Sun and public holidays 9am-5pm.

Accommodation
Following is a selection of accommodation with prices for a double room per night in NZ$, which should be used as a guide only. The telephone area code is 06.

Hotels & Motor Inns
Quality Hotel, 110 Fitzherbert Avenue, ph 356 8059, fax 356 8604 - 154 rooms (private facilities), 2 licensed restaurants, bars, gymnasium, spa, sauna - $110-150.
Sherwood Motor Inn, 252-256 Featherston Street, ph 357 0909, fax 356 9409 - 39 units, restaurant swimming pool, spa - $80-115.
Coachman Palmerston North, 134 Fitzherbert Avenue, ph 356

5065, fax 356 6692 - 30 units, restaurants, sauna, spa - $99.
Alpha Motor Inn, cnr Broadway & Victoria Avenue, ph 357 1129, fax 359 0188 - 39 units, licensed restaurant, spa - $88.
La Mirage Motor Lodge, cnr Linton & Chaytor Sts, ph 358 7074, fax 358 7070 - 22 units, sauna, squash court, gym - $90-165.

Motels
Awatea Park, 243 Fitzherbert Avenue, ph 356 5366, fax 356 6755 - 16 units, spa - $80-110.
A'La Vista Motel, 171 Fitzherbert Avenue, ph 357 1199, fax 357 1194 - 10 units, swimming pool, spa - $79-89.
Avenue Motel, 116 Fitzherbert Ave, ph 356 3330, fax 359 2108 - 13 units, spa - $107.
Birch Trees Lodge Motel, 97 Tremaine Avenue, ph 356 1455, fax 356 1458 - 6 units - $78-95.
Palmerston North Motel, 66 Linton Street, ph 358 0681, fax 356 1753 - 15 units, swimming pool, spa - $85.
The Settlers Motel, 154 Park Road, ph 356 7077, fax 356 7030 - 5 units, spa - $75.

Motor Camps & Cabins
Palmerston North Holiday Park, 133 Dittmer Drive, ph 358 0349 - powered sites $17 x 2, $4.20 children; tent sites $15 x 2, $3.70 children; tourist flats $52 x 2, $10.70 children; tourist cabins (sleep 2-6) $39 x 2, $8 children; cabins (sleep 2-6) $36 x 2, $6.70 children.

Hostel
Peppertree Hostel (YHA), 121 Grey Street, ph 355 4054, fax 355 4063 - $15 per person.

Eating Out
For fine dining it is probably best to reserve a table at one of the licensed restaurants in the hotels and motor inns, but for something a bit more reasonably priced you can try one of the following:
Taj Mahal, 94 Fitzherbert Avenue, ph 356 4235 - **Licensed/BYO** - open Mon-Fri noon-2pm, Mon-Sat 5-10pm - despite the name, has western as well as Indian cuisine - **$15-25** - credit cards accepted.
Bangkok Garden, 276 Church Street, ph 358 0280 - **BYO** - open

daily 11am-2pm, 5.30pm-late - family Thai restaurant - around **$20** - credit cards accepted.

Campbell's Bar & Cafe, 360 Church Street, ph 357 3315 - **Licensed** - open daily 11am-late - wide range of dishes from the servery - **around $20**, but a bottle of wine will escalate the bill - credit cards accepted.

Old Istanbul Turkish Kebab House, 41 The Square, ph 359 3051 - **BYO** - open Tues-Sat 11.30am-2.30pm, Tues-Sun 6pm-late - belly dancers Thurs-Sat - **$25** - credit cards accepted.

Sightseeing

One unusual feature of Palmerston North is that it has 77ha of parkland right in its centre. On its southern side is the Civic Centre, which houses the Council Chambers, Information Centre and a wide variety of shops. The lookout on top of the Civic Centre provides a good view of the square and central business district.

The other main feature of the city is The Esplanade, which covers 25ha and its features are a rose garden, nature trail, aviary, conservatory, miniature railway, mini golf course and children's playground.

Massey University is 5km from the city centre on the main road south. It caters for over 6000 internal students and 10,000 correspondence students. The university is the national centre for Veterinary Sciences, Food Science and Biotechnology.

An overall view of the university can be obtained from the Monro Lookout.

The **Manawatu Art Gallery** at 398 Main Street is open Mon-Fri 10am-4.30pm, Sat-Sun 11.30am-4.30pm 10am-4.30pm, and admission is free. It houses a collection of local art from 1830 to the present, as well as a program of changing exhibitions of international arts and crafts, ph 358 8188.

The **Manawatu Museum**, 396 Main Street, ph 355 5000, has displays of early Maori and Pakeha artifacts. It is open daily 10am-5pm and there is no admission fee. Adjacent to the museum is the **Science Centre** which has the same opening hours, but costs $6 adults, $4 children.

The **National Rugby Museum**, 87 Cuba Street, ph 358 6947, has trophies and souvenirs from all over the world. It is open Mon-Sat 10am-noon, 1.30-4pm, Sun 1.30-4pm, and admission is $3 adults, $1 children.

The eastern entrance to Palmerston North is through the Manawatu Gorge. Jet boat and canoeing trips on the river can be arranged through the Information Centre.

There are many walkways in and around Palmerston North. The most popular walks are the **Riverside Walkway & Bridle Track** going through the city and taking about two-and-a-half hours; the **Tiritea Walkway** is fifteen·minutes' drive from the city and takes about two hours; the **Totara Reserve Walkway** is thirty minutes' drive from the city and takes two hours to walk; the **Coppermine Creek Walk** is fifty minutes' drive from the city in the Woodville area and takes about three hours.

Sport & Recreation

Palmerston North has a wide variety of facilities.

The rainbow-like *Manawatu Sports Stadium* in Pascal Street caters for athletics, badminton, tennis, netball, volleyball, bowls and indoor hockey.

The *Lido Complex* in Park Road next to the Holiday Park has outdoor and indoor swimming pools and spas.

There are four **golf courses** in the city, many bowling greens, and squash and tennis courts.

Roller skating is catered for at *Bell Hall* in Waldegrave Street, and outdoors at Memorial Park in Main Street.

There is a **ten-pin bowling** alley in Tremaine Avenue.

Horse racing is held at the *Awapuni Raceway*, and Trotting and **Greyhound Racing** at the *Manawatu Raceway*, Pioneer Highway.

Outlying Attractions

Foxton Beach is 39km west of the city and is a popular boating, yachting and swimming beach.

The **Rangitikei River** is 80km north of Palmerston North, and jet boat rides and whitewater raft trips are available. Check with the Information Office for details.

The **Pohangina Valley** is 42km north-west and has groves of totara trees. There are camping sites in the reserve and it has several swimming places.

From Palmerston North it is 143km, about a two-hour drive, to Wellington.

Taranaki

This area takes its name from its most prominent natural feature, Mount Taranaki (previously known as Mount Egmont). The Taranaki plains have porous, black, loamy soil which is extremely fertile. The pastures here are unbelievably green and the whole area has a lush appearance. Fingers of natural forests climb up the mountain and disappear into the morning mists.

In 1969, a large gas and condensate field (Maui) was discovered 49km offshore from Taranaki. It came onstream in 1979 and condensate from the field is shipped to Marsden Point, near Whangarei, for refining. Petrochem at Kapuni was founded in 1979 and the production of ammonia-urea commenced in April 1983.

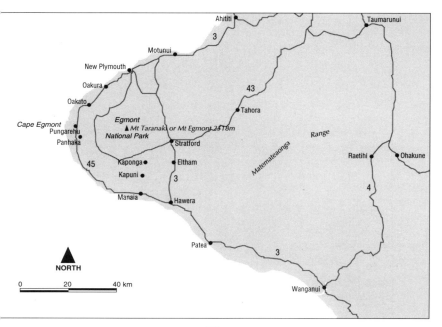

The New Zealand Synthetic Fuels Corporation Limited plant at Motunui was constructed over the years 1982-1985 and the complex achieved full production early in 1986. The Synfuel plant at Motunui processes natural gas from the Maui and Kapuni fields into gasoline. At the design production of 570,000 tonnes per annum, the complex produces the equivalent of one-third of New Zealand's petrol requirements.

The Synfuel plant was the first in the world to utilise a two stage process where natural gas is converted to methanol, and then transformed into petrol using the ZSM-5 catalyst pioneered by Mobil Oil.

Environmental awareness and safety are major considerations in the design and operation of the Synfuel complexes, which incorporate one of the most sophisticated waste-water treatment plants in New Zealand.

New Plymouth

New Plymouth is dominated by Taranaki, 2520m, a dormant volcano. Unlike the volcanoes in Tongariro National Park, Taranaki rises majestically out of lush green meadows, is covered by forest on its lower slopes, and by ice and snow above the treeline except for two or three months of the year. It has a symmetrical shape and looks very like Mt Fuji in Japan. The surrounding countryside is one of the richest dairying districts in New Zealand.

How to Get There

By Air
Air New Zealand Link (Air Nelson) has daily flights to New Plymouth from Auckland and Wellington.
Air New Zealand Link (Eagle Air) has daily flights from Kaitaia, via Auckland.

By Bus
InterCity has daily services from Auckland, Palmerston North and Wellington.

Newmans have daily services to New Plymouth from Auckland and Wellington.

By Road
Auckland - New Plymouth is 368km - approx 5 hours.
Wellington - New Plymouth is 356km - approx 5 hours.
Wanganui - New Plymouth is 163km - approx 2 hours 30 minutes.

Tourist Information
The Visitor Information Office is on the corner of Liardet and Leach Streets, ph (06) 759 6080, and is open Mon-Fri 8.30am-5pm, Sat-Sun 10am-3pm.
Information is also available from *Tourism Taranaki*, 188 Powderham Street, ph (06) 757 9909.

Accommodation
Following is a selection of available accommodation with prices for a double room per night in NZ$, which should be used as a guide only. The telephone area code is 06.

Hotels
Plymouth International, 22 Courteney Street, ph 758 0589, fax 758 9949 - 75 units, restaurant, swimming pool, spa - $75-150.
The Devon Hotel, 390 Devon Street East, ph 759 9099, fax 758 2229 - 100 rooms (private facilities), restaurant, swimming pool, sauna, spa, gymnasium - $110.

Motels
Flamingo Motel, 355 Devon Street West, ph/fax 758 8149 - 30 units, swimming pool, games room - $99-110.
Amber Court Motel, 61 Eliot Street, ph 758 0922, fax 758 6559 - 32 units, swimming pool, spa, games room - $74-94.
Saddle & Sulky Motel, 188-192 Coronation Avenue, ph/fax 757 5763 - 14 units, spa - $78-88.
Coronation Court Motel, 226 Coronation Avenue, ph 757 9125, fax 757 9123 - 21 units, spa - $65-105.
Carrington Motel, 61 Carrington Street, ph 757 9431, fax 757 9602 - 10 units - $65.
Strandon Motel, 464 Devon Street East, ph/fax 758 7762 - 9 units, swimming pool, spa - $70.

Oakura Beach Motel, 53 Wairau Road, Oakura, ph/fax 752 7680 - 7 units - $67.

Motor Camps, Cabins & Caravan Parks

Belt Road Seaside Motor Camp, 2 Belt Road, ph/fax 758 0228 - tent sites $14 x 2; cabins $25-40 x 2; backpackers' accommodation $22pp.

Fitzroy Beach Holiday Park, Beach St, ph 758 2870 - powered sites $16 x 2; tent sites $16 x 2; on-site vans $33 x 2; cabins $38 x 2.

Hookner Park, 551 Carrington Road, ph 753 9506, ph/fax 753 9168 - powered & tent sites $17 x 2; on-site caravan (sleep 4) $30 x 2; cabins $28 x 2.

Hostel

Rotary Lodge Hostel (YHA), 12 Clawton Street, ph 753 5720 - $14 per person.

Local Transport

Car Rental

Hertz, 185 Devon Street West, ph 758 8189; Avis, 25 Liardet Street, ph 757 5736; Budget, cnr Leach & Cameron Streets, ph 758 8039; BP Powderham, 71 Powderham Street, ph 758 4171.

Eating Out

There is a wide variety of restaurants in New Plymouth. Listed below are some you might like to try.

Andre's L'Escargot, 37-43 Brougham Street, ph 758 4812 - **Licensed** - open Mon-Sat for dinner - award-winning restaurant offering French and European cuisine - **$30-50** - credit cards accepted.

Gareth's, 182 Devon Street, ph 758 5104 - **Licensed** - open Mon-Fri noon-1.30pm, nightly 6pm-late - elegant restaurant with dance floor, good food - **$30-50** - credit cards accepted.

Burundi, 55A Egmont Street, ph 758 1112 - **Licensed** - open daily 6pm-late - world cuisine, live music - **$25-45** - credit cards accepted.

The Mill, 2 Powderham Street, ph 758 1935 - **Licensed** - open daily - complete entertainment venue including restaurant/bar, night club with live music and visiting acts - **$15-30** - credit cards accepted.

The Devon Seafood Smorgasbord, Devon Hotel, 390 Devon Street, ph 0800 800 930 - **Licensed** - a great selection of seafood, meat, vegetarian and oriental dishes plus fantastic desserts - open nightly with entertainment - local favourite - **$15-30** - credit cards accepted.

The Carriage, Main Road, Oakura, ph 752 7277 - **Licensed** - open 7 days for lunch, dinner, morning and afternoon teas, or a drink - restored 1918 railway carriage and station - **$25-45** - credit cards accepted.

Sportys Cafe Bar, 50 Sackville Street, Fitzroy (opposite *Pizza Hut*) - **Licensed** - open Sun-Wed 10am-10pm, Thus-Sat 10am-midnight - outdoor garden bars and bbq in summer - **$5** Sunday night roast dinner available.

Sightseeing

The main attraction is **Mt Taranaki**, 2508m, and the surrounding National Park. There are 320km of tracks in the Park with 17 park huts and shelters scattered throughout the area. Three roads lead up to the end of the treeline around 900m. Because of this, even inexperienced bush-walkers can climb to the summit in summer from Dawson Falls or the Plateau with a guide. The Information Offices will be able to put you in touch with an experienced guide. There are dangerous sections on the mountain, and even though it is unusual for snow to lie on the peak in summer, there may be occasional thin sheets of ice in sheltered spots. Walkers should be prepared for bad weather in all seasons.

Egmont Road (which branches off from Highway 3) is the most direct route to the mountain. The North Egmont Visitor Centre (approx 24km from the city centre, ph 756 8710) has an extensive display on the mountain, detailing its formation and the exploration of oil and gas in Taranaki. The Centre is open 9am-4pm daily (Dec 1 to April 30), 10am-4pm Tues-Sun (May 1 to Nov 30).

It is possible to ski on Mount Taranaki, and access to the Manganui ski-field is from Pembroke Road, Stratford. The Mountain House Motor Lodge, PO Box 303 Stratford, ph/fax (06) 765 6100, is also accessible from Pembroke Road, and has a great restaurant.

Dawson Falls (access is from Manaia Road, near Kaponga) offers another route to Mount Taranaki. The Dawson Falls

Tourist Lodge, PO Box 91 Stratford, ph/fax (06) 765 5457, is nestled on the slopes of the mountain and is built in the Swiss style. It has a licensed restaurant and bookings are essential for both meals and accommodation.

Around the Mountain Trip

This is a pleasant drive of around 200km. It follows Highway 45 around the mountain and joins Highway 3 at Eltham.

On the way you pass the Oakuru Beach turn-off. Oakura Beach is patrolled by the local surf lifesaving club during the summer season and offers safe swimming, surfing and windsurfing. After passing through Oakura, you come to the Okato Dairy Factory which produces some of the finest cheese in Taranaki. At Pungarehu you may take Cape Road to view Cape Egmont Lighthouse. Near Pungarehu is Parihaka, once the site of one of the largest Maori villages in New Zealand.

Further along Highway 45, at Manaia, a road branches off to Kapuni which has a natural gas plant and an ammonia-urea plant. These spectacular complexes are an imposing sight, especially at night when they are lit up like Christmas trees.

From Kapuni there is a road to Kaponga and Dawson Falls, or you can drive across to Eltham. The Ferndale Dairies, 11 High Street, Eltham, have a cheese factory and shop that you might like to visit. They are open Mon-Fri 8.30am-5pm.

From Eltham follow Highway 3 to Stratford and back to New Plymouth.

Worth seeing in New Plymouth

Pukekura Park is only ten minutes' walk from the centre of town. The park was created in 1876, covers 20ha, and includes a fernery, display houses, lakes, fountains, a kiosk, sports ground, historic band rotunda, and easy walking tracks. There is also an outstanding public garden of native flora, azaleas and rhododendrons. From the upper lake, near the kiosk, you can get a clear view of Mount Taranaki.

Brooklands Park is lined with walking tracks to adjoining Pukekura Park. Brooklands Bowl is an outdoor amphitheatre which holds 17,000 and is the venue for concerts during the summer months.

The Gables Colonial Hospital is New Zealand's oldest hospital and is situated in Brooklands Park. The medical museum and art gallery are open weekends and public holidays 1-4pm.

The **Taranaki Museum**, War Memorial building, Ariki Street, ph 758 9583, has an extensive collection of Maori art and colonial artefacts. Open Mon-Fri 10.30am-4.30pm, Sat-Sun 1-5pm. Admission is free.

The **Govett Brewster Art Gallery** in Queen Street, ph 758 5149, has one of New Zealand's best collections of contemporary art. The gallery has been closed for renovations and may have new hours when it reopens. Formerly it was open daily 10.30am-5pm, and admission was free.

Pouakai Zoo Park, 590 Carrington Street, about 12km from the city centre, has a good collection of exotic animals and New Zealand native animals and a walk-through aviary of New Zealand birds. Open daily, admission $4 adults, $1.50 children.

Pukeiti Rhododendron Gardens, 2290 Carrington Road, ph 752 4141 are on the fringes of the National Park. The annual Rhododendron Festival is held in October/November each year, but visitors are welcome to the garden all year round. There is a restaurant, souvenir shop and plant stalls. Admission is $8 and the gardens are open daily 9am-5pm.

Dairyland, south of Hawera, ph (06) 278 4537, has traces the history of the dairying industry from its beginnings to the use of the high-tech machinery of today. It is open daily and admission is $2.50 adults, $1 children.

Sport & Recreation

There is something for everyone in New Plymouth - cricket and bowls (both indoor and outdoor), target bowls, ten-pin bowling, horse riding, jet boating, water skiing, canoeing and swimming. Arts and crafts are well catered for, with several outlets specialising in local pottery, locally made glassware, leadlight and weaving. There are also several nightclubs.

Beaches

Surfing beaches include Fitzroy, East End and Black Beaches in New Plymouth; Oakura Beach, Wairau Road, and 'The Kumera Patch', Paora Road, Puniho; Opunake Bay; Skye Williams and Mangahume, Mangahume River Mouth; Ohawe Beach, Hawera.

Windsurfing beaches: Ngamotu and Opunake Beaches are calm enough for beginners; East End Beach, Oakura Beach, and Kina Point in Oaonui are for the experienced only.

Tours

Neumans Sightseeing Tours, ph 758 4622, fax 751 2611, have tours of the city, Mt Taranaki, and the Rhododendron Gardens, and prices range from $20 to $55.

C Tours, ph 751 1711, have a variety of scenic tours ranging in price from $25 to $60.

Beck Helicopters Ltd, Mountain Road, Eltham, ph 764 7073, offer flights over Mt Taranaki and the National Park.

Outlying Attractions

Wanganui

This town is at the mouth of the Whanganui River, 163km from New Plymouth, and approximately half-way between New Plymouth and Wellington. One of its main attractions is the river. The Whanganui is one of New Zealand's longest rivers and several tour operators offer boat trips on its reaches. The town and river are spelt differently because of an early mistake in writing the Maori name.

The Information Office, 101 Guyton Street, ph (06) 345 3286, is open Mon-Fri 8.30am-5pm, Sat-Sun 10am-2pm, and the helpful staff can supply brochures, and can book accommodation and tours, cruises, canoe trips, jetboat rides, etc.

There are quite a few attractions in Wanganui worth visiting, and here is a summary.

Wanganui Regional Museum, in the Civic Centre, Watt Street, is the largest regional museum in New Zealand. It features an outstanding Maori Court with its famous canoes, collections and natural history displays. It is open Mon-Fri 10am-4pm,

Sat-Sun 1-4.30pm. There is an admission charge, ph 345 7443.

Kowhai Children's Playpark on Anzac Parade near the Dublin Street Bridge, is a great place to visit if you have children travelling with you. It has picnic areas, go karts, bumper boats, a maze, many novel slides, carousels, and a Tot-Town Railway which runs on weekends and public holidays.

St Paul's Memorial Church, Anaua Street, Putiki, has Maori carvings and Tukutuku wall panels decorating the entire interior. Guided tours are available and a small donation is requested. A good view of the town can be obtained from **Durie Hill** which curiously is reached by a lift that goes up through the hill to the top. The pedestrian tunnel and elevator is located directly opposite the Wanganui City Bridge at the bottom of Victoria Avenue. On a clear day you can see Mt Taranaki and Mt Ruapehu from the summit, and occasionally across Cook Strait to the South Island.

Holly Lodge Estate is situated on the banks of the river and can be reached by a leisurely cruise on the paddle-wheeler *Otunui* (ph 0800 688 684), which departs daily from the City Marina. The estate has free wine tasting and you can purchase wines and liqueurs, but it also has a craft shop and museum, a large children's play area and a swimming pool. For more information and timetables, ph (06) 343 9344.

Wellington

(see Map page 144)

Wellington (population 400,000 including suburbs) is the nation's capital and seat of government as well as the crossroads between the North and South Islands. It is often called "The Windy City" as it lies on the exposed southern tip of the North Island and calm days are rare. The population is only about one-third that of Auckland.

Like Auckland, it is built on a fine harbour, but there the similarity ends. The heart of Wellington is more compact as the hills around the harbour are steeper, effectively limiting the size of the centre. For years people struggled to build houses on steep blocks higher and higher up the hillsides, but in recent years two main residential areas have been opened up by better roads and railways. The first of these areas reaches up through the Ngauranga Gorge to Porirua on the coast north-west of Wellington, and the other stretches along the Hutt River Valley to the north-east.

Climate

Wellington's climate is tempered by its proximity to the sea. The average daily maximum temperature in January is 20C and in July 11C. Its average annual rainfall is 1240mm and the annual average hours of sunshine are 2159. There is almost always a wind blowing in Wellington.

How to get There

By Air

Travelling by air from overseas is covered in the Travel Information chapter. International Airlines phone numbers are: *Air New Zealand* (04) 388 9737; *Canadian Airlines* 0800 226 234; *Qantas* 0800 808 767; *Singapore* (04) 473 9749; *United Airlines* (04) 472 0470.

Domestic Services

Air New Zealand has daily domestic flights to Wellington from:

WELLINGTON AREA

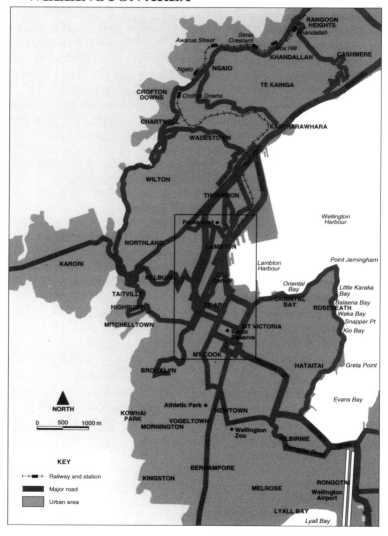

RANGOON HEIGHTS
Khandallah
Simla Crescent
Awarua Street
Box Hill
KHANDALLAH
CASHMERE
Ngaio
NGAIO
TE KAINGA
CROFTON DOWNS
Crofton Downs
CHARTWELL
KAIWHARAWHARA
WADESTOWN
WILTON
THORNDON
Wellington Harbour
Parliament
NORTHLAND
LAMBTON
Point Jernigham
KARORI
Lambton Harbour
KELBURN
CITY Centre
Oriental Bay
Little Karaka Bay
TAITVILLE
TE ARO
ORIENTAL BAY
Balaena Bay
HIGHBURY
ROSENEATH
Weka Bay
MITCHELLTOWN
MT VICTORIA
Snapper Pt
Basin Reserve
Kio Bay
MT COOK
HATAITAI
Greta Point
BROOKLYN
Evans Bay
NORTH
Athletic Park
NEWTOWN
0   500   1000 m
KOWHAI PARK
VOGELTOWN
MORNINGTON
Wellington Zoo
KILBIRNIE
Rongotai Road
KEY
├─■─┤ Railway and station
▮▮▮ Major road
▨ Urban area
BERHAMPORE
KINGSTON
RONGOTAI
MELROSE
Wellington Airport
LYALL BAY
Lyall Bay

Auckland, Bay of Islands, Blenheim, Christchurch, Dunedin, Gisborne, Hamilton, Hokitika, Invercargill, Kaitaia, Mount Cook, Napier, Nelson, New Plymouth, Queenstown, Rotorua, Taupo, Tauranga, Te Anau, Timaru, Wanaka, Wanganui, Whakatane, Whangarei; and less frequent flights from Motueka, Palmerston North, Takaka, Westport.

Ansett New Zealand has daily flights to Wellington from: Auckland, Blenheim, Christchurch, Dunedin, Invercargill, Milford Sound, Nelson, Palmerston North, Queenstown, Rotorua, Te Anau, Whakatane and Whangarei.

Transport from the Airport

The International and Domestic Airports are 8km from the city centre. Super Shuttle, ph (04) 387 8787, has the following services from the airports to the Railway Station: half-hourly 7.15am-9.15am, hourly 9.15am-3.15pm; and half-hourly 3.15pm-5.45pm. Johnstons Shuttle, ph (04) 569 9017, operate a similar service half-hourly 8am-5.30pm. The cost is $5 per person occupying a seat.

   Both companies operate a door to door service on mini coaches between the Airports and the city and all suburbs. Although this service is 'on demand' only, the coaches are usually outside the Airport Terminal for all international arrivals and outside the Domestic Terminal every 15-20 minutes for most of every day. Examples of fares are: Airport to City - NZ$8 for 1 person, NZ$10 for 2, NZ$12 for 3, NZ$14 for 4; Airport to Hutt Central - NZ$23 for 1; to Karori - NZ$14 for 1; to Trentham - NZ$38 for 1.

   The taxi fare from the Airport to the City is around $15.

By Rail

Overlander Express is a daily daytime service between Auckland and Wellington, stopping at Hamilton, Taumarunui and Palmerston North.

The Northerner is an overnight service on the same route as above, running every night except Sunday.

The Bay Express is a daily service between Napier and Wellington, through Palmerston North.

By Bus

InterCity coaches have daily services to Wellington from: Auckland, Hamilton, Napier, New Plymouth, Palmerston

North, Taupo and Tauranga, and services Thurs-Fri & Sun from Rotorua.

Newmans Coachlines have daily services to Wellington from: Auckland, Hamilton, Napier, New Plymouth, Palmerston North, Rotorua, Taupo and Tauranga.

By Car
Wellington-Auckland is 666km - approx 10 hours.
   Wellington-Gisborne is 550km - approx 12 hours.
   Wellington-New Plymouth is 355km - approx 5 hours.
   Wellington-Palmerston North is 145km - 2 hours +.
   Wellington-Rotorua is 462km - approx 7 hours.

Tourist Information
There is an information office at the Ansett Terminal of the International Airport, ph (04) 385 5123, that is open Mon-Fri 7am-6.30pm, Sat-Sun 8am-4pm, and one at the Domestic Airport, ph (04) 385 5123, that is open daily 8am-8pm.

   Wellington City Information Centre is in the Civic Administration Building, 101 Wakefield Street, Civic Square ph (04) 801 4000, and it is open daily 9am-5pm.

   The Automobile Association office is in AA Centre, 342-352 Lambton Quay, ph (04) 473 8738.

   Capital Times is a visitors' information weekly and it is available from most tourist and accommodation outlets, and stands throughout the city and Hutt Valley.

Money Exchange
Trading banks are open Mon-Fri 9am-4.30pm, but trading in overseas currency closes at 3pm. Hotels will change foreign currency travellers cheques.

Accommodation
There is no shortage of accommodation in Wellington, but it is still wise to book ahead. As usual with a big city, it is probably less expensive to stay in the outer suburbs than in the city centre itself.

   Following is a selection of accommodation in the city, with prices in NZ$ for a double room per night, which should be used as a guide only. Many of these establishments have discounted rates for the weekends, and for December-January.

The telephone area code is 04.

Hotels & Motor Inns

Terrace Regency Hotel, 345 The Terrace, ph 385 9829, fax 385 2119 - 110 rooms (private facilities), restaurant, cocktail lounge, swimming pool, sauna, gymnasium - $135.

Harbour City Motor Inn, 92-96 Webb Street, ph 384 9808, fax 384 9806 - 25 units, licensed restaurant, spa - $130.

Portland Towers Hotel, 24 Hawkestone Street, ph 473 2208, fax 473 3892 - 107 rooms (private facilities), licensed restaurant, cocktail bar - $140.

Central City Apartment Hotel, cnr Victoria & Edward Streets, ph 385 4166, fax 385 4167 - 48 suites - $157.

Airport Hotel Wellington, 16 Kemp Street (off Evans Bay Parade), Kilbirnie, ph 387 2189, fax 387 2787 - 120 units, licensed restaurant, cocktail bars, swimming pool - $60-130.

Hotel Willis Lodge, 318 Willis Street, ph 384 5955, ph 384 5952 - 23 units, licensed restaurant - $80-135.

Motels

Capital View Motor Inn, 12 Thompson Street, ph/fax 385 0515 - 21 apartments - $90-110.

Motel 747, 80 Kilbirnie Crescent, ph/fax 387 3184 - 8 units - $90-100.

Trekkers Motel, 213 Cuba Street (or Dunlop Terrace), ph 385 2153, fax 382 8873 - 54 units, 2 licensed restaurants, spa, sauna - $89. (Backpacker bunks $17 per person).

Wellington Motel, 14 Hobson St, ph 472 0334, fax 472 6825 - 5 units - $90-105.

Academy Motor Lodge, 327 Adelaide Road, ph 389 6166, fax 389 1761 - 26 units, spa - $90-115.

Apollo Lodge, 49 Majoribanks Stt, ph/fax 385 1849 -33 units- $85.

Mana Motel, 41 Mana Esplanade, ph 233 8139, fax 233 8137 - 16 units, swimming pool, spa - $86-92.

Halswell Lodge, 21 Kent Terrace, ph 385 0196, fax 385 0503 - 29 units - motel units $110, hotel rooms $69-79.

Carillon Motor Inn, 33 Thompson St, ph 384 8795, fax 385 7036 - 28 units - $69-79.

Hostels

Wellington City YHA (formerly Port Nicholson Youth Hostel), cnr Cambridge Terrace & Wakefield St, ph 801 7280, fax 801 7278 -

$18 per adult, $12 per youth, $9 under 15 years.
Downtown Backpackers, 1 Bunny Street, ph 473 8482, fax 471 1073 - 88 rooms - share $17, Double $40, twin $38, single $30.

Caravan Park
Hutt Park Holiday Village & Motels, 95 Hutt Park Road, Lower Hutt, ph 568 5913, fax 568 5914 - 6 motel units - $78, 5 tourist flats $58, 20 tourist cabins $32-40, caravan sites $20, tent sites $17.

Local Transport
For information on Wellington's bus, train and harbour ferry services, contact Ridewell on 801 7000.

Bus
The main city bus terminal is on the corner of Featherston Street and Lambton Quay, ph 385 9955.

There is a regular service to Eastbourne from the terminal near the Railway Station, ph 562 8154.
Stagecoach Wellington buses travel to all the interesting parts of the city and have a Daytripper Ticket whereby all day travel only costs $5, ph 801 7000.

Train
Suburban and long distance trains depart from Wellington Railway Station. For information and timetables, ph 472 5399 or 0800 802 802.

Suburban services include: the *Upper Hutt-Melling Line*, which travels to Upper Hutt via Kaiwharawhara, Ngauranga, Petone, Western Hutt, Melling, Ava, Woburn, Hutt Central, Epuni, Naenae, Wingate, Taita, Pomare, Manor Park, Silverstream, Heretaunga, Trentham and Wallaceville; the *Paraparaumu Line*, travelling to Paraparaumu via Kaiwharawhara, Takapu Road, Redwood, Tawa, Linden, Kenepuru, Porirua, Paremata, Mana, Plimmerton, Pukerua Bay, Muri and Paekakariki; and the *Johnsonville Line*, to Johnsonville via Crofton Downs, Ngaio, Awarua Street, Simla Crescent, Box Hill, Khandallah and Raroe.

Ferry
The *East by West Ferry* plies between Wellington and

Eastbourne, departing from Queen's Wharf, ph 472 5399 or 0800 658 999.

The *Trust Bank Ferry*, ph 499 1273, has several services daily between Queen's Wharf and Days Bay. Fares are $6 adult single, $3 child single, $33 family return.

Also available are evening harbour cruises, island trips and heritage cruises.

Cable Car

The *Kelburn Cable Car*, ph 472 2199, runs from Cable Car Lane on Lambton Quay to Upland, taking approximately 6 minutes to complete the journey. The Cable Car runs Mon-Fri 7am-10pm, Sat 9.20am-6pm, Sun 10.30am-6pm, and the fares are: adults $1.50 one way, $2.50 return; children $0.70 one way, $1.40 return; family return $8.

Taxi

Some taxi companies have two different rates for their fares. The green (cheaper) rate applies between 6am-8pm on weekdays, with the red (dearer) rate applying outside those hours. Ask the driver before beginning the journey, or check out the light on top of the taxi meter. Taxis are not normally hailed from the kerb. You are expected to go to a taxi rank, of which there are plenty all around the city and airport. Some taxi companies: Black, White & Grey Taxis, ph 385 9900; Capital City Cabs, ph 388 4884; Gold & Black Taxis, ph 388 8888; Olympic Taxis, ph 388 8777; AAA Taxis, ph 388 8833; Wellington Combined Taxis, ph 384 4444.

Car Hire

Avis, ph 801 8108; Budget, ph 385 9085; Hertz, ph 384 3809; National, ph 473 6600.

Eating Out

Wellington is probably the gourmet capital of New Zealand, with many award winning restaurants and cafes. The *Capital Times* includes a lengthy list.

All the better class hotels and motels have restaurants, but if you feel like going out you should be able to find something which suits your taste and budget.

One excellent regulation that the Tourism Council has instituted with the Department of Health is a cleanliness rating which restaurants are obliged to display in the public area of the restaurant. So you know well before hand if it is worth taking the risk with a restaurant or not.

Here is a selection for you to try.

Chevy's, 97 Dixon Street, ph 384 2724 - **Licensed** - open daily 11.30am-late - restaurant/bar with American food - around **$20** - credit cards accepted.

Uncle Cheng's, 70 Courtenay Place, ph 801 9568 - **Licensed** - open daily for lunch and dinner - Szechuan/Cantonese cuisine - **$25** - credit cards accepted.

Dish Cafe and Bar, 90 Dixon Street, ph 384 7544 - **Licensed** - open Mon-Fri 11.30am-2.30pm, Mon-Sat 5.30pm-late - a favourite with the locals, mixed menu - **around $25** - credit cards accepted.

As You Like It Cafe, 32 Riddiford Street, Newtown, ph 389 3983 - **Licensed/BYO** - open Tues-Fri noon-2.30pm, Tues-Sun 6-10.30pm - NZ cuisine with a Shakespearian theme - **$25-45** - credit cards accepted.

Shed Five, Waterfront, Lambton Quay, ph 499 9069 - **Licensed** - open daily 9am-late - winner of *Cheap Eats* Restaurant-of-the-Year - cafe and seafood restaurant - **$45** - credit cards accepted.

Goudy's, 105 Vivian Street, ph 384 6466 - **BYO** - open daily - Spanish, Italian and Southern French cuisine - **$25-45** - credit cards accepted.

Mexican Cantina, 19 Edward Street, ph 385 9711 - **BYO** - open for lunch and dinner - Mexican cuisine - $24 - credit cards accepted.

Rainbow Dragon Chinese Restaurant, Karori Mall, 236 Karori Rd, Karori, ph 476 3455 - **BYO** - open daily for lunch and dinner - Cantonese and Sichuan cuisine - **$24** - credit cards accepted.

Wellington Settlement Restaurant, 155 Willis Street, ph 385 8920 - **BYO** - open Mon-Fri noon-2pm, Mon-Sat from 5.30pm - blackboard menu, pianist plays every night - **$25-45** - credit cards accepted.

Grain of Salt, 232 Oriental Parade, Oriental Bay, ph 384 8642 - **Licensed/BYO** - open Mon-Fri from noon for lunch, nightly 6.30-9pm - award winning NZ cuisine - over **$45** - credit cards accepted.

Museum of New Zealand

Bellissimo Trattoria Italiana, 1st floor, Dukes Arcade, cnr Willis & Manners Streets, ph 499 1154 - **Licensed** - open Mon-Fri noon-midnight, Sat-Sun 6pm-midnight - **$25-45** - credit cards accepted.

Dada Restaurant & Bar, 9 Edward St, ph 385 2916 - **Licensed** - open for lunch Mon-Fri, dinner nightly, brunch Sun - International cuisine - live entertainment - **$25-45** - credit cards accepted.

Il Casino Restaurant & Piano Bar, 108-112 Tory Street, ph 385 7496 - **Licensed** - open for lunch Mon-Fri, dinner nightly - Italian cuisine - **around $40** - credit cards accepted.

La Spaghettata, 15 Edward Street, ph 384 2812 - open for lunch Mon-Fri, dinner Mon-Sat - Italian cuisine - **$25-45** - credit cards accepted.

Turner's Licensed Restaurant, Willis Street Village, 142 Willis Street, ph 385 0630 - **Licensed/BYO** - open nightly from 5.30pm - steakhouse - **$25-45** - credit cards accepted.

Kiwi Rock Cafe, 97 Willis Street, ph 472 1555 - **Licensed** - open from noon till late every day - uniquely New Zealand burgers, etc **- around $20** - credit cards accepted.

McDonalds, 11-13 Courtenay Place; Lambton Quay; Manners Street; 190 Riddiford Street, Newtown; High Street, Lower Hutt; Johnsonville Road, Johnsonville.

Entertainment

Wellington is a city of theatres and galleries and is visited by touring performances and exhibitions. The Michael Fowler Centre, the State Opera House and other theatres, stage world-standard productions throughout the year - see the daily papers for performance times. Wellington is the home of the national ballet company and symphony orchestra, as well as theatres groups.

Cinemas

Embassy, Kent Terrace, ph 384 7657.
Mid-City, Manners Street, ph 384 3567.
Paramount, Courtenay Place, ph 384 3553.
Penthouse, Brooklyn, ph 384 3157.
Regent, Manners Mall, ph 472 5182.
Maidstone, Upper Hutt, ph 528 5136.
Odeon, Lower Hutt, ph 566 4729.

Theatres

Bats, Kent Terrace, ph 802 4175.
Circa, Taranaki Street, ph 801 7992.
Depot, Alpha Street, ph 483 4531.
Downstage, Courtenay Place, ph 384 9639.
State Opera House, Manners Street, ph 384 3842.
Taki Rua, Alpha Street, ph 384 4531.
Michael Fowler Centre, Wakefield Street, ph 471 1573.
Wellington Repertory, Dixon Street, ph 385 4939.

Night Clubs

Allies Cabaret, cnr Dixon Street & Cuba Mall, ph 385 4000.
Arena, 259 Wakefield Street, ph 385 0174.
Club de Ville, Broderick Road, Johnsonville, ph 477 1569.
Metro, Manners Street, ph 385 3870.

Bars

Arizona, cnr Featherston & Gray Streets, ph 495 7867.
Bar Bodega, 286 Willis Street, ph 384 8212.
Bull & Bear, Plimmers Lane, ph 472 6886.
Diva Bar & Espresso, 37 Dixon Street, ph 385 2987.
Ecstasy Plus, cnr Courtenay Place & Tory Street, ph 384 9495.

Kaminsky's Bar, 24 Taranaki Street, ph 384 4281.

The Loaded Hog, 14-20 Bond Street, 472 9160.

Lovelock's Sports Bar, 14 Bond Street, ph 472 9130.

Molly Malone's, cnr Taranaki Street & Courtenay Place, ph 384 2896.

Western Park Tavern, 285 Tinakori Road, Thorndon, ph 472 1320.

Taverns

Back Bencher Pub & Cafe, 34 Molesworth Street, Thorndon, ph 472 3065.

The Featherston Tavern, cnr Featherston & Johnston Streets, ph 472 4045.

The Lord Nelson Tavern, Settlement Arcade, 155 Willis Street, ph 385 1783.

The Old Bailey Bar & Cafe, cnr Ballance Street & Lambton Quay, ph 471 2021.

The Southern Cross, 35 Abel Smith Street, ph 384 9085.

Western Park Tavern, 285 Tinakori Road, Thorndon, ph 472 1320.

Shopping

Downtown Wellington has some interesting shopping centres, and there are a few in the suburbs. The major department store is *Kirkcaldie & Stains Ltd*, Johnston Street. For those interested in art and craft, Wellington is a pure delight.

Shopping Centres/Malls

Most of the activity still centres around Lambton Quay. The Queen's Wharf complex has been a flop unfortunately. Wellington's population has tended to stay static with the loss in population being made up by the influx. Tinakori Road has some very pleasant boutique retailers and is worth the walk albeit steep from the city.

BNZ Centre, Willis Street, City, an underground complex below Wellington's tallest building.

Cuba Mall, Cuba Street, City.

Grand Arcade, Willis Street, City.

Capital on the Quay, Lambton Quay, City.

Gresham Plaza, Lambton Quay, City.

Harbour City Centre, Lambton Quay, City.

James Smith's Corner, 55 Cuba Street, City.
Lambton Square, Lambton Quay, City.
Queen's Wharf, City.

Art and Craft Outlets

The Potters Shop, Kirkcaldie & Stains Building, Johnston Street, City, ph 473 8803.

Janne Land Gallery, 170 Cuba Street, ph 384 2912 - open Tues-Thurs 11am-4.30pm, Fri-Sat 11am-3pm.

Cubacade Antiques and Curios, Cuba Street, City, ph 384 9712.

Clayshapes Gallery, Oriental Parade (opposite the fountain), City, ph 384 4215 - open daily 10am-6pm.

Decade, 10 Majoribanks Street, (Embassy Theatre Complex), City, ph 801 9996 - open Mon-Fri 11am-7pm, Sat 9am-4pm.

Nexus Antiques, Level 2, AA Centre, 342-352 Lambton Quay, City, ph 499 3922 - open Mon-Fri 10am-4.30pm, Thurs to 5.30pm, Sat 10am-1pm.

Thorndon Antiques & Fine China, 109 Molesworth Street, City, ph 473 0173 - open Mon-Sat 11am-4pm.

Walker & Hall Antiques, 93 The Terrace, City, ph 473 9266 - open Mon-Fri 9am-5pm; also BNZ Shopping Complex, 1 Willis Street, City, ph 472 4259 - open Mon-Sat 9am-5.30pm (open later on Fri).

Markets

The Marketplace, Manthel Motors Building, 186-200 Wakefield Street, ph 385 4464, has the downstairs open daily 9am-5pm, but the upstairs section is only open Sat-Sun 10am-5pm.

Wakefield Market, cnr Jervois Quay & Taranaki Street, ph 472 9239, is open Fri 11am-6pm, Sat-Sun 10am-5pm, with more than 140 stalls on three floors.

Thorndon

This historic inner-city suburb, near the Parliament buildings, is a great place for little art and craft shops that have changed very little from the nineteenth century, particularly in Tinakori Road. Situated near the Botanical Gardens, Thorndon also has many restaurants and cafes; Wellington's earliest cemetery, in Bolton Street; Katherine Mansfield's Birthplace, in Tinakori Road (open Mon 10am-2.30pm, Tues-Sun 10am-4pm, adults $4, children $1); and the historically classified Ascot Street, with its workers' cottages from last century. On the corner of Mulgrave and Sydney Street East is the Thistle Inn, the oldest pub on its original site in New Zealand.

Sightseeing

Wellington became New Zealand's capital in 1865, so it is not surprising that politicians and public servants are found here in large numbers. The city's skyline has changed in recent years with many old buildings being torn down and replaced with new structures. The architecture of smaller buildings tends to be in wood as Wellington is in an earthquake zone. Much of the present day harbour shore is reclaimed land, and now Wellington's main shopping street is Lambton Quay, where once large ocean-going ships docked. The city has the bustling air of a place on the move.

One of Wellington's greatest attractions is its harbour. Wellington is a busy port with containers from all over the world arriving here, as well as produce and manufactured goods in transit between the North and South Islands. Row after row of containers can be seen lined up on the wharf like pupils at assembly. Most visitors also pass through here on their way to or from the South Island, as the inter-island ferries ply between here and Picton.

Wellington harbour has several sandy bays, the closest to the city centre being Oriental Bay, which has a boat harbour packed with yachts, motor boats, etc. The people of Wellington also make good use of their harbour and during summer evenings and weekends it is alive with sailing craft of all shapes and sizes. The harbour can best be seen from one of the lookouts, or from the deck of a boat whilst on a harbour cruise.

The **Maritime Museum** is on Queen's Wharf, ph 472 8904, and is open Mon-Fri 9.30am-4pm, Sat, Sun and public holidays 1-4.30pm. It has an extensive collection of maritime memorabilia, including models of ships, paintings, flags, bells, maps, log books and a captain's cabin.

The **Michael Fowler Centre** is on the harbour front. It is a modern conference, exhibition and cultural centre, and is certainly worth seeing as its architecture and setting are superb. Next to it is the Town Hall complex.

Lambton Quay, a vibrant street, is now two blocks back from the harbour. Many of the old buildings have been pulled down and replaced with new towers and open space. The cable car's lower station is found here. The architecture in this commercial and shopping area is modern and imaginative. There are round buildings, beehive-shaped buildings, interesting shopping arcades, plazas, international hotels, etc. Lambton Quay is busy as most Wellingtonians have to walk around it to get from point A to point B as the city is so compact.

Some of the interesting city centre buildings are:
Government Building on Lambton Quay was built from timber in 1876. It is the largest timber structure in the Southern Hemisphere. All 22 chimneys have been removed as they were considered dangerous in the event of earthquakes.

The modern **Government Offices** in Molesworth Street have the nickname of *The Beehive*, for obvious reasons. Next to them, built in traditional style, is the marble Parliament Building. The Chambers are modelled exactly on the British Parliament at Westminster. The General Assembly Library is built in gothic-revival style. Tours of the building leave from the ground floor foyer daily at varying times according to the schedule of the House - contact the tourist information office for details.

The **National Library**, ph 474 3000, is also in Molesworth Street. It is open Mon-Fri 9am-5pm, Sat 9am-1pm. The Alexander Turnbull Section houses the original Treaty of Waitangi, Captain Cook's log, and manuscripts of Katherine Mansfield who was born in Wellington.

Old St Paul's Church, Mulgrave Street, Thorndon (near the railway station) was built in 1865 in Early English Gothic style, adapted to the requirements of a wooden building. It has a magnificent wooden interior and is open for inspection Mon-Sat 10.30am-4.30pm, Sun 1-4.30pm, and admission is free but donations are welcome, ph 473 6722.

St Mary of the Angels, Boulcott Street, built of concrete in the

Gothic style, has been refurbished. It has superb stained glass windows and is worth a visit.

One of Wellington's most famous landmarks is the **Cable Car**. The lower station is just off Lambton Quay (opposite end to the old Government Buildings) and the upper terminal is in Upland Road near the Botanic Gardens. It stops at Clifton Terrace, Talavera Terrace and Salamanca Road on its way to the top. There is a service every 10 minutes (see Local Transport). The cable car is a standing funicular which operates on a driven balance rope system, i.e. there are two cars at the end of a single rope driven by an electric motor and they pass each other on a loop at Talavera Station half-way up the 610m slope. The average gradient is 1:5.6m, and the car rises 120m on the journey. The present system was installed in 1979, replacing the one that commenced operations in 1902.

The Botanical Gardens are home to the Lady Norwood Rose Garden, which is laid out in a formal design with more than a hundred types of roses, areas of wilderness, bush, exotic flora,

Parliament House and the Parliamentary Offices (The Beehive).

formal gardens and lawns. They cover 26ha and include as well a children's play area, duck pond, sound shell, Begonia House, herb garden, Education Centre and tea rooms.

Within the gardens is the **Carter Observatory**, where there are information sessions on weekends, public holidays and on weekdays during school holidays. Adults $4, children $2.

About 700m along Upland Road from the Cable Car Station is **Kelburn Shopping Centre**. It contains a cosmopolitan mixture of restaurants and boutiques.

Museum of New Zealand, the **National Art Gallery** and the **New Zealand Academy of Fine Arts** were all now housed under the one roof on the harbour around from Queens Wharf. The Museum has a wonderful collection of Maori artefacts and some Cook relics, e.g. the figure-head from the *Resolution*. The gallery's collection comprises a large range of sculptures, etchings, and of course, paintings, including some excellent Rembrandts.

The Carillon is in Buckle Street. It is a World War I and II Memorial, and has 49 bells that are played regularly each week.

The **National Cricket Museum** is in the Old Stand at the Basin Reserve on Buckle Street, ph 385 6602, and is open daily October through April 10.30am-3.30pm, weekends May through September 10.30am-3.30pm. The museum has many fascinating exhibits including a curved Addington bat dated 1743; a one piece straight shape bat made by the famous James Cobbett in about 1830; Dennis Lillee's (in)famous aluminium bat; and the Australian blazer worn by the immortal Clarrie Grimmett during the Bodyline series in 1932-33. Admission is $2 adults, $1 unaccompanied children.

The Colonial Cottage Museum, 68 Nairn Street, ph 384 9122, is about 15 minutes walk from the Museum along Buckle and Webb Streets, into Willis Street, then up Nairn Street. The cottage was built in 1858 by William Wallis, a carpenter, and lived in by his descendants until 1972. It provides an opportunity to see the furniture, furnishings and household equipment of the Victorian age, in a faithfully preserved original setting. Open Mon-Fri 10am-4pm, Sat-Sun 1-4.30pm, admission is $3 adults, $1 children.

Down the road from the Museum you can catch a No. 11 or 23 bus to the Zoo in Newtown Park. It is open daily 8.30am-5pm, ph 389 8130. There is a Kiwi House and a miniature train, as well as all the usual animals.

A good view of the city can be obtained from Mount Victoria, 211m. The No 20 Bus from the Railway or Lambton Quay travels there Mon-Fri, and the view from the top is certainly worth the trip. From Mt Victoria you can go down to Oriental Bay, which is a favourite swimming and wind-surfing spot.

There are many more beaches scattered around the Miramar Peninsula.

Sport and Recreation

Golf
Karori Golf Club Inc, South Makara Road, Makara, ph 476 7337.
Manor Park Golf Club, off Western Hutt Motorway at Haywards, ph 563 8794.
Miramar Golf Course, adjacent to Wellington Airport, ph 388 2099.
Whitby Golf Club, Discovery Drive, Whitby, ph 234 7409.

Swimming
There are numerous swimming areas in the 21 bays along Marine Drive, but if you are visiting Wellington in winter, there are three indoor heated swimming centres, all open daily 6am-9pm.
Keith Spry Pool, 15 Frankmore Avenue, Johnsonville, ph 478 9237.
Freyberg Pool & Fitness Centre, 139 Oriental Bay, ph 384 3107.
Wellington Regional Aquatic Centre, 63 Kilbirnie Crescent, Kilbirnie, ph 387 8029.

Facilities for all other sports are available, and details can be found in the Yellow Pages of the Telephone Directory.

Spectator Sports

Rugby Union is played at Athletic Park, Newtown whose exposed elevation between Cook's Strait and the harbour makes it subject to the regular gale; **Rugby League** at either The Basin Reserve or Fraser Park, Lower Hutt; and **Cricket** at the Basin and Hutt Rec, Lower Hutt.

Horse Racing fixtures are held at Trentham, and **Trotting** and **Greyhound Races** are held at Hutt Park.

Outlying Attractions

Wellington's suburbs are broken up into distinct areas by the mountainous terrain, and therefore are in two sections:

1. the Kapiti Coast;
2. the Hutt River Valley and the Eastern Bays.

The Kapiti Coast

Porirua is about 20 minutes north of Wellington on a harbour which opens out into Cook Strait. It is a popular hang gliding area.

Attractions: the *Gear Homestead*, the nineteenth century home of meatworks founder James Gear. It has been restored and is open on the first Sunday of the month 1-5pm; the *Porirua Museum*, on the Porirua-Titahi Bay Road, open Tues-Sun 10am-4.30pm, ph 237 6763; *Aotea Lagoon*; *Melody Farm Music Museum*; and *McArthur Park Seaquarium*, open daily 10am-4pm.

There is a good surfing beach at Titahi Bay, and on the north side of the harbour is the town of Pimmerton.
The **Kapiti Coast** begins 20km from Wellington and stretches north for another 30km. It is a dairying, orchard and market garden area, and its sheltered waters make it a popular place for sailing and fishing. There is a regular rail service between Wellington and **Paraparaumu**, the major town of the area.

Paraparaumu has a good selection of accommodation, restaurants and shopping centres, and the *Southwards Car Museum*.

Boat trips to Kapiti Island can be arranged, ph 298 6085.

Arrowtown area with Coronet Peak in the background,
Central Otago.

Wellington, the capital.

CENTRAL WELLINGTON

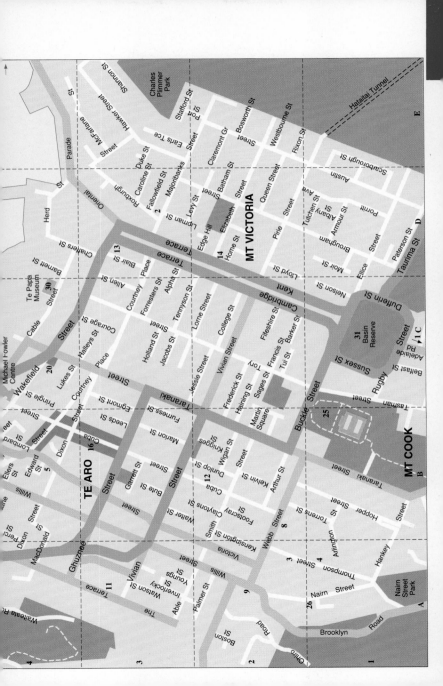

MAP KEY
WELLINGTON CITY

Accommodation

1 Academy Motor Lodge C1
2 Apollo Lodge D3
3 Capital View Motor Inn A2
4 Carillon Motor Inn A1
5 Central City Apartment Hotel B4
6 Downtown Backpackers C7
7 Halswell Lodge C8
8 Harbour City Motor Inn B2
9 Hotel Willis Lodge A2
10 Portland Towers Hotel C8
11 Terrace Regency Hotel A3
12 Trekkers Motel B2
13 Wellington City YHA D3
14 Wellington Motel D2

Shopping

15 BNZ Centre B5
16 Cuba Mall/Manners Mall B3/B4
17 Grande Arcade B5
18 Lambton Quay - Capital on the Quay, Gresham
    Plaza, Harbour City Centre, Lambton Square B6
19 Queens Wharf C6
20 Wakefield Markets C4

Sightseeing

21 Ascot Terrace A8
22 The Beehive (Government Offices) B8
23 The Botanical Gardens A7
24 Cable Car B6
25 The Carillon B1
26 The Colonial Cottage Museum A1
27 Lambton Quay B6
28 Maritime Museum C6
29 Michael Fowler Centre C4
30 Te Papa Museum
    (Museum of New Zealand) C4
31 The National Cricket Museum C1
32 The National Library C8
33 Old St Paul's Church (Anglican) C8
34 St Mary of the Angels (Roman Catholic) B5
35 Thistle Inn C8

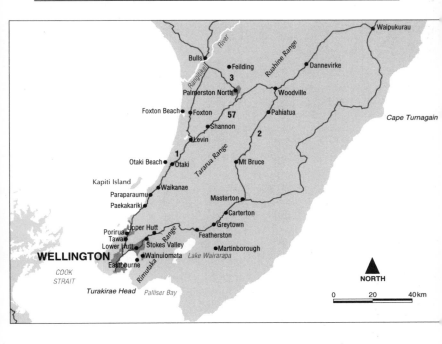

In Otaihanga Road, ph 297 1221, the Southwards Car Museum has one of the largest private motor vehicle collections in the Southern Hemisphere, and it is open daily 9am-5pm. Admission is $4 adults, $1 children.

North of Paraparaumu is *Lindale Tourist Centre*, ph 297 0916, which is open daily 9am-5pm, and has live animal shows at 2pm on weekends and daily during school holidays. The Park also has a cheese factory, farm kitchen, wine bar, honey hive, craft shop, helicopter tours and much more.

South of Paraparaumu is **Paekakariki**, home to *Wellington Tramway Museum* and *Paekakariki Railway Museum*. The Tramway Museum is in Queen Elizabeth II Park, ph 292 8361, and is open weekends and public holidays 11am-5pm. Rides are available across 2km of restored track. The Railway Museum, on SH 1, ph 475 8701, is open for inspection on weekends, but rides are only available three times a year and are advertised in local papers.

The nearby Hemi Matenga Memorial Park Scenic Reserve, the

Nga Manu Bird Sanctuary and the Kaitawa Scenic Reserve all have nature trails. For further information on this part of the world, contact the Kapiti Coast Promotion Council, Paraparaumu, ph 298 8993.

Further along the coast is the *Rangiatea Church* at **Otaki**. It is said to be one of the finest Maori Churches in New Zealand, with carvings and tukutuku wall panels. Construction on the church began in 1849.

Levin lies between the Tararua Ranges and the coast, and has a population of around 16,000. It is 100km north-east of Wellington and is the service centre for the surrounding berry fruit orchards and dairy farms. It is also a textile production centre. The *Kimberley Scenic Reserve* is 8km south of Levin and offers river swimming and picnic areas. The *Waikawa Beach Reserve* is 18km south of Levin on the coast, and offers sea and river swimming. *Waitarere Beach*, 14km from Levin on the Foxton Highway, is where the *Hyderabad* shipwreck lies. This huge sailing ship was driven ashore in 1878.

The Hutt River Valley and the Eastern Bays

Lower Hutt extends from the Petone side of the Wellington Harbour to the Rimutaka Ranges, 30km to the north. The City of Lower Hutt has a population of over 96,000, and includes Petone, Eastbourne, Wainuiomata, Stokes Valley and the Western Hill suburbs, including Kelson, Belmont, Harbourview, Normandale, Maungarakei and Korokoro. An excellent Visitor Information Centre is in The Pavilion, 25 Laings Road, Lower Hutt, ph (04) 566 7218, and it is open every day in summer, and Mon-Sat in winter.

In Laings Road is the *Dowse Art Museum*, **one of the country's finext art galleries with works by local and overseas artists. The museum is open Mon-Fri 10am-4pm, Sat-Sun 11am-5pm, ph (04) 570 6500.**

Nearby, still in Laings Road, are the *Civic Gardens*, which include: the Tutukiwi House, featuring a large selection of New Zealand's sixteen hundred odd species of ferns, as well as a great display of orchids; the sunken Riddiford Gardens with waterfalls; and a children's playground.

In Mitchell Street, near the Lower Hutt Hospital, is the

Mitchell Park Rose Garden, with over 2500 plants laid out in formal gardens. *Percy's Scenic Reserve*, on the Hutt Motorway, has walkways into the natural bushland as well as many native plants and birds.

Petone, the Gateway to the Eastern Bays, lies at the head of the harbour. *The Settlers' Museum*, in The Esplanade, ph (04) 568 8373, has changing displays of Maori and Pakeha settlement of the area, ph 568 8373. The Museum is open Tues-Fri noon-4pm, Sat-Sun 1-5pm, and admission is by donation. It is built on the site of the landing place of the area's first settlers.

The Settlers Market, Jackson Street, is open Sat 10am-4.30pm, Sun 11am-4.30pm.

Eastbourne is a peaceful seaside community about half an hour's drive from Wellington, on the east side of the harbour opposite the city centre. There is an hourly bus service from Wellington Mon-Fri, and the trip takes about 40 minutes. It has several pleasant beaches, and is popular with the boating fraternity. There are also several bush walks around the town.

Eastbourne is a popular arts and crafts centre and has several craft shops and galleries. There is a rough track from there to the Pencarrow Head Lighthouse.

Upper Hutt City is only 25 minutes' drive from Wellington, and although it is an industrial area, careful planning has ensured that there is still plenty of green - there are 32 parks and reserves! Connected to Wellington by a regular train service, Upper Hutt has a population of 37,000.

Attractions include: *Staglands Wildlife Reserve* in the Akatarawa Valley; the *Twin Lakes Lookout* that overlooks the waterworks system in the Kaitoke Regional Park; the *Maori Marae* in Maidstone Park; *Church of St John the Evangelist*, cnr Moonshine Road & Fergusson Drive, which was built in 1863 and has graves of many early settlers of the district; *Silverstream Steam Rail and Vintage Aircraft* at Eastern Hutt Road; and the internationally known racing complex at *Trentham*, which is the venue for the 'Magic Million Yearling Sales' and the 'Wellington Cup Racing Carnival'.

North of Upper Hutt, on the Waikanae Road, is *Staglands Wildlife Reserve***, which has walk-through aviaries and enclosures, a log tearoom, crafts and souvenirs, and barbecue facilities. Visitors can have a go on the flying foxes, or swim in the Akatarawa River. The reserve is open daily 10am-5pm. For more information contact Upper Hutt Promotion & Development Board, ph (04) 527 6041.**

Wairarapa

The hinterland of the Wairarapa is over the Rimutaka hills from Wellington, and is serviced by bus and train.

The only remaining Fell locomotive in the world is at **Featherston**, 32km from Upper Hut. The train originally ran on three rails to climb 265m up the Rimutaka Incline, which is now an interesting walkway.

Martinborough is 18km from Featherston, and was founded by the Hon John Martin who laid the town out like a Union Jack. Until the early 1980s this area was used for sheep and cattle farming. Then it was realised that it was similar to the Burgundy area in France and grape vines were planted. Now Martinborough is recognised for its fine wines which are getting better year by year. Well worth a visit.

At **Greytown**, 13km from Featherston, is Cobblestones, Wairarapa's Regional Early Settlers Museum. The museum incorporates several early buildings and is open daily 9am-5pm.

Masterton is the main centre for the Wairarapa and has a good selection of hotels, motels and restaurants. In March each year the town hosts the world famous Golden Shears International Shearing Championships which lure shearers from all over the world.

The **Mt Bruce** National Wildlife Centre is 28km north of Masterton and has fifteen different aviaries and a nocturnal complex with kiwis, morepork owls and the weta (a large insect).

The Marlborough Sounds and Nelson

This is another area for boating, bush camping and diving, as it has hundreds of little coves, beautiful forests and loads of sunshine (over 2500 hours annually). It is not as spectacular and rugged as the west coast of the South Island, but its mellow beauty and more reliable weather make it an ideal area for a relaxing holiday.

Picton

Picton (population 3500) is a picturesque little town at the tip of Queen Charlotte Sound, and the introduction to the South Island for visitors arriving from Wellington on the Cook Strait ferries. Once a contender for capital of New Zealand, Picton now only seems to come to life when the ferry arrives.

Unfortunately many people leave the ferry and board buses or trains for towns further afield, thereby passing up an opportunity to explore the Marlborough Sounds. If your itinerary falls into this category, at least catch a daylight ferry so that you can see some of the Sounds on the way in or out.

How to Get There

By Ferry

Two passenger ships, the *Aratika* and the *Arahura*, ply between Wellington and Picton and the cruise takes 3 hours aboard the *Arahura* and 3 hours 20 minutes aboard the *Aratika*. Both ships carry passengers and cars, and it is a drive on/drive off service. Adult one-way fares are $44 standard; one-way small car fares are $160 standard; one-way large cars fares are $160 + $20 per half metres over 6m standard. There are Economy, Sailaway Saver and Super Saver reduced fares, but each has its own set of conditions. For further information call the Interislander Reservations Centre, ph 0800 802 802, seven days 7am-9pm.

The normal timetable Wellington-Picton is:

Tues-Sun -	depart 1.30am -	arrive 4.30am
Daily -	depart 9.30am -	arrive 12.30pm
-	depart 2.30pm -	arrive 5.50pm
-	depart 5.30pm -	arrive 8.30pm
-	depart 10.30pm -	arrive 1.50am.

A shuttle service collects passengers from the 12.30pm arrival and transfers them to Picton Railway Station for the 1.40pm departure of the *Coastal Pacific*.

By Air

The airports for the area are at Nelson and Blenheim.

Air New Zealand has daily flights to Nelson from Auckland, Christchurch, Dunedin, Gisborne, Hamilton, Hokitika, Invercargill, Kaitaia, Napier/Hastings, New Plymouth, Palmerston North, Queenstown, Rotorua, Taupo, Tauranga, Timaru, Wanganui and Wellington.

Air New Zealand has daily flights to Blenheim from Auckland, Christchurch, Dunedin, Gisborne, Hamilton, Hokitika, Invercargill, Kaitaia, Napier/Hastings, New Plymouth, Palmerston North, Rotorua, Taupo, Tauranga, Timaru, Wanganui and Wellington.

Ansett New Zealand has daily flights to Nelson from Auckland, Christchurch, Dunedin, Palmerston North, Queenstown, Rotorua and Wellington; and from Invercargill Mon-Fri. They have daily flights to Blenheim from Auckland, Christchurch, Dunedin, Palmerston North, Rotorua and Wellington.

By Rail

The Coastal Pacific service from Christchurch to Picton connects with the Interislander ferry. It is a daily service leaving Christchurch at 7.30am and arriving at Picton at 12.50pm. The reverse trip departs Picton at 1.40pm and arrives at Christchurch at 7pm. Standard one-way fare is $65, but economy, saver and super saver fares are available.

By Bus

Intercity and *Mt Cook Landline* have daily services from Christchurch to Picton.

By Car
Christchurch-Picton is 340km - approx 6 hours 15 minutes.
Greymouth-Picton is 360km - approx 6 hours 25 minutes.
Nelson-Picton is 113km - approx 2 hours 40 minutes.
Blenheim-Picton is 28km.

Visitor Information
The Visitor Information Office is on the foreshore (PO Box 165), ph (03) 573 7477.

Accommodation
Picton has a good range of accommodation, but it is still a good idea to book ahead. Here is a selection, with prices in NZ$ for a double room per night, which should be used as a guide only. The telephone area code is 03.

Hotels
Americano Motor Inn, 32 High Street, ph 573 6398, fax 573 7892 - 26 units, licensed restaurant, cocktail bar, spa, barbecue - $78-85.
Ancient Mariner Motor Inn, Waikawa Road, ph 573 7002, fax 573 7727 - 35 units, licensed restaurant, cocktail bar, swimming pool, spa - $75- 120.

Motels
Harbour View Motel, 30 Waikawa Road, ph 573 6259, fax 573 6982 - 12 units, spa - $67-75.
Marineland Motel, 26 Waikawa Road, ph 573 7634, fax 573 7634 - 4 units, unlicensed restaurant, swimming pool, barbecue - $66.
Aldan Lodge Motel, 86 Wellington Street, ph 573 6833, fax 573 6091 - 11 units, indoor swimming pool, spa - $70-80.
Broadway Motel, 113 High Street, ph 573 6563, fax 573 8408 - 9 units - $63-68.
Sunnyvale Motel, Waikawa Bay (5km from Picton), ph/fax 573 6800 - 6 units, barbecue, catamarans, windsurfers, etc for hire - $55-65.
Bell Bird Motel, 96 Waikawa Rd, ph/fax 573 6912 - 6 units - $55.

Motor Camps & Cabins
Alexander's Motor Park, Canterbury St, ph/fax 573 6378 - camp

and caravan sites $8 adult, $5 child; cabins (sleep 6) $28-38 x 2; cabins (sleep 4) $24-28 x 2; on-site caravans (sleep 2) $24-28 x 2.

Blue Anchor Holiday Park, 78 Waikawa Bay Road, ph/fax 573 7212 - camp and caravan sites $9 per person; flats (sleep 2-5) $55-60 x 2; cabins (sleep 2-6) $35 x 2; cabins (sleep 4-8) $32 x 2; cabins (sleep 4 - backpackers) $22 x 2.

Momorangi Bay Motor Camp, Queen Charlotte Drive, Momorangi Bay, ph/fax 573 7865 - powered sites $16 x 2, unpowered sites $14 x 2; cabins $25 x 2.

Parklands Marina Holiday Park, 10 Beach Road, Waikawa Bay, ph/fax 573 6343 - camp sites $9 per person; powered sites $10 per person; flat (sleep 6) $44 x 2; cabins (sleep 4-6) $35 x 2; on-site caravan (sleeps 4) $35 x 2.

Waikawa Bay Holiday Park, 302 Waikawa Bay Road, ph/fax 573 7434 - powered and unpowered sites $16 x 2; cabins (sleep 2-6) $30 x 2; motel $65 x 2.

Hostel

Wedgewood House (YHA), 10 Dublin Street, ph 573 7797 - $15 per person.

Baden's Picton Lodge, 3 Auckland Street, ph 573 7788, fax 573 8418 - $19 double/twin.

The Villa Backpacker Lodge, 34 Auckland Street, ph/fax 573 6598 - $18 double/twin.

Eating Out

As would be expected because of its location, Picton has many seafood restaurants and cafes, and the Visitor Information Office will be able to point you in the right direction. For a special night out try the restaurant in the *Americano Motor Inn*, ph 573 7040, which is **Licensed** and has many New Zealand specialties on the menu. Prices for a three-course meal range from **$25 to $45.**

Sightseeing

The main sights around Picton are the **Marlborough Sounds**, which have 960km of sheltered waterways. Much of the area has been included in the Marlborough Sounds Maritime Park, which includes scenic and recreation reserves open to the public. You can fish, go boating, canoeing, windsurfing, scuba diving, snorkelling and swimming, or take a bushwalk, or have a picnic. The best way to see the Sounds in a short time is to take one of the cruises that leave from Picton.

The *Cougar Line*, 10 London Quay, ph 573 7925, have three trips daily. The Day Tripper departs at 8am and includes a walk on the most picturesque leg of the Queen Charlotte Sounds Walkway; the Luncheon Cruise departs at 1.30pm and returns around 5pm; and the Afternoon Cruise covers over 65km of native bush with a commentary about the bird life. Other cruise options are available.

Beachcomber Cruises, ph 573 6175, have a range of walks and cruises including: Round The Bays cruise departing daily at 10.15am and 2.15pm; Day tour to the Portage Hotel departing daily at 10.15am, returning around 4.30pm; Magic Mail Run on Mon-Fri departing 11.15am; a one day walk from Torea Bay to Mistletoe Bay leaving at 10.15am daily, returning around 4.30pm. Their address for reservations is PO Box 12, Picton.

There are many other companies that offer boat charters, and details are available from the Visitor Information Office.

Attractions in the town of Picton include the **Smith Museum** on London Quay, which has relics from pioneer and whaling days; and two historic ships at the mouth of the harbour - the *Edwin Fox*, a clipper built in 1853, and the *Echo*, built in 1905.

West of Picton is the town of **Havelock**, at the head of Pelorus Sound. The Pelorus Sound has as much to offer as other places in the area, but it is generally ignored by visitors rushing to more advertised attractions.

Havelock is also known as the mussel capital of the world, and if you want to sample these tasty morsels, call into the Rutherford Hostel in the town and ask Dianne for her home-made bread and mussel chowder.

Titirangi is a golden sandy beach with excellent swimming and other water sports, as well as outer Sounds views and bush walks. The beach can be reached from Picton or Havelock, and has good boat mooring and a wharf. For information contact Dave Drake at the camping ground, ph (03) 579 8006.

There are two scenic drives from Picton.

The shorter of the two is the road to Waikawa Bay/Port Underwood. Take the Waikawa Road past Queen Charlotte College, the Waikawa Marei, Waikawa Bay and on to Karaka Point. The road then goes through Whatamongo Bay, and up Port Underwood Hill, where the sealed road ends. There is a panoramic view from the top of the hill. The road then continues on to Port Underwood, Kakapo Bay, Ocean Bay, Whites Bay and down to Rarangi. From Rarangi take the road to Spring Creek. At the Spring Creek Junction turn left for Blenheim, or right to return to Picton.

If you have time you should also drive along the scenic Queen Charlotte Drive which skirts the sound between Picton and Havelock and offers magnificent views at every turn. The passenger liner the *Mikhail Lermontov* lies beneath the waters of Port Gore in the Marlborough Sounds, but one of its lifeboats is now in the marina at Havelock.

From Picton you can either head down the east coast on SH 1 to Blenheim and Christchurch, or cross over to the west coast via Nelson. If you are heading for the west coast, I suggest you travel via Queen Charlotte Drive to Havelock.

Blenheim

Blenheim (population 18,345) is 28km south of Picton at the junction of the Taylor and Opawa Rivers. It is the largest town in Marlborough, and is famed for its excellent vineyards, the largest in New Zealand. The centre for the farming community of the Wairau plain, Blenheim's industries include paua shell products manufacture and food processing.

Tourist Information
The Information Centre is at The Forum, Queen Street, ph (03) 578 9904.

Accommodation
Following is a selection of accommodation, with prices in NZ$ for a double room per night, which should be used as a guide only. The telephone area code is 03.

Motels

Aorangi Lodge Motel, 193 High Street, ph 578 2022, fax 578 2021 - 17 units, swimming pool, games room, barbecue - $75-99.

Bing's Motel, 29 Maxwell Road, ph 578 6199, fax 578 6159 - 28 units, unlicensed restaurant, swimming pools, tennis courts, games room - $74.

Blenheim Motel, 81 Main Street, ph 578 0559, fax 578 0558 - 9 units, swimming pool - $69.

Cherylea Motel, 73-79 Nelson Street, ph 578 6319, fax 578 6318 - 13 units, adjacent to tavern and licensed restaurant, swimming pool, spa, barbecue - $63-98.

Commodore Court Motel, 173 Middle Renwick Road, ph 578 1259, fax 578 1258 - 18 units, swimming pool, spa, barbecue - $58-75.

Motor Camps, Caravan Parks

Blenheim Grove Bridge Holiday Park, 78 Grove Road, ph/fax 578 3667 - powered and unpowered sites $20 x 2; cabins $35-50; flats $60-75.

Blenheim Motor Camp, 27 Budge Street, ph/fax 578 7419 - powered sites $10 per person; unpowered sites $9 per person; flats and cabins $30-55; backpackers $14.50 pp.

Eating Out

You are in wine country, so you have to have something to wash down with a good red or white - here are a few eateries.

Grove Mill, 1 Dodson Street, ph 578 9119 - **Licensed** - open noon-2pm - small winery with a blackboard menu (wine bar open 9am-5pm) - wine tasting available - **around $15-20** - credit cards accepted.

Twelve Trees Restaurant, Jacksons Road, ph 572 9054 - open from noon daily - winery with inside and outside dining - wine tasting available - **around $20** - credit cards accepted.

Rocco's Restaurant, 5 Dodson Street, ph 578 6940 - **Licensed** - open Mon-Sat noon-2pm, 6pm-midnight - award-winning Italian restaurant with excellent wine list - **$25-45** - credit cards accepted.

Bamboo Garden, 53 Maxwell Road, ph 578 1118 - **Licensed/BYO** - open Mon-Fri noon-2pm, nightly 5.30-9pm - Chinese cuisine -

$25-30 - credit cards accepted.

Gino's, 1 Main Street, ph 578 4755 - **BYO** - open Mon-Thurs 8am-6pm, Fri 8am-late - Italian cuisine, all homemade - around $15-20 - cash only.

Sightseeing

Seymour Square, in the centre of town, is built on land reclaimed from a swamp. It now features fountains, gardens and an historic ship's cannon, called Blenkinsopp's gun. The gun was named after a trader, John Blenkinsopp, who is believed to have fraudulently exchanged land on the Wairau Plain with the Maoris for the gun. The land was later the reason for a skirmish between settlers and the notorious Maori chief, Te Rauparaha. There is a memorial on Highway 1 that marks the site of the battle.

Brayshaw Museum Park has vintage farm machinery and a reconstructed colonial village that includes shops, a bank, a smithy, a miniature railway and a model boating pond.

The **Blenheim Recreation Centre** has indoor and outdoor swimming pools and facilities for roller skating and mini golf. South of Blenheim, about 6km, is the **Riverlands Cob Cottage**, a restored mud-walled and shingle-roofed settler's dwelling from the 1860s. The cottage is furnished in the period. Nearby is **Lake Grassmere** salt works, which provide 80% of New Zealand's table salt.

Kaikoura is 132km south of Blenheim, and 189km north of Christchurch, on SH 1. According to Maori legend, when Maui fished the North Island out of the sea he was sitting on the Kaikoura Peninsula. 'Kaikoura' is Maori for 'to eat crayfish', and there are certainly plenty of them around in the right season, but the main attractions nowadays are whale-watching and swimming with dolphins. The sperm whale is more accessible in this area than anywhere else in the world, and on whale-watching tours it is quite common to also see dolphins, seals, penguins, albatross and other sea birds. Tours are offered by canoe, glass bottomed boats, chartered boats and aeroplanes.

The Visitor Information Office is on The Esplanade, ph (03) 319 5641, or you can contact Dolphin Encounter, 58 West End, Kaikoura, ph (03) 319, 6777; Kaikoura Helicopters, PO Box 5,

The Deluxe Scenic Wine Trail is a good way to experience the region. Three internationally renowned wineries are visited with tours and comprehensive tastings. Departures are from Wellington at 7.30am Lynx, Picton 9.25am and Blenheim 9.50am daily Dec-April, and Saturdays all year. For further information contact Deluxe Travel Line, PO Box 147, Blenheim, ph 578 5467.

For independent travellers, the following is a selection of wineries in the area:

* Hunter Wines (NZ) Ltd, Rapaura Road, ph 572 8489 - open daily, tasting Mon-Sat 9.30am-4.30pm, Sun 11am-3pm.

* Stoneleigh Marlborough Vineyard, Jacksons Road, ph 572 8198 - open daily 10am-4.30pm.

* Cloudy Bay, Jacksons Road, ph 572 8914 - tasting daily 10am-4.30pm.

* Wairau River Wines Ltd, cnr Rapaura Road & SH6, ph 572 9800 - tastings daily 10am-5pm, lunch daily - wineshop and giftware.

* Foxes Island Wines, cnr Rapaura Road & SH6, ph 572 8299 - tastings daily 10am-5pm at Wairau River Wineshop.

* Highfield Estate Winery, Brookby Road, RD 2, ph 572 8592 - tasting and al fresco dining daily 10am-5pm.

* Lawson Dry Hills, Alabama Road, East Blenheim, ph 578 7674 - tasting 10am-5pm daily, evening dining Dec-April.

* Vavasour Wines Ltd, Redwood Pass Road, Awatere Valley, ph 575 7481 - tasting daily 10am-5pm (Oct-March), Mon-Sat 10am-4pm (April-Sept) - 20km south of Blenheim.

* Montana Wines Limited, SH1, 5km south of Blenheim, ph 578 2099 - winery tours on the hour 10am-3pm, winery shop Mon-Sat 9am-5pm, Sun 11am-4pm.

Kaikoura, ph (03) 319 6609; or Air Tours Kaikoura, 8km south on SH 1, ph (03) 319 5986.

Back on land there are a few interesting places to visit, including art galleries, a sea aquarium, Kaikoura Historical Society Museum, and Fyffe House, built by Kaikoura's earliest European settler, George Fyffe. Or you can trek in Mt Fyffe Forest and Puhi Puhi Scenic Reserve.

Kaikoura can be reached by daily bus or train services from Picton, Blenheim and Christchurch.

Nelson

Nelson (population 40,900) is a great place for a holiday, with its lakes, mountains and bush of the Nelson Lakes and Abel Tasman National Parks, the sheltered beaches of Tasman Bay, and the variety of cultural and historical attractions in the city.

Nelson city was New Zealand's first, and was planned and settled last century by the New Zealand Company in London. The first immigrants arrived in 1842, and immediately began to suffer from the effects a plan drawn up by people who had never seen the terrain.

Now the Nelson area, with its sunny climate and fertile soils, is one of the top horticultural producers in the country. It is also New Zealand's smallest wine region, although this industry is expanding every year.

Visitor Information

The Visitor Information Office is on the corner of Trafalgar and Halifax Streets, ph (03) 548 2304.

Accommodation

Following is a selection of accommodation with prices in NZ$ for a double room per night, which should be used as a guide only. The telephone area code is 03.

Hotels

Quality Hotel Rutherford, Trafalgar Street, ph 548 2299, fax 546 3003 - 112 units, licensed restaurants, cocktail lounge, pool, spa, sauna, gymnasium - $115.

Beachcomber Motor Inn, 23 Beach Road, Tahunanui, ph 548 5985, fax 547 6371 - 36 units, licensed restaurant, cocktail lounge, swimming pool, spa - $110.

Trailways Nelson Motor Inn, 66 Trafalgar Street, ph 548 7049, fax 546 8495 - 41 units, licensed restaurant, cocktail lounge - $95.

Leisure Lodge, 40 Waimea Road, ph 548 2089, fax 546 8502 - 26 units, licensed restaurant, cocktail lounge, swimming pool, spa, barbecue, gymnasium - $78-102.

Motels

AA Motor Lodge, 8 Ajax Avenue, ph 548 8214, fax 548 8219 - 13 units - $99-108.

Milton Chalet Motel, 119 Milton Street, ph/fax 548 1524 - 13 units, swimming pool, spa - $67-88.

Amber Court Motor Lodge, 190 Annesbrook Drive, Tahunanui, ph 548 5059, fax 548 6390 - 11 units, spa - $70.

Kings Gate Motel, 21 Trafalgar Street, ph 546 9108, 546 6838 - 11 units, swimming pool - $78-95.

Admirals Motor Inn, 26 Waimea Road, ph 548 3059, fax 548 3057 - 22 units, licensed restaurant next door, swimming pool, spa - $85-95.

Riverlodge Motel, 31 Collingwood Street, ph 548 3094, fax 548 3093 - 11 units - $75-95.

Trafalgar Lodge Motel/Guest House, 46 Trafalgar St, ph/fax 548 3980 - 6 units - $68-78, guesthouse (share facilities) $27 per person.

Motor Camps and Caravan Parks

Nelson Cabins and Caravan Park, 230 Vanguard Street, ph/fax 548 1445 - caravan sites $17; flats (sleep 2-4) $51.50; cabins (sleep 3-4) $41.50.

Richmond Holiday Park, 29 Gladstone Road, Richmond, ph 544 7323, fax 544 4597 - powered and unpowered sites $18; cabins $30-39; flats $60-70; motel $70-85.

Hostels

Paradiso Budget Accommodation, 42 Weka Street, ph/fax 546 6703 - $14-20 per person.

Alan's Place, 42 Westbrook Tce, ph/fax 548 4854 - $14 per person.

Central Nelson YHA, 59 Rutherford Street, ph 545 9988, fax 545 9989 - $17 per person.

Eating Out

Nelson has a good variety of restaurants, something for everyone. Here are some you might like to try.

Appleman's Restaurant, 38 Bridge Street, ph 546 1805 - **BYO** - open daily noon-2pm, 6pm-late - award winning restaurant specialising in seafood - **$25-45** - credit cards accepted.

Junipers Licensed Restaurant, 144 Collingwood Street, ph 548

8832 - **Licensed** - open nightly 6.30pm-1am - award winning restaurant in elegant surroundings - seafood - **$25-45** - credit cards accepted.

La Bonne Vie Seafood Restaurant, 75 Bridge Street, ph 548 0270 - **Licensed/BYO** - open daily 11.30am-2pm, 6pm-late - award winning restaurant that also has meat and vegetarian dishes on menu - **$25-45** - credit cards accepted.

Land of the Pharaohs, 270 Hardy Street, ph 548 8404 - **BYO** - open nightly 6pm-late - genuine Middle Eastern cuisine - **up to $20** - cash only.

Dimitri's Restaurant, 46 Collingwood Street, ph 548 2916 - **BYO** - open Mon-Sat 6pm-late - Mediterranean cuisine - **$30** - credit cards accepted.

Chinatown, 42 Tahunanui Drive, ph 548 6998 - **BYO/Licensed** - open nightly 5.30-10pm - Cantonese and Szechuan cuisine - **$30** - credit cards accepted.

Sightseeing

There are many colonial buildings that reflect the city's rich pioneering history - Bishopdale, home to the Bishop of Nelson since 1868, Isel House, Broadgreen, Fairfield, Melrose, and the Cathedral on Church Hill. The Information Office will supply addresses and access times, if any.

Founders Park, 87 Atawhai Drive, ph 548 2649, is a reconstruction of early Nelson, and is open daily 10am-4.30pm, admission $5. It has the Anchor Inn Restaurant which serves morning and afternoon teas and lunch, a 3D maze for all the family, and a souvenir shop, as well as traditional crafts people and an audio-visual presentation in the Port Nelson Exhibition. It is the major historical attraction in Nelson. Other museums include the *Nelson Provincial Museum*, the *Cawthron Institute Museum* and the *Nelson Harbour Board Museum*.

Nelson is also a centre for the arts as many artists, potters and weavers live in nearby bush retreats. *Craft Habitat*, cnr Richard Deviation, Richmond, 15 minutes' drive south of Nelson, ph (03) 544 7481, has the best range of Nelson's craftwork, offered directly from the studios. Coffee and light meals are available.

A completely different attraction in the area is *Happy Valley 4 x 4 Motorbike Adventures* on Cable Bay Road, Hira, ph 545 0304, fax 545 0347. This company offers escorted trail rides aboard 4-wheel motorbikes or an 8-wheel juggernaut called 'The Argo' that takes the whole family. There are several tours on offer, ranging from $10 for an Argo Adventure to $100 for a Skyline Special. There are different prices for riders and passengers, and reduced prices for children.

From Nelson you might like to continue along the coast via Motueka to Golden Bay at the top of the South Island. You can then return to Motueka and travel along the SH 61, which rejoins SH 6 at Kohatu, or you can head for the west coast through Buller Gorge.

Nelson to Able Tasman National Park and Golden Bay along SH 60.

Follow SH 6 to **Richmond**, 15km from Nelson. Richmond is the service town for the Waimea Plains which support many market gardens and orchards. Fruit juices and wines are produced in this area, and there are also timber and wood chip mills. There are several bushwalks, such as the Hacket, in the nearby Mt Richmond State Forest Park, and swimming is popular in the Lee and Aniseed Valleys.

SH 60 branches off at Richmond for **Motueka**, which is the service town for the Moutere River valley. Hops and tobacco are widely grown along this valley as well as pears, apples, berryfruit and wine grapes. Many of the wineries are open for cellar sales. At the head of the valley is Mount Arthur, which is snow covered in winter, and there is a walking trail up to a hut near the summit. The Visitor Information Office is at 236 High Street, ph (03) 528 6543.

> **One of Moteuka's most popular attractions is Kaiteriteri, a golden sand, almost completely sheltered, beach that offers swimming, water skiing, yachting and fishing.**

The Riwaka and Motueka Rivers attract trout anglers, and the hinterland is a magnet for pig and deer hunters.

If you are into rafting, Ocean River Rafting Co, Marahau, RD 2, Motueka, ph (03) 527 8266, can organise one to four day trips in their specially designed kayaks.

Abel Tasman National Park is the smallest of New Zealand's National Parks, and lies between Tasman and Golden Bays. It is mainly temperate rain forest, with thick bush in the western inland section and beech forests around the coast. Five species of beech are found in the park. The average rainfall is 1250mm on the coast and 2540mm in the highlands. The park abounds in bird life, and pips, paua and mussels are found on the beaches. There is a popular hiking track through the park, The Abel Tasman Coast Track, which begins at Marahau and ends at Totaranui. It follows the coastline for much of its length and provides an easy 3 to 4 day walk. There are five huts and a number of established campsites along the way.

Abel Tasman National Park Enterprises, 234 High Street, Moteuka (next to the Information Centre), ph (03) 528 7801, have many guided walks and cruises in the park, and their Day Cruise Launch will pick up and drop off independent travellers from all bays along the coast.

Golden Bay was visited by Abel Tasman in 1642, but a skirmish with local Maoris resulted in the death of four of Tasman's crew, so he marked the area as Murderers Bay on his map and never put to shore there.

Now Golden Bay is a popular holiday destination with **Takaka** the main centre. Takaka is a small dairying town, but it is close to a number of attractions - the Ngarua Marble Caves, the Anatoki River, famous for its tame eels, and the Pupu Springs, the largest in Australasia.

Collingwood is the last town before the North-west Nelson State Forest Park, a rugged area of land with a network of tramping tracks, including the famous Heaphy and Wangapeka Tracks.

Farewell Spit, New Zealand's longest sandspit, is a 24km promontory that can be reached by 4WD from Collingwood. Attractions include the Pillar Point Lighthouse and a bird sanctuary. Near the base of the Spit there are numerous walks with magnificent views of the coast.

Heaphy Track
The 77km Heaphy Track is best walked east to west (from Collingwood to near Karamea) as most of the climbing is done the first day. The track is rated mild to medium, but has fairly steep climbs. The trip along the track usually takes four to five

days, and there are six huts along the way. It is not as often walked as the Abel Tasman Track, and is recommended only for experienced hikers to undertake without a guide. There are telephones at both ends of the track from where transport can be arranged. Abel Tasman National Park Enterprises, ph (03) 548 0285, and Bickley Motors, Nelson, ph (03) 525 8352, offer transport from Nelson to the Collingwood end of the Heaphy Track as do Northwest Nelson Trampers Service, ph (03) 528 6332, from Motueka. Westport Cunningham Bus Services, ph (03) 789 7177, runs a five day service from Karamea to Westport, and Karaka Tours offer an on-demand service for the same route, ph (03) 789 5080.

The 65km Wangapeka Track is rated strenuous and definitely not for the 'new chum'. There are five huts along the track, it usually takes five days to walk, and is also best walked east to west. More information on both these tracks can be obtained from the Visitor Information Office in Nelson.

If you don't have time to visit the Motueka/Golden Bay area, then from Nelson continue on SH 6 to the West Coast.

Nelson to Westport via the Buller Gorge

The first town you come to is **Richmond**, 13km from Nelson, where the SH 60 branches off for Motueka. The road goes through the rich Waimea Plains, and 34km from Richmond, the SH 61 from Motueka joins the highway. At Kawatiri, 73km from Richmond, the SH 63 branches off for St Arnaud, and the Mount Robert and Rainbow Valley Skifields in the Nelson Lakes National Park. (For information on the skifields, see the Skiing chapter.)

Nelson Lakes National Park has two large lakes, Lake Rotoiti and Lake Rotoroa, and many of its mountain peaks are over 2000m. Mount Travers is the highest at 2338m, and there are still some that remain unclimbed and unnamed. The park offers challenges for mountaineers, rock climbers and trampers. There are many interesting walks in the park ranging from one hour to all day walks around the lakes. There is good trout fishing in the lakes all year, and red deer are present in the park and surrounding forest. St Arnaud is on SH 63, 100km from Blenheim and 26km from Kawatiri Junction on SH 6. Lake

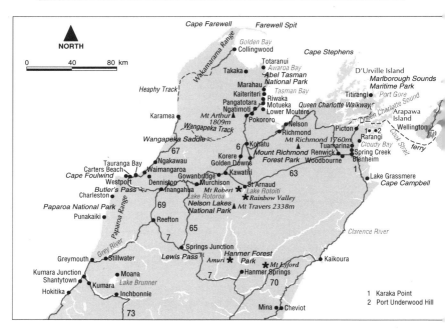

Rotoroa can be reached by turning off SH 6 at Gowanbridge.

St Arnaud village is located on the shores of Lake Rotoiti only an hour's drive from Nelson or Blenheim. It has accommodation to suit everyone's budget, and the Department of Conservation has an excellent information centre there. Nelson Lakes Transport run a Mon-Fri service between Nelson and St Arnaud, ph (03) 521 1858.

SH 6 continues along the Buller River valley to **Murchison** and **Inangahua Junction**. This is an earthquake zone and there were big earthquakes at Inangahua in 1968 and at Murchison in 1929 and 1931. The road is quite spectacular through the Buller Gorge as it is carved into the hill along the side of the river. The trip Nelson-Westport is 226km and takes approx 3 hours 45 minutes.

Westland

The rugged, isolated 483km strip of land between the Southern Alps and the Tasman Sea is so different to the fertile Canterbury Plains and the desert-like tussock-covered uplands of Mackenzie Country, it is hard to believe that they are only about 30km apart. The closeness of the Alps to the coast accounts for the extremely high rainfall (over 5000mm) and the resulting lush vegetation. The Fox and Franz Josef Glaciers pierce the dense bush, making the surrounding scenery unique. It is wild country, yet in the midst of it there are tranquil lakes that mirror the rugged beauty of the Alps. A trip to this area shouldn't be missed.

The main towns are **Westport**, **Greymouth** and **Hokitika**.

How to Get There

By Air
Air New Zealand Link fly daily to Hokitika from Christchurch and Wellington.

By Rail
The Tranzalpine is a daily service between Christchurch and Greymouth, via Arthur's Pass. It is one of the most spectacular train journeys in the world, passing through the farmlands of the Canterbury plains, the gorges of the Waimakariri River, the snow-capped Southern Alps, and the lush rain forests of the West Coast.

By Coach
Intercity has daily services connecting Nelson, Westport, Greymouth, and Franz Josef and Fox Glaciers. There are also daily services to the glaciers from Wanaka and Queenstown.

Mount Cook Landline has services to Westport from Christchurch, Nelson and Dunedin.

By Car
There are several ways to drive to the west coast, and from

south to north they are:

    * Through the Haast Pass from Queenstown/Wanaka area.

    * Through Arthur's Pass from Christchurch.

    * Through the Lewis Pass from Christchurch or Kaikoura.

    * Along the Buller River and through the Buller Gorge from the Picton-Blenheim-Nelson area.

Christchurch-Greymouth is 248km - just under 3 hours.

Picton-Greymouth is 360km - approx 5 hours 25 minutes.

Wanaka-Greymouth is 483km - approx 7 hours.

The scenery is spectacular along all the roads, although it does vary slightly, but wherever you cross through the Alps you are sure to enjoy the drive.

Westport

Westport (population 4563) is actually about 5km off the SH 6 on the eastern bank of the Buller River, protected by Cape Foulwind. As the name suggests, this is the main port for the West Coast. It is home to the local fishing fleet and the bulk carriers that ship cement from the Cape Foulwind cement works, as well as being New Zealand's largest coal exporting town. It is also the service centre for the northern region of the West Coast.

Because mining has played such an important part in the development of the area, a replica coal mine has been built right in town. Coaltown is a walk-through mine complete with sound effects. It is open daily.

Westport also has some good beaches. There is good surfing and diving at Tauranga Bay, and Carters Beach is good for swimming. If you want to try your luck at fossicking, head for North Beach.

At *Cape Foulwind* there is an easy 4km walk to a seal colony, a replica of Abel Tasman's astrolab and a lighthouse.

Westport's Domain has 4ha of native bush, and pathways wander through sub-tropical ferns, rimus and white pine.

Tourist Information

The Visitor Information Office is at 1 Brougham Street, ph (03) 789 6658.

Accommodation

There is not a wide variety to choose from, but here is a selection with prices in NZ$ for a double room per night, which should be used as a guide only.

The telephone area code is 03.

Hotel

Westport Motor Hotel, 207 Palmerston Street, ph 789 7889, fax 789 7885 - 27 units, licensed restaurant, bars - $69-85.

Motels

Chelsea Gateway Motor Lodge, cnr Palmerston & Bentham Streets, ph 789 6835, fax 789 6379 - 14 units - $80-140.

Ascot Motor Lodge, 74 Romilly Street, ph 789 7832, fax 789 6311 - 12 units - $75-85.

Buller Bridge Motel, The Esplanade, ph 789 7519, fax 789 7165 - 11 units, spa, barbecue - $78-90.

Buller Court Motel, 235 Palmerston Street, ph 789 7979, fax 789 7501 - 13 units, barbecue - $70-90.

Westport Motel, 32 Esplanade, ph/fax 789 7575 - 16 units - $58-65.

Motor Camps & Cabins

Westport Holiday Park, 31-37 Domett Street, ph 789 7043, fax 789 7199 - camp sites $8 per person; powered sites $18 x 2; cabins (sleep 2-4) $35 x 2; chalets (sleep 4) $27-37; bunkhouse $12 per person.

Seal Colony Tourist Park, Marine Parade, Carters Beach, ph 789 8002, fax 789 6732 - powered and unpowered sites $19 x 2; cabins $37 x 2; motel units $82-88.

Hostel

Tripinns, 72 Queen Street, ph 789 7367, fax 789 6419 - $17 double/twin.

Outlying Attractions

From Westport, SH 67 follows the coast north to **Karamea**. At Waimangaroa, 16km north, a road branches off to Denniston on the Mount Rochfort Plateau. Denniston has been mined for coal for over 100 years. Magnificent views north to Karamea and as far south as Mount Cook can be obtained from the plateau (weather permitting, of course).

About half-way between Westport and Karamea is the **Charming Creek Walkway**. It is a 3km all-weather track that follows an old coal railway line along the Ngakawau Gorge to the Mangatina Falls. Along the way you will see a swing bridge and tunnel portals. The walk takes about an hour.

Karamea, 88km north of Westport, is a beach resort and the western staging point for the Heaphy and Wangapeka Tracks. *The Forest Service*, which administers the North West Nelson Forest Park, has a base here where information is available on these tracks (see the Marlborough Sounds and Nelson chapter for details). Other attractions in the area are the Oparara Arch, Gabrielle's Mirror and the Honeycomb Hill Cave.

From Westport it is 105km to Greymouth and the drive takes around 1 hour 30 minutes. The scenery along the road is spectacular and the sub-tropical forest grows right down to the bays and beaches.

Charleston is 21km south of Westport and is an old gold mining town which once boasted approximately 100 hotels and three breweries. The old workings can be visited at Mitchells Gully which there are over 16km of tunnels dug by early miners. Visitors can also see a real claim being worked with an overshot wheel driving a stamping battery which crushes the gold bearing quartz rock.

Punakaika and the famous Pancake Rocks are 32km further south. The rocks are in a scenic reserve which has nikau palms, northern rata and black tree ferns. The limestone cliffs here have been pounded by the seas for centuries and weathered by the wind, and as a result the rocks look like pancakes stacked one on top of the other. There are also several blowholes, and some very good photos have been taken here at high tide when the blowholes are at their best. Punakaiki-Greymouth is 45km.

Greymouth

The West Coast's largest town and commercial centre is situated at the mouth of the Grey River, and appropriately named Greymouth (population 11,500). In years past gold and then coal was king here, but now it is timber from the lush forests of the area. Greenstone was once found on the beach - unfortunately not any more - but there are still greenstone carvers in the town. The Point Elizabeth Walkway follows the coast and takes about 4 hours.

The main tourist attraction is **Shantytown**, 20km to the south. This recreation of an old gold mining town of the 1880s has 36 buildings and a working sawmill. You can also pan for gold there, take a ride on the steam train, or on the horse and gig - open daily 8.30am-5pm and admission is $8.

Jetboat rides on the river are another attraction, and these can be arranged through the Visitor Information Office. They will also furnish you with up-to-date information on fishing, as fine trout are caught in the district. They are also the people to arrange visits to the State Coal Mines that operate in the area.

Tourist Information

The Visitor Information Centre is on the corner of Mackay and Herbert Streets, ph (03) 768 5101.

Accommodation

There is quite a good range of accommodation in Greymouth, and here is a selection with prices in NZ$ for a double room per night, which should be used as a guide only. The telephone area code is 03.

Hotels

Ashley Motor Inn, 74 Tasman Street, ph 768 5135, fax 768 0319 - 60 units, licensed restaurant, cocktail lounge, cafe, pool, spa - $95-160.
Revingtons Hotel, 46 Tainui Street, ph 768 7055, fax 768 7605 - 26 units, licensed restaurant, bar - $65.

Motels

Willowbank Pacifica Lodge, SH 6, 3km north of Greymouth, ph

768 5339, fax 768 6022 - 7 units, swimming pool, spa - $78-90.

Charles Court Motel, 350 Main South Road, SH 6, ph 762 6619, fax 762 6594 - 23 units, swimming pool, spa, games room, barbecue - $79-99.

Greymouth Motel, 195 High Street, ph 768 6090, fax 768 6300 - 9 units, barbecue - $70-78.

Aachen Place Motel, 50 High Street, ph 768 6091, fax 768 6958 - 10 units - $75-86.

South Beach Motel, 318 Main South Road, ph 762 6768, fax 762 6748 - 11 units, spa, barbecue - $75-82.

Motor Camps and Cabins

Greymouth Seaside Holiday Park, 2 Chesterfield Street, off Main South Road, ph 768 6618, fax 768 5873 - camp sites $17 x 2, caravan sites $19 x 2; flats (sleep 6) $63 x 2; cabins (sleep 5) $40 x 2; bunkhouse (sleeps 12) $12 per person; on-site vans (sleep 4) $32 x 2.

South Beach Motor Park, 318 Main South Road, ph 762 6768, fax 762 6748 - camp sites $16 x 2; caravan sites $18 x 2.

Hostel

Kaianga-Ra Hostel (YHA), 15 Alexander Street, ph 768 4951, fax 768 4951 - $15 per person.

Round the Lakes Trip

There is a popular trip from here called 'Round the Lakes'. Take the Lewis Pass Highway to Stillwater and turn off to **Moana**, which is an increasingly popular holiday resort on Lake Brunner. Jetboats operate between Moana and Greymouth and visitors can travel one way by jetboat and the other by minibus.

Moana is on the Christchurch-Greymouth Railway line, and is between the Lewis Pass and Arthur's Pass roads. It has a motor camp, and launch trips are available on the lake. From Moana drive to Ruru, Rotomanu, Inchbonnie, Mitchells and Kumara, the site of the first gold discovery on the west coast, and back to SH 6 where you can turn back to Greymouth or go on to Hokitika.

Hokitika is 41km south of Greymouth. It is the former capital of Westland and the site of the 1864 goldrush. The population of this town went from less than 100 in 1864 to 16,000 ten months later, and to 50,000 by 1866. Today the population is around 3500. Hokitika is a service town for this farming area.

The Tourist Information Office is at 36 Weld Street, ph (03) 755 8322, and most of the attractions are located on Tancred Street between Weld and Hamilton Streets.

The Historical Museum in Tancred Street has exhibits of gold and greenstone mining, as well as natural and social history. It is open 9.30am-5pm and a small admission fee is charged.

A good view of the town can be obtained from a lookout on the airport road. Also in the area are a glow-worm dell, a vintage farm museum, and many craft shops.

From Hokitika continue south on SH 6 for 31km to **Ross**, which is also a former gold mining town. A nugget weighing 2.8kg was found here and later given to King George V on his coronation. The Ross Historic Goldfield Walkway takes you around this once thriving town, and there is also a fur factory which makes possum skins into bags and toy koalas, and a taxidermist's wildlife museum.

The Forks is 120km south of Hokitika, and a road leads from there to **Okarito** on the coast where there is a White Heron Sanctuary (August-January only) and a Youth Hostel, ph (03) 753 4082. The hostel is in a former pioneer school building which has been faithfully restored.

From The Forks, it is about 25km to **Franz Josef** and 50km to **Fox Glacier**, both of which are situated in the Westland National Park.

Westland National Park

The park contains dense bushland, spectacular scenery, mirror lakes, and two rumbling, groaning rivers of ice.

The Franz Josef and Fox Glaciers are a few kilometres from the villages. Von Haast discovered the Franz Josef and named it after the Emperor of Austria in 1862. The Fox Glacier was originally called the Albert, but the name was changed as a compliment to Sir William Fox, a Premier of the Colony. Both glaciers are unique in that they are very fast moving (between 1 and 5 metres daily) and the terminal face of the glaciers is in sub-tropical rain forest. This statement, although true, may

Fox Glacier

lead you to expect that they are right in the bush. Actually the bush starts a little bit back so that the actual face is a rather forbidding looking area. Nothing much grows on the sides of the mountains along the glaciers, and they are barren looking places - where man seems insignificant compared to nature. They are definitely sights not to be missed.

The two glaciers are only 24km apart but usually tourists only have time to visit one of them. They are very similar, with the Fox having sharper pinnacles and being slightly more accessible. The Fox is 15km long, 1km longer than the Franz Josef, and finishes just over 200m above sea level, lower than any other glacier in the world outside the polar regions.

A highlight of any visit to the glaciers is to walk on them, and there is a variety of tours available for all fitness levels. For further information contact the Visitor Information Offices at Fox Glacier, ph (03) 751 0807, or Franz Josef, ph (03) 752 0796.

Half and full day helihikes are offered as well as a trip to the Chancellor Hut. You need to be fit to undertake these trips, and they only operate from October to June. From July to

November, heli-skiing trips are offered, but they are only for good skiers, but anyone can take a helicopter flight over the glaciers and Mount Cook. At **Franz Josef** helicopter flights are also offered as well as heli-hikes, and you can drive to the terminal face by car or bus.

Companies which offer some or all of the above are: Alpine Adventure Centre, ph (03) 752 0793; Guided Glacier Walks, ph (03) 752 0763; Glacier Helicopters, ph (03) 752 0755; Pavlova Backpackers, ph (03) 752 0738; and The Helicopter Line, ph (03) 752 0767.

Accommodation

Fox Glacier

Following is a selection of accommodation, with prices in NZ$ for a double room per night, which should be used as a guide only. The telephone area code is 03.

Fox Glacier Plaza Westland Hotel, ph 751 0839, fax 751 0868 - 49 rooms with private facilities (and 26 budget rooms), licensed restaurants, cocktail lounge, games room - $50-130.

Alpine View Motel, in grounds of Fox Glacier Holiday Park, on Lake Matheson Road, ph 751 0821, fax 751 0813 - 6 units - $64-75.

A1 Fox Glacier Motel, Lake Matheson Road, ph 751 0804, fax 751 0706 - 10 units, squash court - $80.

Lake Matheson Motel, Lake Matheson Road, ph/fax 751 0830 - 23 units - $75-80.

Fox Glacier Holiday Park, Lake Matheson Road, ph 751 0821, fax 751 0813 - camp sites $18 x 2; caravan sites $19 x 2; flats (sleep 4) $55 x 2; cabins (sleep 2-6) $30 x 2; hostel (bedrooms sleep 2-6) $34 x 2; bunkhouse $12 per person.

Franz Josef

Franz Josef Glacier Hotel, SH 6, ph 752 0729, fax 752 0709 - 47 rooms (private facilities), licensed restaurants, bistro, cocktail lounges - $180-225.

Westwood Lodge, SH 6, ph/fax 752 0111 - 6 rooms - $130.

A1 Rata Grove Motel, 6 Cron Street, ph 752 0741, fax 752 0741 - 10 units - $60-85.

Glacier Gateway Motor Lodge, SH 6, ph 752 0776, fax 752 0732 - 23 units (all non-smoking), spa, sauna - studio units $95; family

cottages $111-139 (up to 6 people).
Alpine Glacier Motor Lodge & Bushland Court Motel, Cron Street, ph/fax 752 0757 - 2-bedroom family and studio units, barbecue, spa - $70-100.
Franz Josef Holiday Park, SH 6, ph/fax 752 0766 - camp sites $9 per person; caravan sites $19 x 2; flats (sleep 4) $55 x 2; cabins (sleep 5) $42 x 2; cabins (sleep 4) $28 x 2; hostel $17.50 per person; dormitory $13.50 per person.
Franz Josef YHA Hostel, 2-4 Cron Street, ph/fax 752 0754 - $16 per person.

Local Attractions

The Franz Josef Visitor Centre has an audio-visual show that is worth seeing, and admission is charged. The Fox Glacier Visitor Centre has an interesting display gallery which is free.

Between the Franz Josef Visitor Centre and the Waiho River is **St James' Church**, which has great views of the Valley through the altar window.
Lake Matheson, close to the terminal face of the Fox Glacier, is the result of the melting and retreating of the glacier in an earlier age. It is surrounded by beautiful bush land, sheltered from winds, and reflects almost perfectly the majestic Southern Alps, including Mounts Cook and Tasman.

Outlying Attractions

From Franz Josef it's 120km to **Haast** at the start of the Haast Pass Road (opened to vehicles in 1965) to Wanaka.

About 20km from Franz Josef you pass over a very long single span suspension bridge at Karangarua. The road then goes through Bruce Bay, and around Lake Paringa and Lake Moeraki, where the fishing is excellent. The bridge over the Haast River is 737m long but only 4m wide with two passing bays. When the snows melt the river is a raging torrent, but at the end of autumn it is usually only a series of small channels.

The **Haast Pass** forms the boundary between Otago and Westland and is the lowest of the passes (563m) through the Southern Alps. It is 140km from Haast to Wanaka and the trip takes approximately 3 hours 30 minutes. The road winds along the river valley following an ancient Maori greenstone route, and passes through some of the South Island's rugged country.

The Southern Lakes and Fiordland

This is probably the most spectacular area in all New Zealand as it has just about everything. There are high mountains, fiords, beautiful lakes, hot dry summer days and skiing in winter. Queenstown is the main resort and the staging area for most of the trips.

Queenstown

Queenstown (population 3659) is dominated by **The Remarkables,** a craggy mountain range that rises steeply from the shores of Lake Wakatipu. The scenery is so perfect that it could be a painted backdrop in a theatre. Queenstown is a year round resort: in spring there are wild flowers; the summer brings hot, dry weather that is ideal for camping, tramping and fishing; in autumn the deciduous trees turn magnificent shades of red and gold due to the crisp air; and in winter there is snow.

Climate

The mean daily temperatures are: January 22C maximum, 10C minimum; August 10C maximum, 1C minimum. The average number of days on which it rains in January is 8 and in August 7. Queenstown has an average of 6.7 hours of sunshine in January and 3.4 hours in August. It is 310m above sea level.

How to Get There

By Air

Air New Zealand has daily flights to Queenstown from Auckland, Christchurch, Palmerston North, Rotorua and Wellington. *Mount Cook Airlines* fly daily from Mount Cook and Te Anau; and *Aspiring Air* flies from Wanaka.
Ansett New Zealand has daily flights from Rotorua, Wellington and Christchurch.

By Bus

Mount Cook Landline have daily services to Queenstown from Christchurch, Dunedin, Invercargill, Milford Sound, Mount Cook, Wanaka and Te Anau.

InterCity have daily services to Queenstown from Christchurch, Dunedin, Fox Glacier, Franz Josef, Invercargill, Milford Sound, Mount Cook, Te Anau and Wanaka.

By Car

From Christchurch most visitors either travel via Mount Cook, on SH 1 and 8 to Lake Pukaki and through the Lindis Pass to Cromwell, then along SH 6 **or** to Dunedin on SH 1 then on SH 8 to Cromwell **or** SH 1 to Invercargill then SH 6 to Queenstown. From the west coast the most popular route is through the Haast Pass to Wanaka, then SH 89 to Queenstown.

Christchurch-Queenstown is 487km - 8 hours 35 min.(approx).
Mount-Cook-Queenstown is 271km - 3 hours 30 min. (approx).
Dunedin-Queenstown is 281km - 4 hours 20 min. (approx).
Invercargill-Queenstown is 189km - 3 hours 15 min. (approx).
Greymouth-Queenstown is 554km - 12 hours 40 min. (approx).

Tourist Information

The Information Office is in the Clocktower Centre, on the corner of Shotover and Camp Streets, ph (03) 442 4100. It is open daily 7am-6pm and has Travelex Currency Exchange.

Thomas Cook has two money exchanges that are open daily 8am-7pm - on the corner of The Mall and Camp Street, opposite the Post Office, and on the corner of Shotover and Camp Streets.

The Department of Conservation information office is at 37 Shotover Street, ph 442 7933.

Accommodation

As would be expected of a year round resort, Queenstown has loads of accommodation, but it is still wise to book ahead. Following is a selection with prices in NZ$ for a double room per night, which should be used as a guide only. The telephone area code is 03.

CHRISTCHURCH

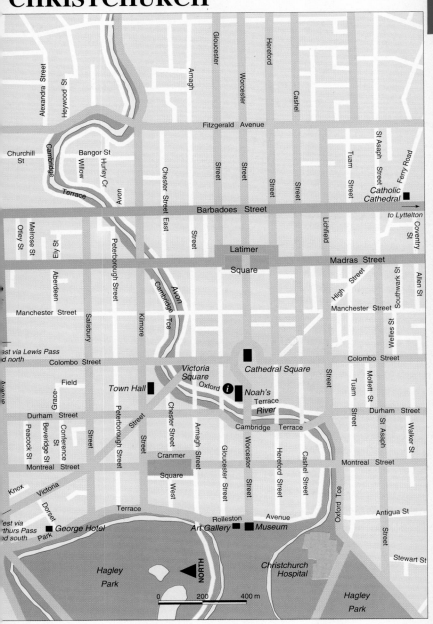

Mt. Aspiring National Park, South Island.

QUEENSTOWN

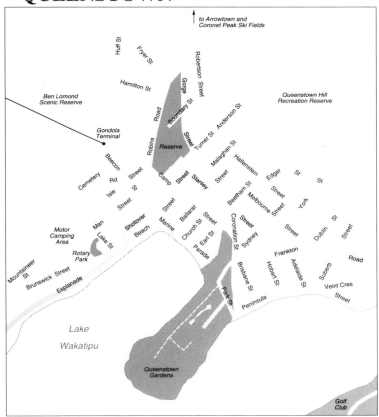

to Arrowtown and
Coronet Peak Ski Fields

Huff St

Fryer St

Robertson Street

Gorge

Hamilton St

Ben Lomond
Scenic Reserve

Queenstown Hill
Recreation Reserve

Boundary St

Road

Anderson St

Turner St

Gondola
Terminal

Robins

Reserve

Street

Malaghan St

Hallenstein

Beecon

Edgar

St

St

Cemetery

Rd

Street

Camp

Street

Stanley

Street

Beetham St

Melbourne Street

Street

York

Isle

St

Street

Street

Ballarat

Church St

Street

Dublin

St

Street

Motor
Camping
Area

Man

Shotover

Street

Coronation St

Street

Lake St

Beach

Marine

Earl St

Sydney

Street

Street

Rotary
Park

Parade

Frankton

Road

Mountaineer
St

Brunswick Street

Esplanade

Brisbane St

Hobart St

Adelaide St

Suberb

Veint Cres

Street

Park St

Peninsula

Lake

Wakatipu

Queenstown
Gardens

Golf
Club

Hotels

Lakeland Queenstown, 14-18 Lake Esplanade, ph 442 7600, fax
442 9653 - 275 rooms (private facilities), licensed restaurant,
swimming pool, spa, sauna, barbecue - $158.
Alpine Village Motor Inn, 325 Frankton Road, ph 442 7795, fax
442 7738 - 51 rooms (private facilities), licensed restaurant, bar,
spa, tennis court - $90-150.
Gardens Parkroyal Queenstown, cnr Earl Street & Marine Parade,

ph 442 7750, fax 442 7469 - 204 rooms (private facilities), licensed restaurant, bar - $155+.

Gold Ridge Hotel - Scenic Circle, Frankton Road, ph 442 6500, fax 442 7896 - 42 units, licensed restaurant, tennis court - $80-144.

Aspen on Queenstown, 139 Fernhill Road, ph 442 7688, fax 442 7677 - 61 rooms (private facilities) and 46 apartments, licensed restaurant, cocktail lounge, swimming pool, spa, sauna - $120-175.

Queenstown Parkroyal, Beach Street, ph 442 7800, fax 442 8895 - 139 rooms (private facilities), licensed restaurant, bar - $155+.

Motels
Melbourne Motor Lodge, 35 Melbourne Street, ph 442 8431, fax 442 7466 - 23 units, 10 guest house rooms, spa - $45-170.

Ambassador Motel, 2 Man Street, ph 442 8593, fax 4428797 - 16 units, barbecue - $95-107.

Amber Motor Lodge, 1 Gorge Rd, ph/fax442 8480 - 11 units - $95.

Four Seasons Motel, 12 Stanley Street, ph 442 8953,fax 4427233 - 15 units, swimming pool, spa, barbecue - $80-100.

Hillside Holiday Motel, 35 Gorge Road, ph 442 9280, fax 4429270 - 10 units, barbecue - $80.

Colonial Village Motel, 100 Frankton Road, ph/fax 442 7629 - 10 units, spa, sauna, barbecue - $75-100.

Motor Camps & Cabins
Queenstown Motor Park, Man Street, ph 442 7252, fax 442 7253 - tent sites $9 per person, caravan sites $10 per person; motel (units sleep 4-6) $78 x 2; flats (sleep 4) $60 x 2; cabins (sleep 3-4) $36 x 2; lodge $46 x 2.

Mountain View Lodge, Frankton Rd, ph 442 8246, fax 442 7414 - tent & caravan sites $7 per person;
hostel (rooms sleep 4) $40 x 2.

Hostel
Wakatipu Lodge (YHA), 80 Lake Esplanade, ph 442 8413, fax 442 6561 - $18 per person.

Local Transport
You can walk to most places in Queenstown, and taxis are available.

Car Hire
Avis, ph 442 7280; Budget, ph 442 9274; Thrifty, ph 442 8100; Hertz, ph 442 4106; Welco, ph 442 3861; National, ph 442 5887.

Eating Out

Queenstown is a true resort town with numerous fine restaurants, and a listing of these is published in *Mountain Scene*, a weekly tourist newspaper that is widely available.

One restaurant that shouldn't be missed is the *Skyline* at the top of the Gondola lift, ph 442 7860. Lunch is served from noon to 1.30pm, dinner 6-9pm, and the restaurant is fully licensed, offering buffet style eating. The Gondola ride and evening meal costs $50 adults, children half price, or one child free with each adult dining from 6pm.

Here are a few others you might like to try.

Beefeater Steakhouse, 40 Shotover Street, ph 442 9149 - **BYO** - open daily 5pm-late - friendly service - **$25-45** - credit cards accepted.

Fishbone Grill, 7 Beach Street, ph 442-6768 - **Licensed/BYO** - open Mon-Fri 11am-2pm, Sat-Sun noon-2pm, daily 5-10pm - **$20-25** - credit cards accepted.

Avanti, The Mall, ph 442 8503 - **BYO** - open daily 7am-late - extensive menu in English and Japanese - **under $20** - credit cards accepted.

Roaring Meg's Restaurant, 57 Shotover Street, ph 442 9676 - **BYO** - open Mon-Sat 6pm-late - table side flambe cooking - **$25-45** - credit cards accepted.

HMS Britannia, The Mall, ph 442 9600 - **Licensed** - open daily 6.30-10.30pm - varied menu in a nautical setting - **$25-45** - credit cards accepted.

Gourmet Express, Bay Centre, Shotover Street, ph 442 9619 - **BYO** - open daily 6.30am-9.30am - American style restaurant-coffee shop - **around $20** (breakfasts for under $5) - credit cards accepted.

Pizza Hut, cnr Camp and Church Streets, ph 442 9670.

Sightseeing

Maoris came to Lake Wakatipu only to collect greenstone from around its shores. They quickly collected the stone and headed back to the coast as there were no fish in the lake or rivers, and practically no birdlife due to the sparseness of the vegetation. The weather was also better nearer the sea.

Nathaniel Chalmers was the first Pakeha to see the lake, in 1853. He was followed by Donald Hay who rafted the length of the lake in 1859 from the southern tip to where Queenstown now stands. At the height of the gold rush around 1860, Queenstown had a population of 10,000 and about thirty vessels plied up and down the lake.

The Mall is the hub of Queenstown and you will always find plenty to look at as you stroll along. Buskers frequent it and there are numerous boutiques and eateries.

For an overall view of Queenstown, Lake Wakatipu and The Remarkables, head for the Skyline Gondola lift which leaves from the end of Brecon Street. This lift was opened in 1967 and rises 445m in 730m, making it one of the steepest lifts in the world. The cabins seat four people, and can transport 750 people an hour to the restaurant at the top. The Gondola operates from 10am daily until late, and costs $10 adult, $3 child, or $20 family.

In the theatre near the restaurant is the incredible audio/visual show **Kiwi Magic**, a thirty minute presentation that runs continuously from 11am-9pm. Admission is $7 adults, $3.50 children.

Underwater World on the wharf at the end of the Mall, is an underwater trout observatory where you can watch the fish in their natural environment, $7 adults, $3.50 children.

In the Gardens there is an open-air **ice skating rink**, ph 441 8000, that is open daily 10am-9pm. Sessions last 2 hours and cost $7 adults, $5 children.

The Motor Museum at 25 Brecon Street has an excellent collection of vintage cars but has changeable hours.

Kiwi and Birdlife Park, ph 442 8059, has kiwis as well as other native birds, in natural surroundings. It is next to the bottom station of the Gondola, and is open daily 9am-5pm - $9 adults, $3 children.

From Queenstown there is a four hour return walk to the summit of the nearby Queenstown Hill (900m), or for the more energetic there is a longer hike to Ben Lomond (1700m), which takes seven hours for the return trip.

Tours

If you want to make the most of a visit to Queenstown you should join some of the many tours available to the district's attractions. There are any number of tours and tour operators in and around Queenstown and perhaps the best way to cover them is under type of tour.

Land Tours

Nomad Safaris, ph 442 6699, and *Outback Tours*, ph 442 7386, offer van tours through Skippers Canyon and prices range from $59 to $69 per person.

Tussock Tours, ph 442 4485, offer a similar tour in their 4WD vehicles for $59 per person.

Lake Trips

Fiordland Travel, Steamer Wharf, ph 442 7500, have trips on the TSS *Earnslaw*, a vintage steamship known as the 'Lady of the Lake'. Tour details are:

morning cruise 9am (summer only) three hours - adult $43, child $10; **midday cruise** 12.30pm one hour - adult $22, child $10; **afternoon cruise** 2pm three hours - adult $43, child $10; **evening cruises** 5.30pm (all year) and 7.30pm (summer only) one hour 45 minutes - adult $26 child $10.

The afternoon cruise incorporates a visit to Walter Peak High Country Farm. Walter Peak is a sheep and cattle farm where you can meet the animals and enjoy a delicious home cooked morning or afternoon tea. The evening cruises can be extended to include dinner at the *Colonel's Homestead Restaurant* at Walter Peak, and the costs then are adult $65 child $32.50. Accommodation is also available at Walter Peak.

There is also a cruise to Walter Peak by launch which departs daily at 9.30am and 2pm.

A yacht, *The City of Dunedin*, leaves for a two hour cruise at 10.30am, 1pm and 4pm - $45 adults, $25 children.

It is also possible to hire boats of all sorts, from wind surfers to sail boats, to jet boats.

Jet Boating & Rafting

Several companies run these types of trips from Queenstown, and listed below are a few of them.

Shotover Jet, ph 442 8570, has a half-hour jet boat ride along the Shotover River for $69 per person

Twin Rivers Jet, ph 442 3257, offer a three-quarter hour ride for $50.

Raft trips can be organised with:

Queenstown Rafting, ph 442 9792, and *Raging Thunder*, ph 442 7318, have trips on the Shotover River for $99 per person, and on the Kawarau River for $79 per person, which includes a shower, a sauna and a meal after the trip.

Extreme Green, ph 442 7100, have trips on the Kawarau River for $69 per person, with no extras thrown in.

Coach Trips to Milford Sound

Several companies operate trips to Milford, and more information and current prices can be obtained from the Visitor Information Centre.

Gray Line have a Milford Sound Tour departing at 8am and returning at 7.55pm, which includes launch trip and coach travel. *Fiordland Travel*, offer a similar tour.

InterCity have a return coach trip and cruise; a coach, cruise and plane trip; and a plane, cruise, plane trip.

Fiordland have a Milford Sound bus trip that departs Queenstown at 7.15am and returns at 8pm. It includes a cruise on the Sound with fly in/bus out or fly in/fly out options.

Flightseeing

Mount Cook Airlines, ph 442 7650, have several flights daily to various attractions, all subject to demand and weather. Some of these are listed below.

Milford Highlights is a ninety minute flight over Cleddau Canyon, Sutherland Falls and the Milford Track, with a landing at Milford, weather permitting.

Magnificent Milford is a three hour flight, the first part of which is the same as the Milford Highlights, and the second part flying over Milford Sound and Mitre Peak with a launch cruise on the sound. Check with the airlines for availability and prices.

The Helicopter Line, ph 442 7820, Queenstown Airport, also have a selection of flights.

The Grand Circle lasts thirty minutes and flies over The Remarkables along the Kawarau River to Arrowtown, Coronet Peak and Lake Hayes, with a landing at 610m for photographs, then return along Skippers Canyon and the Shotover Gorge.

Skippers Canyon and Beyond lasts twenty-five minutes and includes a landing at Skippers Canyon.

The Remarkables lasts eighteen minutes and flies over The Remarkables and Kawarau River with a view of Arrowtown and Lake Hayes and a landing.

Fantastic Lake Wakatipu flies up to The Remarkables spur, 1525m above the lake for a landing to take in the view. This flight lasts twelve minutes.

Similar flights can be arranged through Fiordland Travel, ph 442 7500; Milford Scenic Flights, ph 442 3065; and Southern Lakes Helicopters, ph 442 8133.

Sport & Recreation

There is a bowling green and tennis courts in the Gardens, and squash courts in town.

Golf

There are four golf courses in the area (Frankton, Kelvin Heights, Arrowtown and Millbrook Resort) all of which welcome visitors.

Trail Rides

Hillandale Horse Riding have a three hour escorted ride for experienced riders, with courtesy transport available. *Moonlight Stables* have 2 hour escorted rides for inexperienced riders in the historic Shotover and Moonlight Valleys with courtesy transport also available, departing daily 9.30am and 2pm, ph 442 8892.

Bungy Jumping

Queenstown calls itself the 'Bungy Jumping Capital of the World', and those brave enough should contact A.J. Hackett, ph 442 7100, fax 442 7121, to arrange jumps from either a 43m or a 70m bridge. The really adventurous can book in for a Helicopter Bungy, jumping from 30m+. Costs start from $105, with a lot of goodies thrown in.

Skydiving

Skydive Tandem, The Ultimate Jump, will have you harnessed to an instructor, free fall thousands of feet at 200 kph, and capture the entire adventure on video. If this is for you, contact them on ph 021 325 961, or enquire at the information centre.

Skiing
There are two ski fields close to Queenstown: Coronet Peak, the oldest and best known; and The Remarkables, which is usually open longer.

Coronet Peak has south-west facing slopes and a good mix of faces, bowls and chutes. It offers good skiing for all levels.

The Remarkables is in a sunny valley and covers a huge area with potential for expansion. It has plenty of beginner and intermediate runs. It is ideally suited for families as the lower slopes are gently rounded, while the upper slopes are more challenging and offer magnificent views of Lake Wakatipu and Queenstown.

Heli-skiing is also on offer in the Harris Mountains.
See the Skiing Chapter for more information.

Festivals
Queenstown has a Summer and a Winter Festival, and Arrowtown has an Autumn Festival.

Outlying Attractions
There are a few places just out of Queenstown which are worth seeing, and these can be visited in one day by taking the scenic circuit route past historic **Arthurs Point**, where spectacular views of the Shotover River can be obtained.

The road to Coronet Peak is still reasonable to drive, but the road into **Skippers Canyon** is famous as it rises 915m and has 480 bends in 19km. The trip along this road is noted for its blood curdling bends and precipices as much as for its spectacular scenery. This area once swarmed with gold diggers, but now is only frequented by tourists. This trip is best undertaken on an organised tour as rental car insurance is null and void on this road. Many people raft the river here as it is a ride of a lifetime. It is also possible to fly in by helicopter.

Coronet Peak Ski Resort is 18km from Queenstown and is open in winter 9am-4pm. There is a chairlift to the top station (1524m) which offers 360 degree views. On one side there are rugged, barren mountain peaks and on the other green fields run down to Lake Wakatipu. The lift operates in all seasons. In winter there is good skiing with regular shuttle buses from Queenstown.

Arrowtown, 20km from Queenstown, is one of the few gold rush towns that have changed very little over the years. The present day population is around 1000, but it multiplies during peak holiday times. It does have a few new houses and a hotel, but many of the homes set back from the road behind avenues of deciduous trees are original miners' cottages which have been modernised. Because there are so many deciduous trees in the town it is a picture in yellow and red in autumn. The Arrow River was one of the world's richest sources of alluvial gold and Lakes District Centennial Museum has relics from the gold rush era. There is also a hang gliding simulator near the town.

Other places of interest include Ah Lum's House, the baker's oven, the old gaol, the war memorial, and Millbrook Nursery. Gold panning on the river is popular and pans can be hired from the Gold Nugget and the Old Smithy.

District Walks: Soldiers Hill - 45 minutes return; 3km Hayes Creek Track - 90 minutes return; **Tobins Track** - 2 hours return; **Sawpit Gully Track** - 3 hours return; **Bill Hill** walking track to Macetown - 9 hours; **the Macetown Road** can be used by 4WD vehicles, otherwise it is an 18km full day hike. Return to Queenstown via **Lake Hayes**, one of the most photographed lakes in New Zealand. It is well-known for the colour of its autumn leaves.

Tracks

Many people are combining a trek along the Tracks with a tour of New Zealand, and for more information see the section on *Tramping and Trekking*.

From Queenstown most people head for Te Anau and Milford Sound, which is probably one of New Zealand's most famous attractions, and deservedly so. The road into Milford is exciting and an experience in itself. The trip can be done as a day trip by coach or by coach and air, but if you are driving it is better to stay overnight in Te Anau. From Queenstown take SH 6 south to Kingston and Lumsden.

Kingston is 47km from Queenstown at the southern end of Lake Wakatipu. This town stands on the side of the ancient Maori village of Takerahaka which was built among the rock terminal moraine of the ancient Wakatipu glacier. The main tourist attraction today is a trip on the old steam train, the 'Kingston Flyer' which operates October 1 to April 30 from Kingston to Fairlight. The return trip takes approximately one hour fifteen minutes, and daily departures from Kingston are at 10.15am and 5.15pm, with an extra at 1.30pm on Sundays in January. Passengers are asked to be at the Kingston Railway Station 15 minutes before departure times.

Lumsden is 61km south of Kingston, and only 80km north of Invercargill. This is sheep raising country, but Lumsden is also well known for trout fishing in the Oreti River. From Lumsden follow SH 94 to **Mossburn** where there is a deer farm with more than 2000 animals. The turn off to Manapouri is 45km past Mossburn.

Fiordland National Park

Fiordland stretches 200km from Milford Sound south to Preservation Inlet, and is New Zealand's largest national park. In fact, it is larger than all of the others put together (1,224,603ha), and contains some of the most spectacular scenery in the country. It has fiords that twist and turn until they reach the Tasman Sea, and steep-sided valleys covered in dense vegetation. This is a genuine wilderness area, which receives around 7620mm of rain annually, and snow can fall on the higher peaks at any time.

There is a special significance in the name 'Fiordland', because the land surrounding the fiords is protected within the National Park, but the water is not.

Manapouri is situated on the shores of Lake Manapouri, which has been described as the most beautiful lake in New Zealand, framed as it is by the spectacular Cathedral Mountains. The lake has thirty-five islands, and is about 142 sq km in area, and 433m deep, making it the second deepest lake in New Zealand. The name Manapouri is a corruption of 'manawapora', Maori for 'sorrowing heart', which was actually the ancient name for Lake South Mavora, but mistakenly given to Manapouri by a European cartographer. The actual Maori name for this lake was Roto-ua, 'the rainy lake'. The town of

Manapouri has a population of around 400, and is the gateway to the Doubtful and Dusky Sounds, and the starting point for many walking tracks, hunting and fishing trips.

Fiordland Travel has an interesting tour from Manapouri: travel across the lake, then a coach trip over the **Wilmot Pass** takes visitors to **Doubtful Sound**, the deepest of all the fiords, for a peaceful cruise surrounded by 400 year old podocarp forests. An optional tour of the Manapouri underground power station can also be included. This tour runs daily at 9.30am and when advertised locally at 11.30am, and costs are $150 adult, $40 child. Wilmot Pass was built during the construction of the power station at an estimated cost of $4.85 per 2.5cm, making it the most expensive road in New Zealand. In places the gradient is 1 in 5, making it the steepest passenger road in the country. The road follows the Spey Valley with views of river, forest and mountain. From Wilmot Pass there are incredible views of the Sound stretching to the Tasman Sea.

From Manapouri you can travel across to Te Anau, 19km away, without rejoining Highway 94.

Te Anau

Te Anau (population 3000) is situated on the shore of the lake of the same name. It is the largest of the South Island lakes, and is a holiday resort in its own right as well as being the staging point for trips to Milford Sound. Te Anau has an excellent range of accommodation and shopping facilities.

Tourist Information
The Visitor Information Centre is on Lakefront Drive, ph (03) 249 8900.

Accommodation
Te Anau has loads of accommodation, but it is still wise to book in advance. Here is a selection, with prices in NZ$ for a double room per night, which should be used as guide only. The telephone area code is 03.

Hotels
Te Anau Travelodge, Lakefront Drive, ph 249 7411, fax 249 7947 -

112 rooms (private facilities), licensed restaurants, cocktail lounge, swimming pool, sauna - $95-150.

Luxmore Resort Hotel, Main St, ph 249 7526, fax 249 7272 - 148 rooms (private facilities), restaurant, cocktail lounge - $95-150.

Motels

Explorer Motor Lodge, 6 Cleddau Street, ph 249 7156, fax 249 7149 - 15 units, spa barbecue - $80-103.

Best Western Te Anau Downs Motor Inn, Te Anau-Milford Sound Highway (SH 94), ph 249 7811, fax 249 7753 - 50 units, licensed restaurant (closed May 20 through September 10 each year) - $100-115.

Amber Court Motel, 68 Quintin Drive, ph 249 7230, fax 249 7486 - 9 units, barbecue - $85-90

Lakeside Motel, 36 Lakefront Drive, ph 249 7435,fax 249 7529 - 19 units, barbecue - $80-90.

Aden Motel, 59 Quintin Drive, ph 249 7748, fax 249 7434 - 12 units, barbecue - $68-86.

Edgewater XL Motel & Villas, 52 Lakefront Drive, ph 249 7258, fax 249 8099 - 16 units, barbecue - $78-85.

Motor Camps and Caravan Parks

Fiordland Holiday Park, Milford Road, ph 249 7059 - tent sites $14 x 2; caravan sites $15 x 2; on-site caravans (sleep 4) $28 x 2; flats $58 x 2; cabins $20-35 x 2.

Mountain View Holiday Park, 128 Te Anau Terrace, ph\fax 249 7462 - tent sites $10 per person; caravan sites $10.50 per person; units (sleep 4-6) $77 x 2; cabins (sleep 4) $30 x 2; on-site caravans $40 x 2.

Hostel

Te Anau Hostel(YHA), Milford Road, ph/fax 249 7847 - $16 per person.

Sightseeing

A 30-minute boat trip across the lake will take you to the **Te Anau Glow-Worm Caves**. The Maoris knew of the existence of the caves, but they weren't discovered by Europeans until 1948. These caves are unusual in that they are living caves that are still being eroded away by the Tunnel Burn stream. There are two tours daily at 2pm and 8.15pm throughout the year with additional tours during summer. The tours depart from

Fiordland Travel, ph 249 7416.

The Department of Conservation Visitor Centre, on the lake front, has displays on historical and current uses of Fiordland National Park, information on local tracks, walks, and tourist trips. Also in this centre is the Fiordland National Park Museum

The **Wildlife Centre**, is on the Te Anau-Manapouri Highway, about ten minutes walk from the Conservation Visitor Centre. Here visitors are introduced to takahe, kaka, tui, kea, parakeet and waterfowl, as well as deer.

Lake Trips are available on the yacht *Manuska*, or you can hire a boat and fish. Jetboat rides are also available. Enquire at the Visitor Information Centre.

Southern Lakes Helicopters, ph 249 7167, have a Mount Luxmore flight which hovers along the Hidden Lakes to Mount Luxmore and over the mountains. They also have a Lake Manapouri/Doubtful Sound trip and a Sutherland Falls/Milford Track.

Air Fiordland, ph 249 7505, have scenic flights from the airport, 6.5km from town. They have similar flights to Southern Lakes Helicopters, but in a light aircraft.

The Te Anau-Milford Road

The road from Te Anau to Milford is an engineering feat. It was opened in 1953, but is sometimes closed from June to October due to avalanche dangers, so check with the Tourist Information Centre in Te Anau before proceeding. It is 120km from Te Anau to Milford, and the trip takes about 3 hours, allowing a few stops for sightseeing.

For the first 30km the road follows the lake, then it swings away and winds through beautiful beech forests. The Routeburn and Greenstone Tracks join the road 93km from Te Anau. The road passes through Marion Corner and then Gunn's Camp, 110km from Te Anau. The Hollyford Road branches off at Marion Corner for the start of the Hollyford Track. From Marian Camp it is 17km to the end of the road and the start of the track.

Continuing along to Milford, the road progressively rises to the entrance of the Homer Tunnel. Once through the tunnel the road winds down to Milford Sound and some of the best scenery in the world.

Milford Sound

Described by Rudyard Kipling as the 'eighth wonder of the world', Milford Sound was carved out during an Ice Age. It is 15km long, and is surrounded by very high mounts that are often snow covered. Mitre Peak dominates the scene as it rises directly from the water. The panorama is superb, and as you look around you will see dense forest, glacier ice, strange shaped mountains, deep, clear blue water and often mist.

A trip out on the sound is a must, and there are plenty of opportunities available, aboard a variety of craft. On any of these trips you will see splendid waterfalls, overhanging cliffs, and occasionally, dolphins and seals.

Most people only come for the day trip to Milford, but there is limited accommodation if you wish to stay and enjoy the peace and quite, and the unpolluted air.

Milford Sound

Mitre Peak Lodge, ph 249 7926 - 33 rooms (private facilities), licensed restaurant, cocktail lounges, charter cruises, scenic flights, bushwalks, tramping. This establishment does not take reservations, so for more information and current prices contact the Travelodge in Te Anau, ph 249 7411.

Milford Lodge, ph/fax 249 8071, has 106 beds in double, twin or bunkrooms, restaurant, bar, shops, sauna, barbecue - coach connections to Routeburn, Greenstone, Hollyford, Kepler Tracks, Te Anau and Queenstown every morning at 9.30am - $18-25 per person. Tent and caravan sites available.

Cruises

Milford Sound Red Boat Cruises, PO Box 185, Te Anau, ph (03) 249 7411, fax (03) 249 7947, have been providing a variety of daytime trips on Milford Sound since 1957. *The Lady of the Sounds*, *Lady Stirling* and *Lady Bowen* offer a wide selection of food from quick snacks to a full buffet meal, and complete bar service. Other vessels include *Anita Bay*, used as a service launch to Milford for trekkers completing the Milford Track Guided Trek, *Milford Adventurer* which offers cruises that include a visit to the Milford Sound Underwater Observatory, and *The Lady of the South Pacific*, 38m of luxury that can accommodate up to 67 people on an overnight cruise.

Milford Sound Underwater Observatory

There is a unique coral garden living 10m below the surface of Milford Sound! A part of the many cruises on the Sound is a trip to the underwater observatory, where you take stairs down to the glass walled observation chamber and see the teeming life beneath the waters of the Sound.

Southland

In 1844 the Chief Surveyor of the New Zealand Company described Southland as "a mere bog and unfit for habitation". He was to be proven wrong as the fertile plains produce wool, lamb, beef and dairy products. Southland is chiefly a primary producing area with extensive grazing lands and forests, but with the building of the aluminium smelter near Bluff and the development of the fishing and oyster industries, it has diversified.

In 1861 Southland became a separate province, only to be reunited with Otago a few years later. The principal town of Southland is Invercargill.

Invercargill

Invercargill (population 56,148) lies at the southern end of the South Island. It has an equitable climate with rain spread evenly throughout the year. The city has wonderful parks and gardens and neat houses.

How to Get There

By Air
Air New Zealand has daily flights to Invercargill from Auckland, Christchurch, Dunedin and Wellington.
Ansett New Zealand has daily flights to Invercargill from Auckland, Christchurch and Wellington.

By Rail
The *Southerner* runs daily between Christchurch and Invercargill, stopping at Timaru and Dunedin along the way.

By Bus
InterCity has daily services to Invercargill from Christchurch, Dunedin, Queenstown and Te Anau.

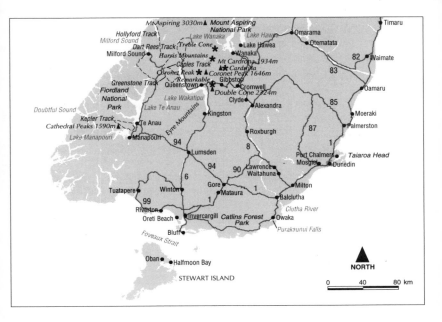

Mount Cook Landline has daily services from Christchurch, Dunedin and Queenstown.

By Car
Dunedin-Invercargill is 217km - approx 3 hours 40 minutes.
Christchurch-Invercargill is 578km - approx 9 hours 30min.
Queenstown-Invercargill is 189km - approx 3 hours 15min.
Te Anau-Invercargill is 159km - approx 2 hours 35min.

Tourist Information
The Visitor Information Office is in Queens Park,
ph (03) 214 6243.

Accommodation
Here is a selection of available accommodation, with prices in

NZ$ for a double room per night, which should be used as a guide only. The telephone area code is 03.

Hotels

Ascot Park Motor Hotel, cnr Tay Street & Racecourse Road, ph 217 6195, fax 217 7002 - 70 rooms (private facilities), 24 motel units, licensed restaurant, cocktail lounge, swimming pool, spa - $145-160 (hotel); $92 (motel).

Kelvin Hotel, 18 Kelvin Street, ph 218 2829, fax 218 2287 - 59 rooms (private facilities), licensed restaurant, cocktail lounge - $108.

Grand Hotel, 76 Dee Street, ph 218 8059, 218 8053 - 57 rooms (private facilities), licensed restaurant, cocktail lounge - $75.

Don Lodge Motor Hotel, 77 Don Street, ph 218 6125, fax 214 0222 - 24 rooms (private facilities), licensed restaurant, cocktail lounge - $60.

Motels

Townsman Motor Lodge, 195 Tay Street, ph 218 8027, fax 218 8420 - 20 units, spa - $80-98.

Balmoral Lodge, 265 Tay Street, ph 217 6109, fax 217 5755 - 27 units & apartments - $90-100.

Bavarian Motel, 444 North Road (SH 6), ph 215 7552, fax 215 7592 - 5 units, barbecue - $85.

Chelmsford Court Motel, 88 Salford Street, ph 217 5807, fax 217 8732 - 4 units, non-smoking - $82-92.

Aachen Motel, 147 Yarrow Street, ph/fax 218 8185 - 12 units - $75-85.

Montecillo Lodge, 240 Spey Street, ph 218 2503, fax 2182506 - 6 units, unlicensed restaurant - $96.

Garden Grove Motel, 161 North Road, ph/fax 215 9555 - 7 units - $75-85.

Motor Camps and Cabins

Beach Road Motor Camp & Tourist Flats, on the road to Oreti beach, ph 213 0400 - camp sites $6 per person; caravan sites $8 per person; flats (sleep 5) $38 x 2; cabins (sleep 1-6) $24 x 2.

Coachman's Caravan Park, 705 Tay Street, ph 217 6046, fax 217 6045 - licensed bar and theatre restaurant - tent sites $8 per person; caravan sites $18 x 2; tourist flats (sleep 4) $69.

Invercargill Caravan Park, A&P Showgrounds, Victoria Avenue, ph 218 8787 - tent sites $7 per person; caravan sites $16 x 2; cabins (sleep 6) $24-30; bunkroom $10 per person.

Hostels
Invercargill Hostel (YHA), 122 North Road, Waikiwi, ph 215 9344 - $15 per person.

Local Transport

Buses
Buses depart from the Post Office area in Dee Street for the suburbs and outlying areas, ph 218 7108.

Car Hire
Hertz, ph 218 2837; Avis, ph 218 7019; Letz, ph 218 8166; Rhodes, ph 218 2836; Budget, ph 218 7012.

Eating Out
All the bigger hotels have restaurants, or you might like to try one of the following.

Kitcheners Family Restaurant, in the Appleby Tavern, Balmoral Drive, ph 218 8235 - Licensed - open nightly for dinner 4.30-9pm - bistro style - **less than $25** - credit cards accepted.

Homestead Cobb & Co Family Restaurant, in the Avenal Hotel, cnr Avenal & Dee Streets, ph 218 3125 - **Licensed** - open Mon-Fri noon-2pm, nightly from 4.30pm - extensive menu - **$25-45** - credit cards accepted.

Ainos Steakhouse & Restaurant, Waikiwi Shopping Centre, North Rad, ph 215 9568 - **BYO** - open Mon-Sat 5-10pm - oldest restaurant in Invercargill - **less than $25** - credit cards accepted.

Cosmopolitan Restaurant, 34 Esk Street, ph 218 2166 - **Licensed** - open Tues-Sat 11.45am-2pm, 6-10pm - fine dining with extensive menu - **$25-45** - credit cards accepted.

Sightseeing
Most people are struck by the fact that the streets are named after Scottish rivers. The city itself is relatively flat and well laid out with many parks and wide streets. **Queens Park**, which spreads over 81ha, is right in the middle of the city with

formal gardens, an aviary, deer park, a beautiful statuary and a children's fountain. It also has an 18-hole golf course, bowling and croquet greens, tennis and squash courts, hockey and cricket grounds, and an indoor ice rink.

In the southern part of the park is the **Southland Museum and Art Gallery**, which was built for the centenary of Waitangi in 1940 and has recently been redeveloped. It has a large collection of Maori art as well as articles belonging to pioneers, sailors and whalers. It also has a Tuatara Lizard House whose occupants belong to an otherwise extinct order of reptiles that is only found in New Zealand. The museum is open daily 10am-4.30pm, and admission is free.

In front of the museum are some specimens from the famous Curio Bay petrified forest. The forest was burnt and buried under lava 160 million years ago and brought to light by sea erosion.

The **Water Tower**, in the Doon Street reserve, is 42.5m and was completed in 1889 from a design by william Sharp, a former civil engineer for the Public Works Department. It is open on Sunday and public holidays 1.30-4.30pm, and offers a great view of the city from the top.

One of the city's landmarks is the brass dome of **St Mary's Basilica**, which was built in 1905. Other buildings of note are St John's and the First Church, and the Town Hall in Tay Street.

Invercargill has a large freezing works that processes 7 million carcasses annually.

Sport & Recreation

Golf
There are courses in Queens Park, Otatara, Green Acres and Oreti Sands.

Swimming
You can swim at the Central Pools, ph 214 3664, at Queens Park Pool & Waterslide, ph 217 5971, and at the beach at Oreti.

Horse Racing
Meetings are held at Southland Racecourse.

Outlying Attractions

Oreti Beach, 9.5km west of the city, is a popular swimming place. A warm current from Australia flows along the beach making the water much warmer than many other beaches in the South Island. Toheroas can be taken from this beach during the open season, but the catch is limited to allow the shell fish to regenerate.

Bluff, 27km south, is the port for Invercargill. A 37ha island has been built in the harbour to provide berths for shipping. Bluff is also the home port of the fishing, crayfishing and oyster fleets. A good view of the Tiwai Point Aluminium Smelter can be obtained from the top of Bluff Hill. Tours of the Smelter are available, free of charge, but bookings are essential, ph 218 5999.

Stewart Island

Stewart Island (population 450) is the smallest and most southerly of the three main islands of New Zealand, and lies 32km from Invercargill across Foveaux Strait. Most visitors expect it to be smaller than it really is. It has an area of 172,000ha, has 755km of rocky, indented coastline, and its highest point is Mt Anglem, 980m. The island has an almost sub-tropical appearance, despite lying between 46 and 47 degrees south. The Aurora Australis, or Southern Lights, are regularly seen at this latitude. Stewart Island is rich in bird and animal life, and is devoid of most of the usual resort infra-structure. It has a genuine, quiet air that will either really appeal to you or you will be glad to leave.

Climate

As Stewart Island is so small there is very little seasonal variation in temperature because of the moderating effect of the sea, but the weather is very changeable, especially in areas exposed to the south and west. Rainfall varies from 5000mm in the south-west to a moderate 1500mm in the north and east. Rain falls on approximately 255 days each year.

How to Get There

It is possible to go there and back in the same day if you don't have a lot of time to spare, and you will be able to see all that there is to see in Oban, and get the general feeling of the island. A stand-by airfare is not much more expensive than the ferry fare, so you may prefer to fly if you don't mind small aircraft.

By Air

Southern Air Ltd, ph 218 9129 (toll free 0 800 658 876) have daily services to Stewart Island and the flying time is 20 minutes. All flights are met by a mini-bus.

By Boat

The *Foveaux Express Catamaran* leaves Bluff Harbour daily, and the trip takes about two and a half hours, and in good weather it can be a pleasant crossing. But, as with all other ferry crossings in New Zealand, that depends on the weather, and the weather in Foveaux Strait can change hourly. Mini-buses meet all ferry arrivals on Stewart Island, and a bus service operates from Invercargill to connect with all ferry departures and arrivals.

Tourist Information

The Visitor Information Office is on Main Road, Half Moon Bay, ph (03) 219 1218.

The Department of Conservation has an office with videos and audio displays on the island's natural history and heritage. Open Jan-Mar daily 8.30am-7pm, April-Dec daily 8.30am-5pm, ph (03) 219 1130.

Accommodation

Not a lot to choose from, but here is a selection with prices in NZ$ for a double room per night, which should be used as a guide only. The telephone area code is 03.

South Sea Hotel, Half Moon Bay, ph 219 1059, fax 219 1120 - 17 rooms with hand basin (bathroom/toilet facilities adjacent), licensed restaurant, cocktail lounge - $80-98.

Stewart Island Holiday Homes, Half Moon Bay, ph/fax 219 1057, (contact address: 131 Chelmsford Street, Invercargill, ph 217 6585) - 2 private self-contained houses sleeping up to 10 - set in secluded bush with views - $60.

Stewart Island Lodge, Half Moon Bay, ph 219 1085 - 4 rooms (private facilities) - DB&B $400 a double.

Rakiura Motel, Half Moon Bay, ph 219 1096 - 5 units - $80.

Local Transport

There are taxis and mini-buses, and you can take a coach tour of the island. Launch trips to the various islands can be arranged with the charter boat operators. Enquire at the Visitor Information Centre or at Stewart Island Lodge.

Sightseeing

Stewart Island offers a real chance to 'get away from it all'. It's a great place for quiet bush walks, hunting whitetail deer and pigs, relaxing, and swimming and skin diving if you don't mind the cold water. A hunting permit is required, and this can be obtained on the island. Many birds inhabit the bush, including the Stewart Island Kiwi.

The main settlement is **Oban** (where the ferry from Bluff docks). Most of the island's population depend largely on the sea for their livelihood, fishing for blue cod, paua and crayfish, or tending the three salmon farms. The **Rakiura Museum** has displays of local history from the days of sealers and whalers through to the mining and saw milling eras. It is open daily 10am-noon, Sunday noon-2pm, ph (03) 219 1049.

There are only 20km of roads on the island, so it is not surprising that one of the most popular pursuits here is walking. The island has over 220km of walking tracks. There is a ten day tramp around the northern circuit, and the Department of Conservation will give you up to date information on track conditions and hut space availability. For the less adventurous, there are plenty of shorter walks around Half Moon Bay.

Titi, or mutton birds (the sooty shearwater) are oceanic birds that are prolific breeders on the offshore islands, and are a protected species. The Maoris consider there birds a delicacy, and they return to the islands each year in April and May to capture the chicks. Only descendants of the original inhabitants are permitted to do so. There is a protected colony at Acker's Point which is within walking distance of Oban.

Fine shells can be found on the beaches around the island, although they are not as plentiful as they once were. Scarlet seaweed is often found too, giving the beaches an unusual appearance.

As well as being a unique experience, Stewart Island is a great place to recuperate after a hectic tour of New Zealand.

Back on the mainland, you can take Highway 99 along the coast to **Riverton** which is another beach and holiday resort, 38km from Invercargill. It is also the home port of a fishing fleet. From Riverton the road goes to **Tuatapere,** then circles back to **Winton** on the Invercargill-Queenstown road. From there you can either go to **Lumsden** and **Te Anau,** to **Queenstown,** or along Highway 96 to **Mataura** and **Gore.**

Gore, 66km north-east of Invercargill, is the largest inland settlement in the South Island. It has a population of around 8500, and is the service centre for a rich farming district. It straddles the Mataura River, which is one of the best stocked brown trout waters in New Zealand. Many illicit whisky stills were found during the last century in the foothills of the nearby Hokonui Ranges, which separate Southland from the Waimea Plains. Gore is the country music capital of New Zealand, and the NZ Gold Guitar Awards are presented here every Queen's Birthday weekend.

Instead of travelling inland to Gore from Invercargill, you can follow SH 92 along the coast to **The Catlins** which is a wilderness area with dense rain forests, plentiful native birds, lonely beaches with towering cliffs, and huge sea caves. The road rejoins SH 1 at Balclutha - see the Otago chapter for a detailed description of the route.

Otago

Otago is divided into two main areas, Coastal Otago and Central Otago. The coastal strip can be divided into three sections: North Otago, which was the birthplace of the frozen meat industry; East Otago, between Dunedin and Oamaru, a popular holiday area; and South Otago, around Balclutha and The Catlins.

Dunedin is the principal city and port of the region. Its Scottish ancestry is revealed in its architecture and it is often called the Edinburgh of the South. Christchurch has a city square, but Dunedin's centre is an unusual octagonal-shaped garden reserve in which is found a statue of the Scottish poet, Robbie Burns.

Hunting and fishing are popular pastimes in Otago and the lakes can be fished July-September, but not the streams or rivers, which close in April except for the lower reaches of the Clutha and Taieri, which are open until September. Wild animal hunting (deer, chamois, thar and pigs) is allowed all year, but a permit is needed to hunt in the forests. This can be obtained from rangers in Dunedin, Lawrence, Naseby or Hawea. For all waterfowl, except Canada geese, the hunting season finishes on July 27. Upland birds can be hunted through September.

Christchurch to Dunedin on SH 1

Travelling south from Christchurch along SH 1, you will cross the fertile Canterbury Plains and see some of New Zealand's best sheep country. The border between the Canterbury and Aorangi Regions is the Rakaia River, approximately 55km from Christchurch.

The first major town you will come to is **Ashburton**, which has a population of around 14,000. It is 87km south of Christchurch in the centre of the largest wheat growing area in New Zealand. It has a flour mill and a freezing works. The Ashburton Domain was formerly a semi-desert area that has been turned into a lush garden with a beautiful lake. Fishing is a popular recreational sport as the nearby rivers abound with fish. Another popular sport is trotting, as Ashburton is one of the major trotting centres in the country. Apart from that, it is only 57km from the Mt Hutt ski-field, and in winter many skiers use Ashburton as a base when visiting the snowfields. Heading south the next town you come to is Temuka.

Temuka is the pottery centre of the south, and a fisherman's paradise, as the rivers in the area are swarming with trout and quinnat salmon. Earthenware pottery from Temuka graces tables all over the world, and if you are interested in pottery, this is a good place to stop off. 18km south is Timaru.

Timaru is 163km south of Christchurch. It is the port for, and centre of, the frozen meat industry of the South Island. It has two meat works, a brewery, a tannery, textile mills and food processing factories.

There is a sign-posted scenic drive which covers most places of interest, and affords the visitor good views of the coast and mountains.

Timaru was once a whaling station and a 914m breakwater was built of local bluestone to form an artificial harbour. Caroline Bay, with its gently sweeping beach, is protected by this breakwater. It is a popular resort in summer when holiday-makers come to enjoy its warm, protected waters.

Worth seeing are: The South Canterbury Museum in Perth Street; the Aigantighe Gallery in Wai-iti Road; and the Botanic Gardens in Queen Street.

The *Pleasant Point Railway and Historical Museum*, ph 688 9694, is 19km north-west of Timaru, and is reached by the 'Fairlie Flyer' which leaves from the centre of the town for the 3km run to the Pleasant Point Railway Station.

About 63km south of Timaru is the Waitaki River, the border between the provinces of Canterbury and Otago. This river offers salmon and trout fishing and jet boating.

North Otago

The next town that you will come to is **Oamaru**, 250km from Christchurch and 120km north of Dunedin. It is the most important town of North Otago, and is often called 'The White

Stone City'. The cream-white stone quarried at Weston, 7km away, was used to build most of the main buildings of the town, e.g. the National Bank, the Bank of New South Wales (now an art gallery), the old post office, courthouse and athenaeum. Other places of interest include the Public Gardens in Chelmer Street; the Wallaby Park in Chelmer Street, ph (03) 434 8060; the North Otago Museum in Thames Street; and the Historic Farm Buildings in Totara Estate Centennial Park, 8km south of town on SH 1.

The Oamaru Information Centre is at 1 Thames Street, ph (03) 434 1656. South of Oamaru the highway leaves the coast again for some kilometres, and rejoins it near **Hampden**. Close to Hampden a track leads through Boulder Park to the beach where the **Moeraki Boulders** lie scattered across the sand. This geological phenomena weigh tons and are just over a metre in diameter.

At **Palmerston**, 26km south of Hampden, SH 85 from Alexandra joins SH 1. Palmerston has a population of around 850, and should not be confused with Palmerston North in the North Island. A further 54km south lies Dunedin.

Dunedin

Dunedin (population 118,890) is built on steep hills around Otago Harbour. It has beautiful parks and gardens, and is a picture in the springtime when the azaleas and rhododendrons are in bloom. The 'Edinburgh of the South' has many stately stone buildings as well as modern tower blocks. It is an elegant city where the arts flourish.

Climate

Average temperatures: June-August (winter) 6.8C; September-November (spring) 11C; December-February (summer) 26C; March-May (autumn/fall) 11C. The wettest month is July, and the windiest period is in November. Dunedin has an average rainfall of 775mm, and it rains on average 167 days each year.

How to Get There

By Air
Air New Zealand has daily flights to Dunedin from Auckland, Christchurch, Invercargill and Wellington.
Ansett New Zealand has daily flights to Dunedin from Auckland, Christchurch, Invercargill and Wellington.

By Rail
The *Southerner* travels between Christchurch and Invercargill, stopping at Dunedin. It is a weekday service, but weekend trains run during the summer school holidays.

By Bus
InterCity has daily services to Dunedin from Christchurch, Invercargill, Queenstown and Te Anau.
Mount Cook Landline has daily services to Dunedin from
    Christchurch, Invercargill, and Sun-Fri services from Queenstown and Wanaka.

By Car
Christchurch-Dunedin is 361km - approx 5 hours 40 minutes.
Invercargill-Dunedin is 217km - approx 3 hours 30 minutes.
Mount Cook-Dunedin is 329km - approx 4 hours 50 minutes.
Queenstown-Dunedin is 281km - approx 4 hours 20 minutes.
Wanaka-Dunedin is 276km - approx 4 hours 20 minutes.

Visitor Information

Dunedin Visitor Information Office is at 48 The Octagon, ph (03) 474 3300. It is open Mon-Fri 8.30am-5pm, Sat-Sun 9am-5pm.

Accommodation

Dunedin has a wide range of accommodation, and here is a selection, with prices in NZ$ for a double room per night, which should be used as a guide only.
The telephone area code is 03.

Hotels
The Southern Cross Hotel, cnr Princes & High Streets, ph 477 0752, fax 477 5776 - 134 units, restaurants, brasserie, 24-hour

cafe, cocktail lounges - $192-310.

Cargills, 678 George Street, ph 477 7983, fax 477 8098 - 50 rooms (private facilities), restaurant (entertainment Fri-Sat), cocktail lounge - $113-195.

Abbey Motor Lodge, 900 Cumberland Street & 680 Castle Street, ph 477 5380, fax 477 8715 - 38 rooms (private facilities) + 12 motel units, restaurant, cocktail lounge, indoor swimming pool, spas, sauna - $95-270.

Shoreline Hotel, 47 Timaru Street, ph 455 5196, fax 455 5193 - 36 rooms (private facilities), restaurant, cocktail lounges (entertainment) - $99.

Motels

Leisure Lodge Motor Inn, Duke Street, ph 477 5360, fax 477 5460 - 76 units, licensed restaurant - $145.

Larnach Castle Lodge, Otago Peninsula, ph 476 1616 - 12 rooms (private facilities), licensed restaurant - $120.

Academy Court & Dunedin Motels, 624 George Street, ph/fax 477 7692 - 14 units and 6 3-bedroom apartments - $85-95.

Alcala Motor Lodge, cnr George & St David Streets, ph/fax 477 9073 - 23 units, spa - $82.

Chequers Motel, 119 Musselburgh Rise, ph 455 0778 - 6 units - $60-65.

Arcadian Motel, 85-89 Musselburgh Rise, ph 455 0992, fax 455 0237 - 11 units - $60-65.

Bayfield Motels, 210 Musselburgh Rise, ph/fax 455 0756 - 9 units, barbecue - $60-65.

Harbour View Motel, 20 Canongate, ph 477 7972, fax 477 7982 - 6 units - $60-70.

Beach Lodge Motel, 38 Victoria Road, ph 455 5043, fax 455 4411 - 18 units - $69-75.

Hostels

Manor House, 28 Manor Place, ph 477 0484, fax 477 8145 - 7 rooms $17-20 per person; 4 bunkrooms (sleep 22) $15 per person.

Stafford Gables Hostel (YHA), 71 Stafford Street, ph 474 1919, fax 474 1919 - $16 per person.

Motor Camps & Caravan Parks

Aaron Lodge Holiday Park, 162 Kaikorai Valley Road, ph 476 4725, fax 476 7925 - camp sites $18 x 2; caravan sites $20 x 2;

DUNEDIN

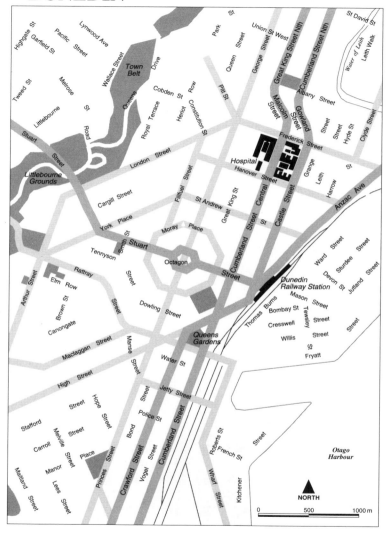

flats (sleep 5) $51-58 x 2; cabins (sleep 3-5) $30-33 x 2.
Farmlands Caravan Park, Waitati Valley Road, ph 482 2730 - caravan sites $18 x 2 (no tent sites); cabin (sleeps 4) $28 x 2.
Portobello Tourist Park, 27 Hereweka Street, Portobello, ph/fax 478 0359 - tent sites $17 x 2; caravan sites $19 x 2; on-site caravans $35 x 2.
Tahuna Park Seaside Camp, Tahuna Park, St Kilda, ph/fax 455 4690 - tent sites $18 x 2; caravan sites $18.50 x 2; cabins (sleep 5) $46 x 2; cabins (sleep 6) $32 x 2.

Local Transport

Car Hire
Thrifty, ph 486 1993; Budget, ph 474 0428; Avis, ph 4775973; Hertz, ph 477 7385.

Bicycle Hire
10-speed bikes can be hired at the Information Centre, and come with a self-guide book for Otago Peninsula.

Eating Out
There are plenty of eateries to choose from in Dunedin, and following are some you might like to try.
Shamrock's Restaurant, Clarendon Hotel, 28 Maclaggen Street, ph 477 9095 - **Licensed** - open nightly 6-9pm - specialises in seafood - **$25-45** - credit cards accepted.
Settlers Restaurant, Quality Hotel Upper Moray Place, ph 477 6784 - **Licensed/BYO** - open noon-2pm, 6-9.30pm - NZ cuisine - **$25-45** - credit cards accepted.
Peppermill, 199A Stuart St, ph 477 3930 - **BYO** - open Wed-Mon 6pm-late - Italian style cuisine - **$25-45** - credit cards accepted.
Little India Bistro & Tandoor, 82 St Andrew Street, ph 4776559 - **BYO** - open Mon-Fri 11.30am-2.30pm, Wed-Mon from 6pm - **under $25** - credit cards accepted.
City Limits, 412A George Street, ph 477 2463 - **BYO** - open Mon-Fri 11am-2pm, Mon-Sat 6pm-late - cafe and restaurant with mixed menu - **under $25** - credit cards accepted.
Bacchus, The Octagon, ph 474 0824 - **Licensed** - open Mon-Sat 11am-1am - wine bar with good food, plus cheaper bar food - great selection of South Island whites - **under $25** -credit cards accepted.

University of Otago, Dunedin

Sightseeing

Most of the city sights can be seen on a walking tour, but if you enjoy cycling, you might like to hire a bike from the Visitor Information Office. The best place to start the tour is at **The Octagon**. This park area in the centre of town has two main features: the Star Fountain which plays music at 12.30pm, 6pm,

7.30pm and 9.30pm in summer (it is illuminated at night); and the statue of Robbie Burns.

The Octagon is also the site of the **Dunedin Public Art Gallery**, ph 477 4000, which has a collection of paintings by New Zealanders and Australians, including works by artist Frances Hodgkins who was born in Dunedin. The gallery is open daily 10am-5pm and admission is $4 adult, $2 child.

Dunedin has several interesting old buildings with turrets, towers, gables and spires, which can be best seen on a walking tour, and these are listed below.

The **Municipal Chambers**, built 1878-80, face the Octagon as does **St Paul's Cathedral. First Church**, with its spectacular spire, is in Moray Place, the true octagonal street one block back from The Octagon. **Knox Church** in George Street was built in 1876, **Fortune Theatre** in 1869, and the **Southern Cross Hotel** in 1883.

Olveston House, 42 Royal Terrace, was built in Jacobean style in 1906. The 35-room home of a successful merchant and philanthropist now houses a collection of international antiques. It is open daily 9.30am-5pm and admission is $10 adults. One hour guided tours commence at 9.30am, 10.45am, noon, 1.30pm, 2.45pm and 4pm, ph 477 3320 to make a booking.

The University of Otago, founded in 1869, was the first university to be established in New Zealand, and holds a central place in the life of the city. It is a grey stone building with a distinctive clock tower, set in lawns on the banks of the Waters of Leith.

The **Otago Museum**, 419 Great King Street, has a good collection of Pacific and Maori art, ancient civilisations and natural history. Open daily 10am-5pm and entrance is by donation. Discovery World, in the Museum, is a hands-on science centre with fun displays, and admission is by donation.

The **Otago Early Settlers Museum**, 220 Cumberland Street, has a collection of items from the city's pioneering days. It is open daily 10am-5pm and admission is $4 adult.

The **Botanic Gardens** have both formal gardens of roses, azaleas and rhododendrons, as well as greenhouses and native bush. The Rhododendron Dell, planted in 1914, is well-known. The scenic belt overlooking the city is worth visiting, and Queen's Drive takes you through it. Panoramic views of the city can be obtained from Mount Cargill Lookout, Signal Hills and from the Rotary Park Lookout.

The **Port of Dunedin** caters for ships with a draught of up to 8m, and Port Chalmers handles the larger ones as well as offering docking facilities.

Speights Brewery has daily one hour tours with sampling at the conclusion. Bookings are essential, ph 477 9480.

Cadbury Confectionery Ltd have one hour tours of their chocolate factory, but again bookings are essential, ph 474 1126.

Wilson's Distillers Ltd, New Zealand's only whisky distillery is open for daily tours, ph 473 0677.

Sport & Recreation

Harbour Cruises
The MV *Monarch* has a variety of cruises on the harbour and to view albatrosses, seals, penguins and cormorants, ph 477 4276 for details and prices.

Sail Southern Spirit has regular 4 hour cruises on Otago Harbour, with passenger involvement in the sailing. Contact the Visitor Information Office for details.

Horse Riding
Bums'N'Saddles, ph 488 0097, and Castle Discovery, ph 478 0592, offer horse treks.

Swimming
There are enclosed and open-air waterslides, an olympic pool and restaurant at Moana Pool, ph 474 3513 for opening times.

Golf, tennis, fishing, sailing and rafting are some of the many recreational facilities available.

Tours

Dunedin Citisights is a tour of the city's buildings and points of interest aboard a double decker bus. Tours depart daily from the Visitor Centre at 10am and 3.30pm and costs are $15 adult, $8 child.

At noon a tour leaves for Larnach Castle and the Peninsula - $28 adult, $15 child. For more information contact Newtowns on ph 477, 5577, fax 477 8147.

Outlying Attractions

The nearby beaches of **St Clair** and **St Kilda** offer a change of pace from the city, but the water is rather cold. St Clair has a heated salt water swimming pool on the beach front, open November to March.

Glenfalloch Woodland Garden is also worth a visit as this 11ha garden nestles in a valley filled with trees, rhododendrons and azaleas. There are walks through the gardens, a tropical aquarium, children's playground, chalet tearooms and potter's cabin.

The Otago Peninsula is one of Dunedin's greatest treasures, and can be visited on a 66km round trip from Dunedin. There are many points of interest - historical, wild and scenic.

At **Taiaroa Head**, at the northern end of the peninsula, is the Royal Albatross Colony, where the birds nest closer to human habitation than anywhere else. The albatross observatory is open every day, but prior bookings are essential, ph 478 0499 or 478 0498. The viewing season opens on November 24 and closes on September 16 of the following year (earlier if the chicks have moved out of sight).

There is also a Pa site, and a lighthouse, and on the headland is **Historic Fort Taiaroa**, with a network of tunnels and a fully restored Armstrong Disappearing Gun, plus ammunition chambers, and an historical display of Taiaroa Head since Colonial times, including life-size models depicting the life of the soldier. There are also uniforms and photographs and memorabilia of the past. Prior bookings are also necessary for the Fort, and can be made at the same telephone numbers as above, or at the Visitor Information Office.

At **Penguin Place** there is the opportunity to see yellow-eyed penguins (the rarest penguin in the world), fur seals and spotted shags. **Larnach's Castle** is a landmark on the peninsula, and is open for inspection. It has beautiful wrought iron lace on the verandahs and the front fence. Two lions and two eagles guard the outside stoop. Inside, it has elaborate carvings and rare timber panelling. For more information and opening times, ph 476 1616.

The **Taieri Gorge Limited** train trip is definitely worthwhile. The train leaves from the historic Dunedin Railway Station daily at 1.30pm (March 21-September 30) or 3.30pm (October 1-March 20) returning at 5.30pm and 7.30pm respectively. The scenery through the gorge is spectacular, and the train stops two or three times to allow passengers to take photos. Tickets can be purchased at the Booking Office in the Dunedin Railway Station, ph 477 4449.

Highway 1 swings away from the coast south of Dunedin and travels 42km to **Milton**. From there you can continue on SH 1 south to Balclutha and Invercargill, or you can take SH 8 to Alexandra and Cromwell, then branch off for Wanaka.

South Otago

About 10km south of Milton is Lovells Flat Sod Cottage which has been restored and furnished in colonial style.
   A side road branches off and follows the shore of Lake Tuakitoto with its prolific water birds, then you pass through Kaitangata, a coal mining centre, before arriving at Balclutha, the main town of South Otago.
   Balclutha is on the Clutha, New Zealand's second longest river but the one with the greatest volume of water. The river has been harnessed by a huge hydro-electric scheme at Roxburgh. The Clutha River is a fisherman's paradise because it abounds in rainbow and brown trout.
   There is a seven-span bridge across the river at Balclutha and this has become its landmark. The South Otago Museum, 1 Renfrew Street, is worth a visit and is open Mon-Fri 10am-4pm, Sun 1-4pm. From Balclutha there are two ways of getting to Invercargill, either taking SH 1 inland through Gore, or SH 92 following the coast.

Invercargill via the coast
Owaka is 30km from Balclutha and is the gateway to **The Catlins**, a wilderness area with rain forest walkways, plentiful native birds, and lonely beaches with towering cliffs and huge sea caves. Close to Owaka are the **Purakanui Falls** which are a ten minute walk from a loop road. At the falls the water

cascades down three rock terraces.

The attractions along SH 92 are well sign-posted so you will have no trouble finding them. There are quite a few so there may only be time to detour to some of them.

Listed below are the main sights:

Jack's Bay Blowhole
Tautuku Beach
Cathedral Caves -   underwater at high tide
Waitawa
Porpoise Bay
Penguin Bay -   penguin parade
Lake Wilkie
Cannibal Bay -   False Island
Curio Bay -   petrified forest
Waipapa Point -   shipwrecks.

Invercargill via Gore

This trip only takes two hours. It passes through **Gore**, which is on the Mataura River where the Southland Plains and the Waimea Plains join. Gore is a service town for the prosperous area, and has an annual Country & Western Music Festival in June. The largest cereal mill in the Southern Hemisphere is found in Gore.

Mataura, 11km to the south, has an important paper factory and nearby falls. From there it is only another 53km to Invercargill - see Southland for detailed information.

Central Otago

Central Otago is a vast hilly area which was the scene of the gold rush of the 1860s. It can be reached three ways:

1. By turning off SH 1 at Palmerston and travelling along SH 86 (Pigroot Road) to Keyburn and then SH 85 to Alexandra.

2. By taking SH 87 from Dunedin through Mosgiel which also joins SH 85 at Keyburn.

3. By travelling south to Milton and taking SH 8 to Alexandra. This is a picturesque route that passes through the old mining towns of Waitahuna, Lawrence and Roxburgh. Roxburgh is now the centre of a stone fruit growing area and there is a large dam and power station near the town.

Alexandra

Alexandra (population 4685) is the heart of Central Otago and its origins go back to the Dunstan Goldrush of 1862. It is a thriving town servicing a rural community.

It has an annual rainfall of less than 330mm and relies on irrigation to supply water for the town and the orchards in the area. Its dry climate, brilliant sunshine and central position bring numerous tourists to the area. The surrounding countryside is desert-like with stark high cliffs of tan and ochre.

Tourist Information

Central Otago Visitor Information Centre is at 22 Centennial Avenue, ph (03) 448 9515.

Accommodation

Following is a selection of available accommodation, with prices in NZ$ for a double room per night, which should be used as a guide only. The telephone area code is 03.

Hotel

Centennial Court Motor Inn, 96 Centennial Avenue, ph 448 6482, fax 448 9012 - 33 units, restaurant, cocktail lounge - $72-92.

Motels

Avenue Motel, 119 Centennial Avenue, ph 448 6919, fax 448 6918 - 10 units, spa - $68-80.

Alexandra Motor Lodge, 85 Centennial Avenue, ph 448 7580, fax 448 7089 - 9 units - $68-75.

Almond Court Motel, 53 Killarney Street, ph 448 7667, 448 6283 - 8 units, swimming pool, barbecue - $63-70.

Kiwi Motel, 115 Centennial Avenue, ph 448 8258, fax 448 6201 - 6 units, barbecue - $63-70.

Alexandra Garden Court Motel, Manuherikia Road, ph 448 8295, fax 448 8200 - 5 units, swimming pool - $68.

Al Park View Motel, cnr Bantry & Shannon Streets, ph/fax 448 7400 - 5 units - $70-75.

Motor Camps & Cabins

Alexandra Holiday Camp, Manuherikia Road, ph 448 8297, fax 448 8294 - tent sites $16 x 2; caravan sites $20 x 2; cabins $20-35. *Pine Lodge Holiday Camp*, Ngapara Street, ph 448 8861, fax 448 8276 - tent sites $7.50 per person; caravan sites $16.50 x 2; units (sleep 4) $27 x 2; cabins $31 x 2.

Hostel

Riverside Hostel (YHA), 4 Dunorling Street, ph 448 8152 - $14 per person per night.

Sightseeing

The landmark of the town is a large illuminated clock, 12m in diameter, on Knobbies Hill overlooking the town. This clock can be read from 8km away. There are several fine buildings in the town, including the old Courthouse which opened in 1879, and the Bendigo Hotel.

There are many walkways around the town and out into the surrounding area. They are clearly marked.

Horse riding trips, fishing safaris and rafting expeditions are offered in season. In winter, ice skating and curling on Manorburn Dam are popular sports, and spectacular hoar frosts often occur.

In springtime the flowering fruit trees are a sight to behold as pink and white blossoms can be seen for miles. The annual Blossom Festival in September-October attracts thousands of people to the town to see the spectacular floats and displays. In the surrounding hills carpets of wild thyme and mountain herbs can be seen.

The town's modern amenities compare favourably with those of the larger New Zealand towns.

From Alexandra it is only two hours' drive to Queenstown, Wanaka or Hawea. SH 8 goes past the outskirts of Clyde.

Clyde is an old gold mining town that has changed little from a century ago. It still has the original shops, cottages, churches and hotels. A visit there is like stepping back in time, except for the massive Clyde Dam. Many craftsmen live in Clyde and their wares can be seen at the beautifully restored Oliver's estate. You can hire a bicycle and ride along the old gold seekers' trails, or swim in the river. Lake Dunstan was formed by the dam. The highway goes on to join SH 6 (turn left for Queenstown) just before Cromwell.

Cromwell is situated at the junction of the Karawarau and Clutha River, and part of the old section of the town has been flooded by Lake Dunstan. Cromwell has a 25m indoor heated pool if you feel like a dip. From Cromwell you can take SH 6 to Wanaka, Haast Pass and the West Coast, or continue on SH 8 to the Mount Cook area.

Wanaka

Wanaka (population 1122) is situated on Lake Wanaka, 70km from Queenstown on SH 89. It actually belongs to Central Otago and is just over 50km from Cromwell. Wanaka lies in a rather harsh area. Even the early Maoris didn't have large permanent settlements in this vicinity as it is broken, hilly country cut by deep river gorges, giving it an isolated feeling.

During the gold rush of the 1860s, bushmen came to Wanaka seeking timber for the gold-fields. They found some good stands, and floated it down the Clutha River to Cromwell. There were no significant gold finds around the lake, but some gold was discovered in the Cardrona Valley between Wanaka and Queenstown. Evidence of the workings can still be seen in the area - old tailings, sluice races, stone huts, etc. Some gold was dredged near Albert Town, which was a busy ferry terminal for miners crossing the Clutha. Albert Town is one of the few gold towns to survive.

Climate

The climate here is like the landscape. It is extreme and varies considerably between summer and winter. The average annual rainfall in Wanaka itself is only 635mm, but at Mount Aspiring Station only 40km away, the average is around 2500mm. Over the length of the lake the vegetation changes from tussockland to beech forest, and then to sub-tropical rain forest. The summers are hot and dry, and the winters are cold with frost. The surrounding hills are covered in snow in winter. Summer temperatures often reach 38C, and in winter temperatures often drop below -10C. Frosts of 0C have been recorded when the surrounding hills are snow-covered.

How to Get There

By Air
Mount Cook Airlines and *Ansett New Zealand* service Wanaka via Queenstown, with Aspiring Air providing feeder services to Wanaka connecting with most Queenstown arrivals and departures.

By Bus
Mount Cook Landlines travel to Wanaka from Christchurch and Dunedin.
InterCity has services from Queenstown and Franz Josef.

By Car
Queenstown-Wanaka on SH 89 is 71km - approx 1 hour 20 minutes.
Dunedin-Wanaka is 276km -approx 4 hours 20 minutes.
Christchurch-Wanaka is 428km - approx 6 hours 20 minutes.
Haast-Wanaka is 148km - approx 3 hours.
Greymouth-Wanaka is 483km - approx 7 hours.

Tourist Information
The Wanaka Visitor Information Office is in Ardmore Street, ph (03) 443 1233.

Accommodation
The prices in Wanaka are generally lower than in Queenstown and can offer better value for money. Following is a selection with prices in NZ$ for a double room per night, which should be used as a guide only. The telephone area code is 03.

Hotels
Edgewater Resort Hotel, Sargood Drive, ph 443 8311, fax 443 8323 - 100 rooms (private facilities), restaurant, cocktail lounge, tennis courts, spa, sauna, mini golf - $145-225.
Wanaka Motor Inn, Mt Aspiring Road, ph 443 8216, fax 443 9108 - 36 units, restaurant, cocktail lounge - $108-135.

Motels

Bay View Motel, Mt Aspiring Road (2km from town towards Glendhu Bay), ph 443 7766, fax 443 9194 - 7 units - $80-97.

Alpine Motel, 7 Ardmore Street, ph 443 7950, fax 443 9031 - 18 units, barbecue - $65-98.

Brookvale Manor, 35 Brownston Street, ph 443 8333, fax 443 9040 - 10 units, swimming pool, spa, barbecue - $78-85.

Pleasant Lodge Holiday Park, Glendhu Bay Road, ph/fax 443 7360 - 7 units, swimming pool, waterslide, spa, barbecue - $70.

Fairway Lodge, cnr McPherson Street & SH 89, ph 443 7285, fax 443 9178 - 16 units, swimming pool - $70-95.

Lakeview Motel, 68 Lismore Street, ph/fax 443 7029 - 6 units - $65-70.

Archway Motel, 64 Hedditch Street (off SH 6), ph 443 7698, fax 443 8642 - 15 units, barbecue - $68-75.

Wunderview Motel, 122 Brownston Street, ph 443 7480, fax 443 8100 - 6 units, spa, barbecue - $70.

Motor Camps & Cabins

Glendhu Bay Camp, 1 Mt Aspiring Road, ph/fax 443 7243 - tent sites $7 per person; caravan sites $8 per person; cabins (sleep 4) $26 x 2; backpackers $13 per person.

Pleasant Lodge Holiday Park, Glendhu Bay Road, ph/fax 443 7360 - tent sites $17 x 2; caravan sites $18 x 2; cabins $30 x 2; tourist flats (sleep 6) $55 x 2; motel units $70.

Wanaka Holiday Park, 212 Brownston Street, ph/fax 443 7883 - powered and unpowered sites $9 per adult; tourist flat $50-58 x 2; cabin $30 x 2.

Hostels

Altamont Lodge, Mount Aspiring Road, ph 443 8864 - $22 per person.

Wanaka Hostel (YHA), 181 Upton Street, ph/fax 443 7405 - $15 per person.

Sightseeing

In summer the lake is the hub of all activity, and in winter it is the ski-fields.

Lake Wanaka is a glacial lake, torn out of the mountains at the end of the last ice age. The southern end of the lake is surrounded by the harsh, dry hills of Central Otago, while at the northern end, lush forests creep down the steep foothills of the snow-covered Southern Alps towards the shores.

The lake is 56km long, 5km wide, and more than 328m deep. There are three islands in it - Ruby Island, Ram Island and Pigeon Island. It is alive with boats and swimmers during the hot summer months.

The town beach (Roys Bay) is a popular swimming place, as is the willow-lined Glendhu Bay 11km further around the western shore. The road to Glendhu Bay continues on to the Mount Aspiring National Park, 46km away. In the summer months paddle boats, windsurfers, canoes and dinghies can be hired on the lakeshore. The water is safe for swimming and paddling, and there are marked lanes for water skiing and jetboaters at Bremner Bay, Roys Bay and towards Ruby Island.

Tramping
There are numerous walkways and tracks branching out from the town catering for all levels of fitness. Following are some examples.

* Wharf to Eely Point - an easy walk around the lake edge following tracks and footpaths - one hour return.

* Mount Iron - an easy walk that climbs to 250m above the town, providing good views over the lake and Clutha River outlet - one and a half hours return.

* Wharf to Waterfall Creek - goes along the waterfront to the south-west corner of Roys Bay, then by formed track to Waterfall Creek - 2 hours return.

* Wharf to Wanaka Station Park - access from park to Waterfall Creek track - one hour return.

* Lake outlet to Albert Town - flat walk along the Clutha bank, with the option of returning by the same route, or by Mount Iron Road and Anderson Road - 1.5 hours return.

Scenic Flights
Aspiring Air, Wanaka Airport, ph 443 7943, offer flights in single and twin-engined aircraft. Examples are:

Milford Sound - one hour twenty minutes.

Mount Aspiring - forty-five minutes.

Mount Cook - one hour forty-five minutes.

The Adventure Centre
Situated at 99 Ardmore Street, Wanaka, ph 0800 684 468, fax

443 8589, this Centre can arrange bookings for all the excitement deemed necessary for exhilaration. Examples are:

* *Deep Canyon Experience* - plunge, abseil, jump, swim - $145 including lunch.

* *Alpine River Guides* - kayak expeditions with tuition. Full or half day - $60-98.

* *Mt Iron Saddle Adventures* - 2 hour guided rides through Kanuka Forest - $45 adult.

* *Jet Boat Charters* - 2½ hour Clutha River Eco tour - $65; 3½ hour Matukituki River Eco tour - $75. Charters also available.

* *Alpine Biking* - superb views on challenging descents. Heli biking and overnight trips available. Half-day $65, full day $85 (includes bike hire).

* *Pioneer Rafting* - half-day to full day adventures or 2-8 day expeditions - from $75.

* *Planes of Fame* - from the NZ Fighter Pilots' Museum - joyrides $140.

* *Mt Aspiring Guides Heli-hike* - Helicopter flight to the tops of ridges then guided walking at own pace - $350 per person per full day.

* *Wanaka Paragliding Tandem Flights* - intro and rating course from $156.

* *Wanaka School of Rock Climbing* - professional instruction and guiding - $85 half-day; $125 day sport course.

Maze and Puzzle Centre

The centre is on the main highway, 2km from Wanaka, and is open daily 8.30am-5.30pm. The maze has 1.5km of confusing over and under passageways, and the average time to conquer it is at least 40 minutes. There are emergency gates for those who run out of time or patience.

The Puzzle Centre has probably the largest display of puzzles in the world for you to try, then you can enjoy delicious Devonshire Teas in the cafeteria, ph/fax 443 7489.

Other activities in Wanaka include: horse trekking, deer park visits, guided fishing, hunting, launch cruises, motor boat hire, pedal boat hire, jet ski hire, yacht hire, kayak and canoe hire, sailing, golf, bowls, squash and tennis. Enquire at the Information centre for full details.

Mt. Aspiring National Park, South Island.

Outlying Attractions

Mount Aspiring National Park

It starts north-west of Wanaka and stretches almost to the northern tip of the lake. Mount Aspiring, 3036m, is the highest peak in the park which contains peaks of the Southern Alps, bush-covered foothills and stony river flats. The park extends from the Haast Pass to the Fiordland National Park.

There are two distinct groups of vegetation in the park: beech forests on the lower levels of the mountains on the western slopes, with rata and kamahi higher up; and grasslands above the forests. The grasslands have suffered badly from the introduction of red deer, goats and chamois, but controlled hunting keeps their numbers down.

There is a good road leading to the park. Tracks and bridges have been constructed in some areas and in other parts, permits are required before trampers and climbers can enter. Check with park headquarters before setting off on any treks. **The inexperienced are better off booking for one of the guided walks on the Milford, Hollywood or Greenstone Tracks.**

Many tourists give Wanaka a miss in the autumn when it's too cold for water sports and too early for snow, but they are missing out on magnificent scenery because the whole of the area is beautiful when the cold, dry climate decks the deciduous trees out in beautiful autumn tones.

The bracing air makes it an ideal time for walking and tramping around the lake.

The arrival of the snow heralds the return of the crowds. There are two international standard ski-fields within half an hour's drive of Wanaka - Cardrona and Treble Cone. Both these fields offer long months of spring skiing. There is also heli-skiing on the Harris and Richardson Mountains. For more information see the **Skiing** Chapter.

Treble Cone is 29km from Wanaka off the Glendhu Bay Road, and is one of the most scenic ski-fields in the world. The view down to Lake Wanaka is magnificent. It is one of the highest ski-fields in the South Island, with runs to 2074m, providing challenges for experienced skiers.

Cardrona is about 25km from Wanaka (between Wanaka and Queenstown) and from the top of the ridge it is possible to see the back of Coronet Peak. It was the first area in New Zealand to have a quad chair. This field has a lot of gently sloping terrain, but there are a few steeper runs if you look for them. The Cardrona Valley gold-fields offer many reminders of the gold rush days, and you can even try your luck at panning.

Lake Hawea is only an hour's drive from Wanaka along the Haast Pass Road. It offers good fishing, mountain climbing, hunting and water sports. The level of this lake was raised 20m when the dam was built at Roxburgh down river.

The **Haast Pass Road** follows the western shore of Lake Hawea for quite a while, and then climbs high above the lake affording fine views of the Hunter Mountains to the north, and of Goat Island right below. The road climbs over a narrow strip of ancient moraine and back down to the north-eastern shore of Lake Wanaka. This road is the lowest of the passes across the Southern Alps, and follows the lakes and river valleys for most of its journey to the west coast.

Aorangi (Mount Cook) Region

The Aorangi Region takes its name from the Maori word for Mount Cook. The translation for Aorangi is "cloud piercer", an apt name for the mountain. South Island natives pronounce the name Aoraki, and there is a legend that says the mountain was named after the eldest son of Raki, the sky parent of creation.

The Aorangi region is bordered by the Rakaia River in the north (56km south of Christchurch), the Waitaki River in the south (20km north of Oamaru) and by the Southern Alps around Mount Cook in the west.

How to Get There

By Air
Mount Cook Airlines have daily direct flights to Mount Cook from Christchurch and Queenstown.

By Bus
Mount Cook Landline and *InterCity* have daily services to Mount Cook from Christchurch and Queenstown.

By Car
Christchurch-Lake Pukaki is 273km - approx 4 hours 20 minutes.
Pukaki to Mount Cook is 60km - approx 45 minutes.
Queenstown-Mount Cook is 271km - approx 5 hours.

To get to Mount Cook from Christchurch by car, take the Main South Road and follow SH 1 to Ashburton.
South of the Rangitata River, turn off onto SH 79 to Geraldine.
Geraldine has a country village atmosphere. It is surrounded by forests and has many craft shops, as well as being the only town in New Zealand with a linen flax mill. West of Geraldine (8km) is Barker's Winery where you can sample some berry wines - open 9am-6pm Tues-Sun.

Continue on SH 79 to **Fairlie**, which is the gateway to Mackenzie Country. In winter the town is invaded by skiers headed for the Fox Peak ski-fields in the Two Thumb Range. From Fairlie take SH 8 to Tekapo. The road winds through narrow valleys between brown hills up to Burke's Pass, the entry to Mackenzie Country.

Mackenzie Country

This tussock upland country is very good sheep pasture. Although most people find it rather desolate looking, it does have its own appeal. Mackenzie Country is a wide inland basin over 300m above sea-level. It is approximately 129km long and between 24km and 80km wide. Flowing through it are many creeks and rivers which eventually become the Waitaki River.

The basin takes its name from a sheep rustler named Mackenzie. This Scot was working on The Levels sheep station near Timaru as a shepherd in the 1850s, and often explored the surrounding countryside with his dog, Friday, and his pack-bullock. On one of his forays he discovered the high tussock basin known today as Mackenzie Country.

In 1855, he stole 500 sheep and hid them in this basin before selling them in Otago and Southland. The next year he stole some more, but unfortunately for him he was followed. He managed to elude his would-be captors, and turned up at Lyttelton where he was arrested. He was tried and gaoled, and after several escapes from prison, he received a pardon and left New Zealand. The publicity surrounding his trial brought the existence of the basin to the notice of those seeking land. The overseer, John Sidebottom, who was responsible for Mackenzie's arrest, lodged the first application for 30,000ha in the basin. He was granted the licence but, as he failed to stock the land within six months of the lease being granted, it was cancelled. In 1857 the land was divided among other runs.

From Burke's Pass, the road winds through the brown hills to **Tekapo**. This large lake is 707m above sea-level and, like other glacier-fed lakes, is a milky turquoise colour. This is due to powdered rock, ground by the glaciers, being fed into the lake. On the summit of Mount John, 1029m, 2km west of Tekapo, is an observatory and satellite tracking station. On the lake shore is a much photographed statue of a sheepdog. The *Church of the Good Shepherd*, right next to the lake, is well worth a visit as the view through   Mt Cook

the window above the altar is breath-taking. No stained glass window can compare with the vista here.

The countryside remains unchanged after Tekapo, mile after mile of brown tussock country with not a tree in sight. The weather matches the harsh landscape as it is hot in summer, and snow and frost lie in winter.

Mackenzie Hydro Park

Back in 1904, P.S. Hays realised the potential of the area for producing hydro-electricity. In his eighty page study he identified the importance of the Mackenzie Basin lakes to any scheme on the Waitaki, and recommended bringing the water from Lake Tekapo across country by canal or conduit, a feat that was beyond the expertise of the country at that time.

Construction of the first dam and power station on the Waitaki River began downstream near Kurow in 1928 and the first power was generated in 1934. In 1938 work commenced on a tunnel beneath the south end of Lake Tekapo, but World War II intervened and the scheme was not completed until the early 1950s, when much work was undertaken in this area. Firstly, the level of Lake Tekapo and Lake Putaki was raised by the building of dams, and then the Benmore project got underway. A large dam 110m high and 823m wide was built across the valley, resulting in a man-made lake of 8000ha with a shoreline of 116km. Every effort was made to beautify the shores and provide amenities for boating, camping and picnicking.

Following the success of that scheme, work was started on linking Lakes Tekapo, Pukaki and Ohau and the creation of a new lake, **Lake Ruataniwha**. The Twizel township was constructed to house the headquarters for this project in 1969.

Twizel has developed into a service centre for the surrounding runholders, and the tourist areas of Tekapo, Mount Cook and Omarama. The Visitor Information Office is in Wairepo Road, ph (03) 435 0802. The town has squash and tennis courts, a swimming pool with hydro slide, and a roller skating rink.

Nearby Lake Ruataniwha was officially opened in 1982 and has been developed as a tourist area. It has a motor camp, boat ramps, picnic areas, and an international standard rowing course stretching over two kilometres. Many trees have been planted along the shores, and the lake is stocked with fish.

Accommodation

The telephone area code is 03.

Lake Tekapo

Lake Tekapo Alpine Inn, SH 8, ph 680 6848, fax 680 6873 - 80 units, licensed restaurant, cocktail lounge, swimming pool, barbecue - budget $55; standard $80; superior $130.

Parkhead Motel, Pioneer Drive (lake frontage), ph 680 6868, fax 680 6869 - 4 units, barbecue - $82.

Lake Tekapo Motels & Motor Camp, Lakeside Dr, ph 680 6825, fax 680 6824 - motel $70-80; flats (sleep 5 & 6) $55 x 2; cabins (sleep 2-6) $30 x 2; power sites $9 per person; tent sites $8 per person.

Twizel

Mackenzie Country Inn, cnr Wairepo & Ostler Road, ph 435 0869, fax 435 0857 - 108 units, restaurant, cocktail lounge - $90-150.

Mountain Chalets, Wairepo Road, ph 435 0785, fax 435 0551 - 27 units, spa - $75-85.

High Country Holiday Lodge, 23 Mackenzie Dr, ph 435 0671, fax 435 0747 - 109 beds (share facilities), 9 motel units, restaurant, bar, self-catering facilities, backpacker accommodation - $15-70.

Omarama

Countrytime Resort Hotel, SH 8, ph 438 9894, fax 438 9791 - 51 units, licensed restaurant, cocktail lounge, swimming pool, spa, sauna, tennis court, barbecue - $90-120.

Heritage Gateway Hotel, SH, ph 438 9805, fax 438 9837 - 90 units, licensed restaurant, cocktail lounge - $101.

Sierra Motel, Omarama Avenue (SH8), ph 438 9785, fax 438 9789 - 6 units - $55-85.

Glenburn Holiday Park, SH 83 (shores of Lake Benmore), ph/fax 438 9624 - ensuite tent/caravan/campervan sites $20 x 2; ensuite cabins $30; farm cottages $40-60.

Omarama Holiday Park Ltd, Junction SH 8 and 83, ph 438 9875 - tent and caravan sites $18 x 2; flats (sleep 4) $57 x 2; cabins (sleep 4) $30 x 2; on-site caravans (sleep 4) $35 x 2.

Sport & Recreation

Fishing

Common game species are rainbow and brown trout, quinnat

and sockeye salmon. An licence is required, and can be picked up at any fishing shop. If you would like a guide, contact Walter Speck of Mid Southern Tracks Ltd, at 14 Pioneer Drive, Lake Tekapo, ph/fax (03) 680 6774, or Glentanner Park in Mount Cook, ph (03) 435 1855.

Skiing
There are three commercial fields adjacent to the Park - Dobson, Tekapo and Ohau. All the fields are easily reached by private and/or public transport (see **Skiing** chapter).

Boating
Concrete launching ramps have been provided on all lakes, and jetties, harbours and moorings have been constructed. Motor boats and yachts are forbidden on Lake Alexandrina, and motor boats on the Wairepo Arm. The Tekapo, Pukaki and Ohau rivers are subject to level fluctuations due to power generation. All the lakes are subject to quick weather changes because of their proximity to the Alps.

Hunting
If killing defenceless animals is your bag, Mid Southern Tracks Ltd at Lake Tekapo, ph/fax (03) 680 6774, can help you to find the time and the place.

Golf
Courses are at Tekapo, Twizel, Omarama, Otematata & Kurow.

Tramping
There are plenty of tracks around the park and experienced trampers can contact the Forest Service or the Department of Conservation for information and maps. Alpine Recreation, PO Box 75, Lake Tekapo, ph (03) 680 6736, fax (03) 680 6765, have a 3-day guided trek across Ball Pass with two nights accommodation at Caroline Hut, the only private hut in the Mount Cook National Park. Price is NZ$625 per person.

Mountaineering
If you would like to explore the high country around here with a guide, you could contact Alpine Recreation, ph (03) 680 6736, fax (03) 680 6765. They have a 'learn as you climb' 4 day trip which teaches the basics of rock, snow and ice climbing, glacier

travel, rope work, navigation, weather assessment and emergency survival. The trip is based at Caroline Hut, the only private hut in the Mount Cook National Park. Costs range from NZ$850 per person (minimum 2 people) to NZ$1250 for a one on one guide.

Mount Cook

The road to Mount Cook branches off SH 8 at Pukaki, and most tourists can't wait to catch their first glimpse of Aorangi, the cloud piercer.

The road closely follows the shore of the lake virtually all the way up to Mount Cook Village, and on a clear day, as you drive along, not only will you see the 3764m Mount Cook in the distance, but also La Perouse (3079m), The Footstool (2765m) and Mount Sefton (3157m) on the left, and to the right and slightly behind is Mount Tasman (3497m). These majestic mountains are definitely worth photographing but they can be rather elusive as they have a habit of playing hide and seek with the clouds, and then disappearing for a day or two at a time. So, if you see them on the way in, photograph them straight away or it may be too late. On my first trip there I didn't, thinking I had the next two days to take photos, but they didn't re-appear.

The road swings away from the lake near the end of the journey and then the small Mount Cook Village comes into view. It is dominated by The Hermitage hotel.

Tourist Information

The Mount Cook Visitor Information Office is in Bowen Drive, ph (03) 435 1818.

Accommodation

Hotels & Motels

Four different places to stay, but they all have the same telephone number - (03) 435 1809. Prices quoted here are in NZ$ exclusive of GST, for a room per night, and should be used as a guide only.

The Hermitage Hotel - 104 rooms (private facilities), 3 licensed restaurants, cocktail lounges, sauna, spa - $245-280.

Mount Cook Chalets (check in at The Hermitage) - 20 units that sleep up to six people - $110 up to 4 people.

Mount Cook Motels (check in at The Hermitage or Mount Cook Travelodge) - 12 units (self contained), 4 studios, 8 doubles - $120-140.

Mount Cook Travelodge - 57 rooms (private facilities), house bar, entertainment, guest lounge, tennis court - $170.

Motor Camp & Cabins

Glentanner Park, 23km from Hermitage on Lake Pukaki, ph (03) 435 1855, fax 435 1854 - tent sites $13 x 2; caravan sites $14 x 2; cabins (sleep 4-10) $30-55 x 2; flats $60 x 2.

Hostel

Mount Cook Hostel (YHA), cnr Bowen & Kitchener Drives, ph (03) 435 1820, fax 435 1821 - $18 per person.

The **Mount Cook National Park** stretches for 70km along the Southern Alps and contains twenty-two mountain peaks over 3000m. Its mountain scenery is unsurpassed. The area has many glaciers, but the Tasman is the longest. With a length of 29km and a width of up to 3km, it is the longest glacier in the world outside the polar regions.

The *Hermitage Activities Desk* can arrange for flights over the mountains and to the glaciers. These flights are not inexpensive, but a flight is really the best way to gain an appreciation of the spectacular scenery of the region and Mount Cook shouldn't be missed, weather permitting of course. Glentanner Park can arrange helicopter flights, as can Mount Cook Line, ph (03) 435 1849.

Mount Cook Village is right in the mountains, and on a clear day the views are superb. Mount Cook, with its permanent snow, seems to peek around the skirts of its neighbouring mountains, and you have to walk a little way up the track for the best views. Mount Cook was first climbed in 1894, and it has claimed several lives.

The mountain air is invigorating and you will undoubtedly have the urge to walk and see as much as possible. There are easy walking tracks as well as harder climbs, so no matter your level of fitness you will be able to enjoy the area.

The Hermitage has a garden dedicated to alpine plants so you will be able to see these without walking far. Behind the Hermitage are the remnants of a beech forest and the trails in this area offer excellent examples of the local vegetation. The mountain buttercup, huge lupins, snow tussock, mountain daisies, and the Mount Cook lily, can be seen in spring.

The rangers at Mount Cook National Park Headquarters just down the road from The Hermitage, will be only too pleased to advise you on the different walks. If you want to do some longer trips you may want to hire a guide.

Whatever you decide to do, I am sure you won't be disappointed with what you see, as this area has some of the best mountain scenery in the world.

Alpine Guides Ltd (PO Box 20) have an office in the village, ph (03) 435 1834, and can organise day treks. They also hire out equipment. They have three exciting adventures for the serious skier - *Ski The Tasman*, *Wilderness Heli-skiing*, and *Methven Heli-skiing* - which cost $600 per person per day.

If you want to walk the Copland Track across the alps, they will guide you over the snow and ice section, and then return to the village bringing the equipment with them. Due to erosion over the last couple of years however, this is no longer a hiking route, but more for serious mountaineers.

You will still need to arrange transport from the other end of the trail on SH 6.

If you would like to see a working sheep station, you might head for Glentanner Park, 20km from Mount Cook Village. The property carries 8500 prize merino sheep and offers horse riding, cross-country trail riding, trout fishing, hunting and excursions into the back country.

From Mount Cook head south back to Pukaki from where you can either return the way you came, or travel via Twizel and Omarama to Queenstown through the Lindis Pass (approx four hours), or go back to the east coast along the Waitaki River valley. Omarama is well known as a fine gliding area and several records have been set there.

Canterbury

Mention Canterbury and immediately Canterbury Plains and Canterbury Lamb spring to mind. The vast fertile Canterbury Plains are a delight to behold, and sheep still dot the landscape, but the farmers have diversified, and you will see some cattle, horses, and even commercial deer runs, as well as fruit and vine growing. The majority of the fields are divided by hedge-rows, giving the whole of the plains a neat, ordered appearance.

The settlement of Canterbury was organised by the Canterbury Association in the 1840s with the main body of settlers reaching Lyttelton at the end of 1850. The settlers had to present a certificate of morality from their parish church in an attempt to keep adventurers out. They spread out from Christchurch to take up holdings on the plains and in the hill country of the province, and soon began raising sheep and wheat. Other towns began to spring up, but Christchurch has remained the largest town and hub of the South Island.

Christchurch

(see Map page 288)
Christchurch (population 306,000) is the most English-like city in New Zealand and its parks, gardens and river make it a delightful staging place for a trip through the South Island.

It nestles at the base of the hills of the Banks Peninsula and was a swampy plain 150 years ago, but it has been transformed into a garden city with solid grey stone buildings interspersed with modern high-rise. The heart of the city is Cathedral Square, and the city centre is laid out in neat rectangles surrounded by parklands and the Avon River.

How to Get There

By Air
Travelling from overseas is covered in the Travel Information

chapter. *International Airlines* phone numbers are: Air New Zealand, ph (03) 379 5200; Ansett New Zealand, ph (03) 371 1146; British Airways, ph (03) 379 2503; Japan Airlines, ph (03) 365 5879; Qantas Airways, ph (03) 379 6500; Singapore Airlines, ph (03) 366 8003; United Airlines, ph (03) 366 1736.

Domestic Services

Air New Zealand has daily direct flights to Christchurch from Auckland, Blenheim, Dunedin, Hamilton, Hokitika, Invercargill, Napier/Hastings, Nelson, Palmerston North, Queenstown, Rotorua, Te Anau, Timaru and Wellington.
Ansett New Zealand has daily direct flights to Christchurch from Auckland, Dunedin, Invercargill, Rotorua and Wellington.
Flights are available from all other airports in New Zealand, connecting with flights from the above cities.

Christchurch International Airport is 11km out of town and there is a half-hourly bus service to the city, 6.30am-9pm Mon-Fri; hourly 7.30am-8.30pm Sat; and hourly 7.30am-6.30pm Sun. The fare is NZ$2.70 adult, NZ$1.35 child.

A door to door service is also provided by Super Shuttle who operate a mini coach between the airport and city and all suburbs. This service is classified as 'on demand', but there are usually coaches outside the airport for all international arrivals. Airport to the city costs NZ$10 for one person; NZ$6 per person for 2 people; NZ$5 per person for 3 people; NZ$4 per person for 4 to 7 people; $30 for 8 or more people. Bookings and further information ph (03) 365 5655.

By Rail

The Southerner runs between Invercargill and Christchurch Mon-Fri, stopping at Gore, Balclutha, Milton, Dunedin, Oamaru, Timaru and Ashburton.

The daily *Coastal Pacific Express* runs between Picton and Christchurch, and the daily Tranz Alpine Express runs between Greymouth and Christchurch, via Arthurs Pass.

By Bus

InterCity has daily services from Dunedin, Greymouth, Invercargill, Mount Cook, Nelson, Queenstown and Te Anau.
Mount Cook Landline has daily services from Dunedin, Invercargill, Mount Cook, Nelson, Picton, Queenstown, Te Anau and Wanaka.

By Car

Picton-Christchurch is 350km - approx 6 hours 15 minutes.
Dunedin-Christchurch is 362km-approx 5 hours 40 minutes.
Mount Cook-Christchurch is 331km - approx 5 hours.
Queenstown-Christchurch is 486km - approx 8 hours.

Tourist Information

The Visitor Information Centre in the city is on the corner of Worcester Boulevard & Oxford Terrace, ph (03) 379 9629. It is open Mon-Fri 8.30am-5pm, Sat-Sun 8.30am-4pm, with extended hours in summer.

There is also an information office in the International Terminal that is open for all inbound flights, and one in the Domestic Terminal that is open Sun-Fri 6.30am-10.30pm, Sat 6.30am-8pm.

Accommodation

There is no shortage of accommodation in Christchurch, but it is still wise to book ahead. Following is a selection of what is available, with prices in NZ$ for a double room per night, which should be used as a guide only.

The telephone area code is 03.

Hotels

Noahs Christchurch, cnr Worcester Street & Oxford Terrace, ph 379 4700, fax 379 5357 - 208 rooms (private facilities), licensed restaurants, cocktail lounges - $260+.

The Chateau on The Park, 189 Deans Avenue, Riccarton, ph 348 8999, fax 348 8990 - 200 rooms (private facilities), licensed restaurants, cocktail lounges, adjacent Hagley Park with golf and tennis - $175.

Quality Hotel Durham Street, cnr Durham & Kilmore Streets, ph 365 4699, fax 366-6302 - 161 rooms (private facilities), licensed restaurants, cocktail lounges, sauna, spa, gym - $155+.

George Hotel of Christchurch, 50 Park Terrace, ph 379 4560, fax 366 6747 - 54 rooms (private facilities), licensed restaurants, tennis court - $155+.

Pavilions Christchurch, 42 Papanui Road, ph 355 5633, fax 355 3554 - 70 units, licensed restaurant, swimming pool, spa - $145-225.

Commodore Airport Hotel, 447 Memorial Avenue, ph 358 8129, fax 358 2231 - 105 units, licensed restaurant, cocktail lounges, swimming pool - from $146-165.

Autolodge Motor Inn, 72 Papanui Road, ph 355 6109, 355 3543 - 74 units, licensed restaurant, cocktail lounge - $150.

Carlton Mill Lodge, 19 Bealey Avenue, ph 366 1068, fax 365 2331 - 34 units, licensed restaurant, bar - $80-140.

Motels

Australasia Motor Inn, cnr Hereford & Barbadoes Streets, ph 379 0540, fax 366 4700 - 25 units, licensed restaurant, cocktail lounge - $119.

Alcazar Motor Inn, 22 Riccarton Road, ph 348 0909, fax 348 9876 - 34 units, licensed restaurant - $90-120.

Canterbury Court Motel, 140 Lincoln Road, ph 338 8351, fax 338 8391 - 20 units - $85-95.

Coachman Motel, 316A Riccarton Road, ph/fax 348 6651 - 10 units - $70-95.

Earnslaw Motel, 288 Blenheim Road, ph/fax 348 6387 - 10 units, spa - $70-75.

Cashel Court Motel, 457 Cashel Street, ph/fax 389 2768 - 6 units, swimming pool - $58-70.

Aalton Motel, 19 Riccarton Road, ph 348 6700, fax 348 0185 - 10 units, spa - $80-90.

Middlepark Motel, 120 Main South Road, ph 348 7320, fax 348 6794 - 13 units, 7 cottages - $70-84.

Pineacres Motel Motor Park & Licensed Restaurant, Main North Road, Kaiapoi, ph/fax 327 5022 - 6 units, cocktail lounge, swimming pool - motel $65; studio $60; tourist flat $50; cabin $40; powered site $9 per person; tent site $8 per person.

Motor Camps, Caravan Parks and Cabins

All Seasons Holiday Park, 5 Kidbrooke Street, off Linwood Avenue, ph 384 9490, fax 384 9843 - tent sites $9 per adult; caravan sites $10 per person; flats (sleep 5) $55 x 2; cabins $30-40.

Amber Park Caravan Park, 308 Blenheim Road, ph/fax 348 3327 - caravan sites $18 x 2; flats (sleep 2-5) $44-50 x 2.

Meadow Park Holiday Park, 39 Meadow Street, off Main North Road, ph 352 9176, fax 352 1272 - tent and caravan sites $20 x 2; flats (sleep 2-6) $50-52 x 2; cabins (sleep 2-6) $33 x 2; cottage (sleeps 2-6) $57 x 2; motel $85 x 2.

Hostels

Christchurch City Central, 273 Manchester Street, ph 379 9535, fax 379 9537 - $18

Cora Wilding Hostel (YHA), 9 Evelyn Couzins Avenue, Richmond, ph 389 9199 - $15 per person.

Rolleston House (YHA), 5 Worcester Street (cnr Rolleston Avenue), ph 366 6564, fax 365 5589 - $17 per person.

Local Transport

Bus

The Christchurch Transport Board operates a regular bus service in the city and suburbs. For details of the routes and timetables contact Businfo, ph 366 8855. The Big Red Day Pass allows a full day's travel on Christchurch bus routes, and is available from the bus driver, the Bus Kiosk in the Square or the Visitor Centre, $4 single, $10 family.

Car Hire

Hertz, ph 366 0549; Avis, ph 379 6133; Budget, ph 366 0072; McDonalds, ph 366 0929; Renny, ph 366 6790; Economy, ph 359 7410; Avon, ph 379 3822.

Bicycle Hire

Bikes can be hired from *Rent-a-Bike*, 141 Gloucester Street, ph 365 7589; and *Trailblazers Cycle Hire*, 86 Worcester Street, ph 366 6033.

Taxis

Blue Star Taxis, ph 379 9799; First Direct, ph 377 5555; Gold Band Taxis, ph 379 5795; Supershuttle, ph 365 5655.

Eating Out

Christchurch has a plethora of eateries to suit all tastes and budgets. Here is a selection.

The Bridge Restaurant, 128A Oxford Terrace, ph 366 9363 - **Licensed** - open daily noon-2.30pm, 6pm-late - award-winning French cuisine - **$25-45** - credit cards accepted.

Americano's, 167 Hereford Street, ph 365 5360 - **Licensed** - open daily 6pm-very late - American/Mexican cuisine - **around $25** - credit cards accepted.

Great China, Carlton Courts, 2 Papanui Road, ph 355 8500 - **BYO** - open nightly 5.30pm-late - Cantonese cuisine - **around $25** - credit cards accepted.

Steel Magnolias, 132 Armagh Street, ph 379 9177 - **Licensed** - open Mon-Sat 9.30am-late - cafe with varied menu and live entertainment - $25 - credit cards accepted.

The Loaded Hog, 39 Dundas Street, ph 366 6674 - Licensed - open Mon-Wed 11am-11pm, Thurs-Sat 11am-1am - boutique brewery with dishes for **around $8** - credit cards accepted.

Spagalimis, Victoria Street, ph 379 7469 - **Licensed** - open Mon-Sat 11.30am-10.30pm - family Italian/pizza - **$20** - credit cards accepted.

Kurashiki, 1st Floor, Worcester & Colombo Streets, ph 366 7092 - **Licensed** - open daily 11.30am-2pm, 5.30pm-late - Japanese cuisine - **around $25.**

Bardellis, 98 Cashel Mall, ph 353 0000 - **Licensed** - open Mon-Sat 10am-late, Sun 10am-3pm - inside/outside tables - winner of Cheap Eats award - **around $20 (dinner)** - credit cards accepted.

Pegasus Arms Restaurant, 14 Oxford Terrace, ph 366 0600 - **Licensed** - open Mon-Sat noon-3pm, 6-11pm - brasserie overlooking Avon - **$25-45** - credit cards accepted.

Dux de Lux Vegetarian Restaurant, cnr Hereford & Montreal Streets, ph 366 6919 - **Licensed** - cafe style - **around $20** - credit cards accepted.

Entertainment

As with any city its size Christchurch has its share of cinemas, nightclubs, discos, etc, but one of the most popular venues deserves a mention here - **Christchurch Casino**. It is situated at 30 Victoria Street, ph 365 9999, and has 350 slot machines, money wheels, keno, blackjack, roulette, baccarat, Sic Bo and Caribbean stud poker. Admission is free to everyone aged 20 and over who is dressed appropriately (no jeans or track shoes). Hours are Mon-Wed 11am-3am, 11am Thurs-3am Mon.

Nga Hau E Wha (*Marae of the Four Winds*) is the country's largest urban marae, with two large meeting houses, and is at 250 Pages Road, ph 388 7685. Tours of the complex are available daily 11am and 2pm, and local guides tell of the myths and legends of their ancestors. Admission is $5.50 adults, $3.50 children.

The marae also hosts *A Night of Magic*, which includes a traditional welcome ceremony, marae tour, hangi feast and a cultural concert. Costs are $55 adults, $30 children, and bookings are essential. Evening tours plus concert (no dinner) cost $25 adults, $15 children. Both these events are held nightly.

Sightseeing

The heart of the city is **Cathedral Square** with the gothic revival Anglican Cathedral in its centre. It is Christchurch's landmark as its 63m copper sheathed spire can be seen from all over the city. The cathedral should be the first stop-off as a good view of the city can be obtained from its tower balconies.

The cathedral is open Mon-Sat 8.30am-6pm (until 9pm Oct-March), Sun 7.30am-8.30pm. Free guided tours are available, ph 366 0046 for more information and times . Cameras may be used (camera permit $2) except during services. The tower is open from 8.30am Mon-Sat, and from 11.30am on Sun, and admission is $2 adult, $1 child, $5 family, with funds raised being used for maintenance of the Cathedral. Sunday services are held at 8am, 10am and 7pm.

The Wizard, a noted orator, entertainer and fun-maker, performs at 1pm on weekdays in Cathedral Square. He is occasionally absent due to inclement weather or some other reason known only to him, but his postcards and upside-down maps are available from the Visitor Centre.

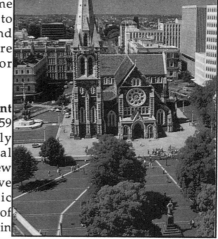

The **Provincial Government Buildings**, built between 1859 and 1865, are the only remaining provincial government buildings in New Zealand and are distinctive for their fine Gothic architecture. This system of government was abolished in

Cathedral Square

1876. Situated beside the Avon River in Durham Street, the buildings are open Mon-Sat 10.30am-3pm, Sun (Oct-April) 2-4pm, and arrangements can be made for guided tours, ph 366 1100.

The Arts Centre of Christchurch is located on the west end of Worcester Street. The neo-gothic stone buildings were once the home of Canterbury University, but now they are a gathering place for artists, craftspeople, musicians and performers.

Activities and attractions include: the Court Theatre; Southern Ballet Theatre; the Academy Cinema; weekly recitals in the Great Hall; the Dux de Lux Restaurant; Annie's Wine Bar and Restaurant; Le Cafe; craft studios; the Bookshop; and the smallest music shop in New Zealand. Check *The Press* for details of live shows. On Saturday and Sunday there is a weekend Market from 10am-4pm, with arts, crafts, food and live entertainment. For more information contact the Arts Centre Visitor Centre, ph 366 0989.

Canterbury Museum, Rolleston Avenue at the entrance to the Botanic Gardens, is open daily 9am-5pm. It has displays of natural history, Maori culture and Antarctic exploration. The Antarctic display is the largest in the world, which is not surprising as Christchurch is a major staging point for Antarctic expeditions. Featured is a lot of equipment used by Amundsen, the unlucky Scott, and Shackleton.

The **Botanic Gardens** can be entered through the iron gate next to the Museum. The gardens have many show houses dedicated to different species of plants, and they are open daily from 7am to one hour prior to sunset. Conducted tours of the gardens are available on the "Toast Rack", an electric vehicle that operates daily from outside the tea kiosk, 11am-4pm, in fine weather. *The Gardens Information Centre* is open 10.15am-4pm daily Sept-April, 11am-3pm daily May-August, ph 366 1701. The restaurant/tea kiosk serves lunches and teas and is open 10am-4.30pm daily, ph 366 5076.

A popular way to view the Botanic Gardens and Hagley Park, is from a boat on the Avon. Single and double canoes and paddle boats can be hired from the Antigua Boatsheds, 2 Cambridge Terrace, ph 366 5885, open daily 10am-4pm.

Robert McDougall Art Gallery, Rolleston Avenue behind the museum, ph 365 0914, is open daily 10am-5.30pm (summer), 10am-4.30pm (winter). The gallery was built in 1932 and has permanent collections of paintings, drawings, prints, sculptures and ceramics by British, Oriental, Australian, European and New Zealand artists. Only portions of the permanent collection are displayed at any one time. Admission is free, but a charge is made for special exhibitions.

Hagley Park, which surrounds the Botanic Gardens, is divided into two main sections by the road to Riccarton. The park covers an area of approximately 180ha, and is used for cricket, softball, tennis, golf, rugby, hockey, soccer, netball, bowls, croquet, jogging and cycling.

The Bridge of Remembrance over the Avon River at Cashel Street is a World War I memorial. Adjacent to the bridge are plantings of trees gifted to the city, known as Friendship Corner.

The Town Hall is in Kilmore Street on the banks of the Avon River, overlooking Victoria Square. It is acknowledged as the finest town hall in New Zealand, and opened in 1972. It is also one of the country's finest conference centres, with an auditorium seating approximately 2650 as well as the James Hay Theatre accommodating 1000. Other facilities include conference rooms, restaurant and banquet room, and coffee shop. Visitors are welcome on weekdays 9am-5pm, Sat-Sun 10am-5pm, and guided tours can be arranged for groups except when the complex is under hire, ph 366 8899.

Nearby is the much photographed Floral Clock.

Victoria Square was once the Market Square, and is now a floral and green oasis in the central city. The Avon River flows under quaint bridges where the Bowker and Ferrier Fountains have diverse but complementary displays beside statues of Queen Victoria and Captain Cook. During the summer months music and entertainment fill the Amphitheatre in front of the Park Royal and Town Hall complex.

The Roman Catholic Cathedral of the Blessed Sacrament in Barbadoes Street, near the corner of Moorehouse Avenue (close to the railway station), was designed by F.W. Petrie, a New Zealand architect, in the Classic Revival style. Built early this century it is considered one of Christchurch's finest buildings.

On the northern outskirts of Christchurch is **Willowbank Wildlife Reserve**, 60 Hussey Road, Harewood, ph 359 6226. The Reserve is a specialist in breeding endangered species, and has a farmyard, zoo, and the ultimate New Zealand Experience, which offers an opportunity to view native flora and fauna, a pre-European Maori village and the Kiwi forest. Food and meals are available in the licensed restaurant. The Reserve is open daily 10am-10pm and admission is $10 adult, $4.50 child, combined tour and evening dining costs $32.50.

Orana Park Wildlife Trust, New Zealand's most extensively developed open range wildlife reserve, is situated on McLeans Island Road, just north-west of the airport. As well as the usual lions, cheetahs and giraffes, the reserve has a Kiwi House (for the feathered variety), native bird aviaries, and in the Reptile House the Tuatata (New Zealand's Living Fossil) can be viewed. A daily bus tour leaves the Square at 11am, or pick-up can be arranged, ph 379 8755. The reserve's Serengeti Restaurant is fully licensed and offers excellent dining and views. Orana Park is open daily 10am-5pm, with last admission at 4.30pm, and admission is $12 adult, $6 child. For more information and feeding times, ph 359 7109.

The **Yaldhurst Transport Museum**, opposite the Yaldhurst Hotel, School Road, 12km from Christchurch, has displays of many rare and fascinating relics. It also has one of the finest collections of horse-drawn vehicles in the southern hemisphere. The Museum is open daily 10am-5pm and admission is $6.50 adult, $2.50 child, ph 342 7914.

Air Force World, Main South Road, Wigram, ph 343 9532, has displays showing New Zealand's involvement in military aviation from 1913 to the present days. They include 15 significant aircraft, ground equipment, a History Hall, video presentations, and an art gallery. The museum is only 15 minutes drive from Cathedral Square, or take Buses nos 8, 25 or City Circuit. Open daily, admission is $9 adults, $4 children, $20 families.

Ferrymead Historic Park is a Heritage Park, covering over 40ha in the Heathcote Valley, at 269 Bridle Path Road, Heathcote, ph 384 1970. The Tramway provides a 1.5km link between the two main areas of the Park, and operating vehicles include restored electric trams and an 1881 Kitson Steam train.

The Hall of Wheels has changing exhibitions on the changing technology; the Hall of Flame has an extensive display of fire appliances and fire fighting equipment.

The Moorhouse township is named after one of Canterbury's early VIPs who played a major part in building the first railway at Ferrymead. The town has an operating bakery, printshop, cooperage, furniture restoration and construction, and livery stables, as well as a church, schoolhouse, gaol and houses of historical interest. Open daily 10am-4.30pm, and admission is $6 adults, $3 child 5-15 years, $1 child 3-4 years, with family concessions available. Tram and train rides at weekends cost $2 for multi-rides. Access is along Ferry Road, and first turn over the Ferrymead Bridge, or take Buses no 3 or City Circuit.

International Antarctic World is five minutes' walk from Christchurch International Airport and 15 minutes from the City Centre, ph 358 9896. It has sound and light shows that recreate Antarctica in all its moods, a unique Antarctic aquarium with live fish, hands-on exhibits, and the Antarctic Shop, with themed merchandise that includes many exclusive products. There is also a cafe and bar. The Centre is open daily 9.30am-8.30pm October through March, 9.30am-5.30pm April through September;admission is $12 adult, $6 child, $28 family.

Mount Cavendish Gondola is on the Port Hills overlooking Christchurch, and the ride provides a 360 degree view of the Southern Alps, the Canterbury Plains, Lyttelton Harbour and its port, and the extinct volcano that formed Banks Peninsula. At the top there is a Time Tunnel that presents the sound and feel of centuries-old Maori and European settlement. Nearby is the first-class Montebelos Restaurant for lunch or dinner, and the Red Rock Cafe. *Free shuttle buses* are available from the Visitor Centre, or take Bus no 28, and the attractions are open daily 10am-late (summer) noon-late (winter). The Gondola Ride costs $12 adult, $6 child, $29 family. The Time Tunnel costs $4 adult, $2 child, $10 family.

Mona Vale is a reserve and stately home situated on the Avon River 1.7km from the city centre. The historic home is surrounded by beautiful gardens with fountains and exotic trees and plants. Entry is from Fendalton Road, adjacent to the railway crossing. Cars can drive through to the Irvine Street exit, and there is ample parking space. The grounds are open daily 8am-7.30pm (October-March), 8.30am-5.30pm (April-September), and the homestead is open Sun-Fri 10am-3.30pm. **Punts** on the Avon operate daily, from the landing stage in front of the homestead, 10am until evening Sun-Fri, contact the Visitor Information Centre for details. Other punting trips on the Avon are available, leaving from the Information Centre, from opposite the Town Hall Restaurant, and from the Thomas Edmonds Restaurant. Costs are $10 per person for a 20 minute trip, $12 for a 30 minute trip, and $20 for a 45 minute trip.

Lyttelton, the port for Christchurch, can be reached by road either by taking Evans Pass (19km journey from the city centre) or by driving through the Road Tunnel which is 1.6km in length (11km journey). For those without their own transport, Bus no 28 leaves for Lyttelton from Cathedral Square.

Lyttelton Harbour is the flooded crater of a long extinct volcano, and its beautiful bays offer safe swimming and water sports. The steam tug *Lyttelton* is often moored in Lyttelton and makes some harbour cruises. There are two islands in the harbour, Ripapa and Quail, and there are regular launch connections to Diamond Harbour, on the other side of the bay. Ripapa Island has had a varied history. It has been a Maori fortress, a prison, a quarantine station, a coastal defence fort, and a prisoner-of-war camp for the German Sea Raider, Count Felix Von Luckner.

Tours

Land Tours

Christchurch Tramway, ph 366 7830, has an explorer-type tour with nine stops along the way. It is a continuous service with departures every 15 minutes from 9am until 6pm, later in the summer months. Tickets are bought from the conductor on board and costs are: adults - 1 hour pass $5, 4 hour pass $6, all day pass $7; children under 15 - 1 hour pass $2, 4 hour pass $3, all day pass $4.

A2B Tours, ph 358 7579, have half-day tours within the city and suburbs, and full day trips to Hanmer Springs, Akaroa, Arthurs Pass, Mount Cook, Milford Sound, etc.

Canterbury Leisure Tours, ph 0800 484 485, have half-day tours around the hills and harbour, Orana wildlife park and also historic town tours. They also have a range of full day tours including a trip around Banks Peninsula.

Walkaway Tours, ph 365 6672, offer walking, coach and private car tours from two hours to a full day.

Mount Cook/Grayline, ph 0800 800 904, have a half-day Roundabout Tour of the city, Lyttelton and Port Hills, and tours further afield to Banks Peninsula and Kaikoura.

Water Tours

Canterbury Cat Cruises, ph 304 7641, have 2 hour Akaroa Harbour cruises daily at 11am & 1.30pm.

Canterbury Sea Tours, ph 326 6756, have a coastal tour past bird colonies, penguins, dolphins, seals and through a volcanic sea cave around Banks Peninsula. They leave daily at 9.30am and 2pm from Sumner.

Ripapa Island-Lyttelton Harbour is a 2 hour cruise and guided historic walk on Ripapa Island, and it leaves Lyttelton Jetty B at 2pm daily during the school holidays and in summer, ph 328 8368.

MV Tuhoe sails from Kaiapoi Wharf. Enquire at the Information Centre as to schedules, or ph 327 5003.

Steam Tug Lyttelton has regular sailings Nov-April. Enquire at the Information Centre.

Rangitata Rafts Ltd, ph 0800 251 251, can supply 5km of white water rafting on a grade 5 river.

Flightseeing
Garden City Helicopters, ph 358 4360, have full and half-day flights over local attractions.
Pionair Adventures, ph 0800 733 388, offer flights in a DC3.
Wigram Barnstormers, ph 025 426 528, offer flights in a Tiger Moth or a Boeing Stearman.
Air Adventures NZ, ph 379 5780.

Sport and Recreation

Beaches
The Pacific coastline provides the province of Canterbury with a number of extensive beaches, all providing good swimming, surfing, windsurfing, yachting and fishing. Sharks don't seem to be a problem, but the tidal currents can be dangerous, so swimming in designated, patrolled areas is recommended.

Ballooning
Up, Up & Away Ltd, ph 358 9859, ascend from North Hagley Park opposite the George Hotel.

Bungy Jumping
Available at *Thrillseekers Canyon*, Hanmer Springs, ph 315 7046.

Car Racing
Supa Karts, 100 Moorhouse Avenue, ph 374 9425.

Fishing Guides
Rakaia Salmon Safaris (Geoff Scott), ph 302 7444.

Deep Sea Fishing
Bluefin Charters, Akaroa Harbour, ph 304 8686.

Golf
Most of the golf courses in the area welcome visitors as green fee players. Some have clubs for hire.
Ascot, Ascot Avenue, North New Brighton, ph 383 1105 - 18-hole, par 3 course.
Christchurch, Horseshoe Lake Road, ph 385 2738 - 18-hole championship course.
Hagley, North Hagley Park, ph 379 8279 - 12-hole course, restricted hours.

Harewood, McLeans Island Road, ph 359 8853 - 36 hole championship, electric carts, driving range.
Rawhiti, New Brighton, ph 388 7408 - full-size course.
Russley, 428 Memorial Avenue, ph 358 4612 - 18-hole championship course, club hire, electric carts.
Waitikiri, Waitikiri Drive, Burwood, ph 383 0729 - 18-hole championship course.
Windsor, Waitikiri Drive, Burwood, ph 383 1403 - 18-hold course in picturesque setting.

Horse Riding
Cobden Riding School, 274 Russley Road, ph 358 5278.
Parkgrove Horse Treks, Marshlands/Spencerville, ph 385 2508.

Squash
Sockburn Squash Centre, Takaro Avenue, Sockburn,
ph 348 5092.
Pioneer Sports Stadium, cnr Rose & Lyttelton Streets, Spreydon,
ph 332 2676.
Queen Elizabeth II Park, Travis Road, North Beach, ph 383 4313.

Swimming Pools
Centennial Pool, Armagh Street, ph 366 8917.
Queen Elizabeth II Park, Travis Road, North Beach, ph 383 4313.
Jellie Park Aqualand, Ilam Road, ph 351 8774.
Waltham Road Lido Pool, Waltham Road, Waltham,
ph 366 0725.
Wharenui Coronation Pool, Elizabeth Street, Riccarton,
ph 348 6488.
Sockburn Park Pool, Main South Road, Sockburn, ph 348 5092.

Ten Pin Bowling
Garden City Bowl, Iversen Terrace, ph 366 3323.

Outlying Attractions

Akaroa & Banks Peninsula
Akaroa is 84km from Christchurch on Banks Peninsula, and it is a popular resort on the shores of Akaroa Harbour. 'Akaroa' is Maori for 'Long Harbour', and the name was given to the settlement by the large numbers of Maoris who populated the peninsula.

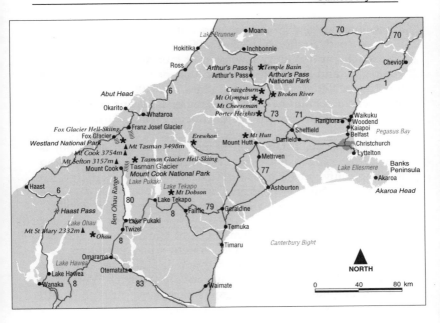

The township was first settled by the French, as evidenced by the quaint old buildings and the street names. The Langlois-Eteveneaux house dates back to the 1840s, and forms part of the Early Settlers Museum, with colonial costumes and whaling displays. It is open daily 10am-5pm (winter), 10am-6pm (summer).

Historic Akaroa lighthouse is a local landmark and it is open Sun 1-4pm and daily during January.

Okains Bay has an interesting Maori and Colonial Museum that is open daily 10am-5pm, and it has rare Maori artifacts, a Maori meeting house and historic remnants of the district. Admission is $4 adults, $1 children.

Wineries

Canterbury's first grape plantings were made by the early French settlers, but it is only since the 1970s that the area has really developed a reputation for fine wines.

Amberley Estate Vineyard was established by Jeremy Prater in 1979 with 4ha of vines, 50km north of Christchurch. Amberley specialises in dry white table wines, and vineyard lunches are available indoors and outdoors daily 11am-5pm. Reserve Road, Amberley, ph 314 8409.

French Farm Winery is located at French Farm Bay, Banks Peninsula, and it revives the tradition of winemaking where the French settlers first planted vines in 1840. The winery has an excellent restaurant that serves regional cuisine, and is open daily 10am-6pm. French Valley Road, French Farm, ph 304 5784.

Giesen Wine Estate planted its first vines in 1981, but is now producing a wide range of quality wines including Riesling, Sauvignon Blanc and Chardonnay. It is open Mon-Sat 10am-5pm, Sun 11am-5pm, and barbecue facilities are available. Burnham School Road, 32km south of Christchurch, ph 347 6729.

Larcomb Wines are 18km south of Christchurch, and the first vines were planted in 1980. White wines produced now are Briedecker, Riesling, Gewurztraminer and Pinot Gris, and there is also a red Pinot Noir. Lunches are available 11am-5pm, and evening meals by prior arrangement only. Cnr Main South & Larcombs Roads, Rolleston, ph 347 8909.

Central Canterbury

Ashburton is 85km south-west of Christchurch, and is the commercial centre for the farming communities of central Canterbury. It has a population of 15,000, and facilities include a golf course, indoor heated swimming pool and a racecourse.

Methven, 34km from Ashburton, is a popular winter resort serving the Mt Hutt Skifield. It is also the base for mountaineering, deerstalking and fishing. The **Rakaia Gorge**, 17km north of Methven, is a very popular picnic spot.

Arthurs Pass

Arthurs Pass is a village that is renowned for its spectacular mountain, river and forest scenery, and it is 153km from Christchurch. In 1865, Arthur Dudley Dobson was sent to find a new route to the West Coast, to provide access to the goldfields, and in appreciation the pass was named after him.

Beneath the pass runs the 8.5km Otira railway runnel, still the only rail link across the South Island.

The village is surrounded by the Arthurs Pass National Park, which has an area of 98,000ha mainly covered in beech forest, interspersed with cascading waterfalls. Mount Rolleston (2272m) towers over the western side of the gorge opposite Temple Basin, a popular skiing resort. Other ski resorts around here include Porter Heights, Broken River and Mt Cheeseman.

The National Park Visitor Centre in Arthurs Pass village, ph (03) 318 9211, can provide all the information needed for tramping, hunting, picnicking, etc.

Northern Canterbury

To get there from Christchurch take SH 1 to Waipara and then SH 7. The route will take you along the North Canterbury coast through Kaiapoi, 19km north of Christchurch. The Rangiora /Oxford Bus from Christchurch travels through this area.

Kaiapoi was an important trading centre in the 1850s when waterways allowed boats and paddle steamers to supply goods to the early settlers.

The Domain, Scott Rose Garden and reserves along the riverside are great spots for picnics.

The historic MV *Tuhoe*, a restored coastal trader, sails on most Sundays from Kaiapoi Wharf to Kairaki and return, subject to tide and weather conditions. The trip takes 1½ to 2 hours, ph 327 5003.

Kaiapoi River offers good fishing for trout, salmon and whitebait. Facilities in the town include an 18-hole golf course, heated swimming pool, boat ramps, and a museum that is open Sun-Thurs 2-4pm.

Rangiora is 27km north of Christchurch, and is the centre of a prosperous agricultural, pastoral, fruit-growing and horticultural area. There are several large forests in the area, including the largest forest nursery in the South Island.

The district has some fine examples of wooden colonial architecture, including St John's Anglican Church (1875) and St Stephen's Church of Tuahiwi (1865). Rangiora has a replica cob cottage and a museum that is open Sun and Wed 1.30-4pm.

Facilities in the town include a heated swimming pool, squash courts, racecourse and golf course where visitors are welcome, ph 313 6666.

Waiau Ferry Bridge

The nearby Ashley River is good for swimming and fishing, and there are popular beaches at Waikuku and Woodend.

Ashley Gorge is set on the middle reaches of the Ashley River, 59km from Christchurch. It has good river swimming, bush walks, horse trekking, picnic and camping facilities. The town of Oxford is 10km away.

Hanmer Springs is 134km north of Christchurch, in the outlying spurs of the Southern Alps surrounded by vast forests. It is the South Island's principal thermal resort, and the Hanmer Springs Thermal Reserve ranks with the best in New Zealand. It includes three thermal pools, an active heated pool, children's paddling pool and four spout pools. Towels and costumes are available for hire, and the complex is open daily (except for Christmas Day) 10am-9pm. Admission is $7 adult, $3 child, and family and all day passes are available, ph (03) 315 7511.

Hanmer Springs has a good range of accommodation and eateries, and there are plenty of sightseeing tours available. More information is available from the Visitor Information Centre on the corner of Amuri Avenue and Jacks Pass Road, Hanmer Springs, ph (03) 315 7128.

The surrounding 6880ha of forest has many walking tracks catering for all ages and degrees of fitness. Conical Hill, only a short distance from the village, offers panoramic views of the countryside. Other popular walks include Mount Isobel, Waterfall Track, and a 3km forest track that follows an old coach route built last century. Disabled folk can take a wheelchair walk that begins at the Forestry Information Centre.

Other attractions in the area include the nearby Amuri Skifield, a golf course, swimming, squash, horse trekking, bowls, croquet, jetboating, safari tours, rafting and bungy jumping from the Waiau Ferry Bridge.

The Clarence, Waiau, Hanmer and Percival rivers offer excellent fishing and summer swimming, as well as numerous picnic spots.

From Hanmer Springs it is only 70km to the **Lewis Pass**, another popular bush walking area.

Skiing

Skiing is a very popular winter sport in New Zealand probably because the ski fields are relatively close to the larger towns. There are fourteen commercial ski fields and a dozen club fields spread throughout the country. The majority are found in the South Island, but there are two areas with ski fields in the North Island - Mount Ruapehu in the Tongariro National Park in the centre of the island; and Mount Taranaki near New Plymouth. In the South Island there are ski fields spread all over. They vary from small private fields with only rope tows, to the large commercial fields with excellent facilities, as well as the in-between range of smaller commercial fields.

The snow in New Zealand varies from area to area and from year to year, but generally speaking it is dry and powdery in the South Island for most of the season, and the spring corn lasts until the end of October-beginning of November at some fields. The higher slopes on Mount Ruapehu do offer powder snow skiing at times, but it is not as dry as in the South Island.

New Zealand also offers excellent off-piste skiing close to the ski resorts, as well as on the glaciers and in the undeveloped mountains. Heliskiing is becoming more popular with the passing of each year, and for the intermediate to advanced skier there is a range of heliskiing options. All heliskiing guides are highly trained and specialised in the area of mountain safety and guiding. The helicopter pilots, too, are some of the most experienced in the world. Holiday ski packages with many different options are available from *The Ski Travel Company* who have an office in Sydney, Australia, ph (02) 9977 7677.

All prices given for lifts, lessons, hire equipment, accommodation, etc, in the following sections are in **NZ$**.

North Island

There are two commercial ski fields in the centre of the North Island on Mount Ruapehu: Whakapapa behind The Grand Chateau, and the Turoa field above Ohakune. These fields have exciting terrain with lava cliffs and gullies which extend the best skiers, as well as gentler slopes for learners. At the summit of the mountain is the crater lake, the sides of which are steep and dangerous, and care should be taken not to approach too closely. Unless you are an experienced mountaineer, it is not advisable to descend to the lake, the temperature of which varies with volcanic activity, but is always hot! The view from the crater edge is fantastic - neighbouring Ngauruhoe and Tongariro, and in the background Lake Taupo stretching off into the distance. On a clear day you can also see Mount Taranaki, 120km away. The ski season usually lasts well into November on the southern slopes of the mountain.

Whakapapa

The oldest ski field on the mountain and the largest in New Zealand, Whakapapa is 364km from Auckland, 341km from Wellington, and 26km from National Park.

It is approximately 8km from The Grand Chateau along a sealed road, and a regular bus service operates in winter between The Grand Chateau and the field. The field faces north and has an area of over 400ha. It is renowned for its sunny spring skiing. There are many privately owned ski club huts around the base of the chairlift.

The field is open daily 8.30am-4.30pm, early June to mid-November.

Lifts

1 express quad chairlift, 1 quad chairlift, 4 double chairlifts, 4 T-bars, 4 platters, 7 beginners tows - vertical rise 675m. The top station is at 2300m. Lift capacity is 23,000 skiers per hour. The longest run is 4km.

Trails

25% beginner; 50% intermediate; 25% advanced.

Facilities

The field has 4 cafeterias, a licensed restaurant, ski school, ski repair, ski hire, ski patrol, snow making, snow grooming, first aid emergency service, full professional creche.

Snowphone 090 099 333; Information (07) 892 3738.

Prices

Lifts - full day $49 adult, $25 child; half day $39 adult, $20 child; learners $37 adult, $19 child; season pass $850 adult, $420 child.

Rental - full ski $26 adult, $16 child per day; full board $47 per person; board only $41 per person. All equipment and clothing can be hired.

Lessons - Ski school: group lesson $20 per person; private lesson $60 per person; starter pack $48 adult, $28 child. Boarding school: group lesson $20 per person; private lesson $60 per person; starter pack $90 adult, $78 child.

Accommodation

The closest accommodation is Whakapapa Village, 8km from the field, and *The Grand Chateau* is the best known accommodation there. It is a 64 room hotel with a licensed restaurant, lounges, swimming pool and tennis court, and rooms cost from $157.50 per night, ph (07) 892 3809. Also in the village is the *Skotel Holiday Resort*, ph (07) 892 3719, with 57 units, licensed restaurant, cocktail lounges, spa pool, sauna and rooms from $90 per night.

Other places are a bit further away from the ski field. Here is a selection with prices in NZ$ for a double room per night during the peak season, which should be used as a guide only. The telephone area code is 07.

Discovery Motel, cnr SH 47 & SH 48, ph 892 2744, fax 892 2603 - 22 units, licensed restaurant, spa - $50-75 (summer), $85-125 (winter).

Howard's Lodge, Carroll Street, National Park, ph/fax 892 2827 - 39 rooms (12 with ensuite), barbecue - $70-90 (winter).

Eivin's Lodge & Motor Camp, SH 47 (17km north-east of Chateau turn-off), ph 386 8062, fax 386 7659 - 40 rooms (no private facilities), barbecue - $25 x 2; camp sites $9 per person.

The Ski Haus, Carroll Street, National Park, ph/fax 892 2854 - 17 bunk rooms (sleep 2-6) (shared facilities), licensed restaurant, spa pool, bar - B&B $35-50 per person (double); hostel $15-20 per person; campervans $5-8 per adult.

National Park Lodge & Motel, Carroll Street, ph/fax 892 2993 - 12 rooms - motel units $50-140, backpackers $12-25.

Motor Camps and Cabins

Discovery Caravan Park, (see above) - caravan sites $8 per person; cabins (sleep 2) - $42 x 2.

Tongariro Motor Camp, adjacent to Eivins Lodge (see above), ph 386 8062 - BYO restaurant - caravan sites $9 per adult.

Whakapapa Camp, 250m above Chateau, ph 892 3897 - caravan and tent sites $9 per adult; flat (sleeps 4) $47 x 3; cabins (sleep 4-6) $33 x 3; backpackers $12 per person; lodge $16.50 per person.

Turoa

Turoa ski field is 17km from Ohakune, 366km from Auckland, and 317km from Wellington. It is on the south-east side of the mountain with south and south-west facing slopes. The field has 20km of marked runs close to the lifts, but the off-piste skiing for advanced skiers is through gullies, ice falls and on a glacier. The slopes are wide and great for intermediate skiers. The road to the ski field is fully sealed. There is a shuttle bus to the field from Ohakune. The season usually lasts from mid-July to early November. The skiable area is 370ha.

Lifts

2 quad chair, 2 triple chairs, 3 T-bars, 4 platters - vertical rise 720m. Top station is at 2,322m. Lift capacity is 10,400 skiers per hour.

Trails

20% beginner, 55% intermediate, 25% advanced.

Facilities

3 cafes, snack shack, bar, snow making, snow grooming, ski hire, ski patrol offering free guiding service, information office, child-care centre, ski school.

Snowphone 090 099 444; Information ph (06) 385 8456.

Prices

Lifts - full day $48 adult, $25 child; half day $39 adult, $20 child; learners $22 adult, $12 child; season pass $899 adult, $449 child.

Rental - full ski $25 adult, $15 child; full board $40 per person.

Lessons - Ski school: group lesson $26 per person; private lesson $70 per person; learners pack $45 adult, $29 child. Boarding school: group lesson $26 per person; private lesson $70 per person; learners pack $95 adult, $70 child.

Accommodation

Ohakune is known as the 'Gateway to Mt Ruapehu' and has an Information Centre on Clyde Road. Information is also contained in the local weekly paper *The Ruapehu Bulletin*.

The town is also home to quite a few good restaurants and bars, and the Information Centre will be able to point you in the right direction.

Here is a selection of accommodation with prices for a double room per night in NZ$, which should be used as a guide only. The telephone area code is 06.

Ruapehu Homestead, SH 49, Rangataua, ph/fax 385 8799 - 8 rooms, licensed restaurant, spa - $60-135.

The Hobbit Motel, Lodge, Restaurant & Bar, cnr Goldfinch & Wye Streets, ph 385 8248, fax 385 8515 - 17 units and 36-bed lodge, licensed restaurant, bar, spa - from $75-95.

Acacia Lodge Motel, 4 Moore Street, ph 385 8729, fax 385 8347 - 13 units, spa - from $65-75 (summer - winter rates on application).

Ohakune Court Motel, 101 Goldfinch Street, ph 385 8183, fax 385 8590 - 18 units, swimming pool, spa, barbecue - from $70-105 (seasonal rates apply).

Tukino

This club field is 392km from Auckland, 315km from Wellington and 32km from Waiouru. It is usually open from early July to the end of September. Skiable area - 19ha.

Lifts

2 rope tows - vertical lift is 250m.

Trails

65% beginner, 30% intermediate, 5% advanced.

Facilities

There is a ski club on the field.

Snowphone (06) 585 6294, Information ph (04) 234 6961. Contact: 11 Grendon Road, Titirangi. No ski hire.

Milford Sound, Fiordland National Park, South Island.

Fox Glacier, Westland.

Manganui

This field on Mount Taranaki (2517m) is another club field, and it is 22km from Stratford on the Pembroke Road. It also can be reached from the Egmont Road, which branches off SH 3. It is 24km from New Plymouth to the end of this road. From there you can walk across to the field, which is usually open from mid-June to mid-October. Skiable area - 59ha.

Lifts
1 T-bar, 3 rope tows - vertical lift is 420m

Trails
5% beginner, 30% intermediate, 65% advanced.

Facilities
Ski hire is available at The Mountain House in Stratford at the base of the mountain.

Snowphone (06) 765 7669, Information (06) 765 5493. Contact: Box 3271, New Plymouth.

Prices
Lifts - $25 adult ($20 weekdays), $20 child, $25 student.

Accommodation
Stratford or New Plymouth (see Taranaki chapter for details).

South Island

Skiing in the South Island is big business with twenty-one commercial and club ski fields. Three major ski festivals are held during the season in Queenstown, Canterbury and Wanaka.

Nelson Lakes National Park

There are two ski fields in the park, Mount Robert and Rainbow Valley. To get there from Nelson, travel along SH 6 and the turn-off for the fields is at Kawatiri where SH 63 branches off for St Arnaud, 26km from SH 6. From Picton take SH 1 to Blenheim then travel along SH 6 to Renwick, and then

SH 63. Nelson-St Arnaud is approximately 130km, and Blenheim-St Arnaud is approximately 100km. Lake Rotoroa can be reached by turning off SH 6 at Gowanbridge. Many people drive out from Nelson and Blenheim for the day to ski at these fields. At weekends there is a constant stream of cars on the road going out in the morning and returning at night.

Nelson Lakes Transport have a daily service between Nelson and St Arnaud during the winter, ph (03) 521 1858.

There are two large lakes in the park, Lake Rotoiti and Lake Rotoroa, and many of its mountain peaks are over 2000m. Mount Travers is the highest at 2338m, and there are mountain peaks still unclimbed and unnamed. St Arnaud village is located on the shores of beautiful Lake Rotoiti.

Mount Robert

Mount Robert is a club field about 15km from St Arnaud, and the access track takes about 1½ to 2 hours to walk. It is usually open from July to mid-September. Skiable area - 450ha.

Lifts
4 rope tows - vertical lift is 300m.

Trails
10% beginner, 70% intermediate, 20% advanced.

Facilities
Limited ski hire on field. Helicopter shuttle runs on weekends.
Snowphone (03) 548 8336. Contact: Box 344, Nelson.

Accommodation
St Arnaud is the closest village and accommodation is available in lodges, hostels and the camping ground.

The Yellow House, ph (03) 521 1850, has low priced backpacker accommodation.

Rainbow Valley

Rainbow Valley ski field is 56km from St Arnaud, and 100km from Nelson and Blenheim. It offers great terrain for intermediate skiers and has some challenges for those more advanced. The field is open June to September and is accessed by 15km of unsealed road. The skiable area is 350ha.

Lifts
1 double chair, 1 T-bar, 2 rope tows - vertical lift is 322m.

Trails
25% beginner, 55% intermediate, 20% advanced.

Facilities
Accommodation, restaurants, ski hire, ski school, tobogganing and ice skating. Snowphone 090 034 444, Information ph (03) 521 1861. Contact: Private Bag, St Arnaud.

Prices
Lifts - full day $44 adult, $24 child; half day $33 adult, $17 child; learners $22 adult, $13 child; season pass $699 adult, $299 child.
Rental - full ski $30 adult, $24 child; full board $42 adult, $35 child.
Lessons - Ski school: group lesson $30 adult, $15 child; private lesson $50 per person; starter pack $61 adult, $45 child. Boarding school: group lesson $30 adult, $15 child; private lesson $50 per person; starter pack $61 adult, $45 child.

Accommodation
For accommodation on the field, contact the information number above. St Arnaud is the closest village.

Canterbury

Canterbury has three commercial and seven club fields, with the most upmarket being World Cup host Mount Hutt, which is always the first field to open in New Zealand each year.

Mount Lyford
This is the newest of New Zealand's ski areas, and it is situated 140km north of Christchurch. The skiable area of 446ha is made up of two fields that are separated by a ten minute drive around the mountain - Lake Stella and Terako. Mount Lyford is usually open May to September.

Available within forty minutes' drive of the fields are chalet accommodation, golf, ice skating, fishing and hot pools.

Lifts
4 Pomas, 3 rope tows, 1 fixed grip tow - vertical lift is 420m.

Trails
30% beginner, 30% intermediate, 40% advanced.

Facilities
Cafe/restaurant, ski hire, snow board hire, heliskiing, toboggan/luge hire, ski school, shuttles from Christchurch, Kaikoura and toll gate, ski touring. Snowphone 090 034 444, Information ph (03) 315 6178. Contact: Private Bag, Waiau.

Prices
Lifts - full day $35 adult, $30 child; half day $30 adult, $25 child; season pass $325 adult, $260 child. Road toll - $5.

Accommodation
Mount Lyford village is 4km west of the field and has chalet accommodation. Hanmer is 60km to the east and may be the best bet (see above).

Amuri

A club field situated on Mount St Patrick above the Hanmer Basin, Amuri is known as a very friendly field. It is 17km from the spa town of Hanmer, and the access road goes right to the field. Amuri is usually open July to September. The skiable area is 52ha.

Lifts
1 Poma, 2 rope tows - vertical lift is 300m.

Trails
10% beginner, 60% intermediate, 30% advanced.

Facilities
Ski hire, snowboard and mono-ski hire, snow groomer, ski school, day lodge. Snowphone (03) 366 5865, Information ph (03) 315 7125. Contact: Box 129, Hanmer.

Accommodation
Fraemoh's Lodge is on the field, or there are plenty of places to stay in Hanmer. Here is a selection, with prices for a double

room per night, which should be used as a guide only. The telephone area code is 03.

Motels

Larchwood Motel, 12 Bath Street, ph/fax 315 7281 - 16 units, swimming pool, barbecue - $78-170.

Hanmer Resort Motel, 7 Cheltenham Street, ph 315 7362, fax 315 7581 - 15 units - $80-110.

Greenacres Motel, 86 Conical Hill Road, ph/fax 315 7125 - 13 units, spa, barbecue - $78-109.

Alpine Spa Lodge, 1-11 Harrogate Street, ph/fax 315 7311 - 28 units, swimming pool, spa, barbecue - $70-85.

Forest Peak Motel, 4 Torquay Terrace, ph/fax 315 7132 - 10 units - $58-92.

Willowbank Motel, 121 Argelins Road, ph 315 7211, fax 315 7010 - 9 units, - $55-65.

Motor Camps and Cabins

AA Tourist Park, Jacks Pass Road, ph/fax 315 7112 - sites $17 x 2; flats (sleep 5) $56 x 2; cabins (sleep 6) $40 x 2.

Mountain View Holiday Park, Main Road (400m from Thermal Pools), ph/fax 315 7113 - tent sites $17 x 2; flats (sleep 6) $57-65 x 2; cabins (sleep 3-5) $33-43 x 2.

The Pines Motor Camp, Argelins Road, ph 315 7152 - tent sites $13 x 2; caravan sites $16 x 2; cabins (sleep 4) $32 x 2; on-site caravans $30 x 2.

Temple Basin

Temple Basin is 44km from Arthur's Pass and 157km from Christchurch. Arthur's Pass is 737m above sea-level and is surrounded by National Park. The field is usually open from late June to the end of September. The walk to the field from the road takes approximately one hour, but your goods go up on a lift. There is on field accommodation in two modern lodges. The skiable area is 17ha.

Lifts

4 rope tows - vertical lift is 417m.

Trails

25% beginner, 50% intermediate, 25% advanced.

Facilities

Canteen, ski hire, limited snowboard hire and video hire.
Snowphone (03) 366 5865, Information ph (03) 332 1725.
Contact: Box 1228, Christchurch.

Craigieburn Valley

Craigieburn is a club field, more suited to intermediate and advanced skiers. The field is usually open July to September and the turn-off from SH 73 is 1km past the Broken River exit. The skiable area is 101ha.

Lifts

3 rope tows - vertical lift is 503m.

Trails

70% intermediate, 30% advanced.

Facilities

Day lodge, accommodation lodge, shuttle services. No ski hire on field.
Snowphone (03) 366 5865, Information ph (03) 348 2842.
Contact: Box 2125, Christchurch.

Broken River

Broken River is a club field 128km from Christchurch and 46km west of Springfield. It is usually open June to October. It is a long walk from the car park to the skiing area - naturally uphill - but there are three accommodation houses near the tows so if you are staying a week you will only have to do it once. There is a goods lift from the car park for your gear. You can cross the ridge line to Craigieburn and Cheeseman fields, and lift tickets from either field are accepted.

Lifts

4 rope tows.

Trails

15% beginner, 50% intermediate, 35% advanced.

Facilities

Day lodge, canteen, snow grooming - no ski hire on field.

Snowphone (03) 366 5865, Information ph (03) 389 1803. Contact: Box 2718, Christchurch.

Accommodation

For on-field accommodation contact the *Gnomes Ski and Sport Shop*, Main West Road, Darfield, ph (03) 318 8433. *The Darfield Hotel*, ph 318 8325, has 6 bedrooms (3 with private facilities) and a restaurant, and the room rate is B&B $70 a double.

Mount Cheeseman

Mount Cheeseman is a club field 112km from Christchurch and 45km from Springfield. The access road is not as good as the one to Porter Heights, but the T-bar is only a short walk from the carpark. Mount Cheeseman is usually open July to September. The skiable area is enormous.

Lifts

1 T-bar, 1 platter, 1 grip tow - vertical lift is 293m.

Trails

10% beginner, 40% intermediate, 50% advanced.

Facilities

Day lodge, ski hire, snow grooming, ice skating pond, skate hire. Snowphone (03) 366 5865, Information ph (03) 379 5315. Contact: Box 22178, Christchurch.

Accommodation

On-field accommodation in two large huts, or at nearby Springfield.

Porter Heights

This is the closest field to Christchurch (approximately 89km) and it is only 30km from Springfield on SH 73. It is a commercial field that has some of the longest continuous slopes in the country, and is less crowded than Mount Hutt. The season usually lasts from early July to mid-October as it gets a lot of sun. The road to the ski field is second only to the one to Coronet Peak, and that makes a welcome change. The skiable area is 230ha.

Lifts
3 T-bars, 2 platter - the vertical lift is 670m.

Trails
20% beginner, 40% intermediate, 40% advanced.

Facilities
Lodge with accommodation and restaurant, ski school, ski hire, snowmaking, snow grooming. Daily transport from Christchurch by Snowman Shuttle. Snowphone 090 034 444, Information ph (03) 379 7087. Contact: Box 536, Christchurch.

Prices
Lifts - full day $44 adult, $25 child; half day $34 adult, $20 child; learners $30 adult, $20 child; season pass $695 adult, $395 child.
Rental - full ski $25 adult, $15 child; full board $45 per person; board only $35 per person.
Lessons - Ski school: group lesson $25 adult, $15 child; private lesson $45 adult, $40 child; starter pack $48 adult, $30 child. Boarding school: group lesson $25 adult, $15 child; private lesson $45 adult, $40 child, starter pack $65 adult, $45 child.

Accommodation
Porter Heights Ski Club Lodge, PO Box 2473, Christchurch, ph (025) 340 909, or (03) 379 2600 - only 5 minutes below the field car park - dinner/breakfast available - transport to and from the field is available. Other accommodation is available in Springfield - *Springfield Hotel*, West Coast Road, ph 318 4812.

Mount Olympus

Mount Olympus is a club field in the Craigieburn Range, 128km from Christchurch and 12km from Lake Ida. Take the Lake Coleridge turn-off from SH 72 and then there is another turn-off to Lake Ida near Lake Coleridge. It is 11km from Lake Coleridge to the carpark. The field is in a basin between two peaks and looks down on the Ryton River. Accommodation is available in the lower hut as well as some on the upper mountain. When the snow is down to low levels, it is advisable not to attempt the top kilometre of the access road without 4WD. The field is usually open July to October. The skiable area is 60ha.

Lifts
3 rope tows, 1 fixed grip, 1 beginners tow - vertical lift is 441m.

Trails
10% beginner, 55% intermediate, 35% advanced.

Facilities
Canteen, lunch hut, ski patrol and ski instruction. Snowphone (03) 366 5865, Information ph (03) 329 1823. Contact: Box 25055, Christchurch.

Mount Hutt

Mount Hutt is the principal ski field of Canterbury and has the longest season in the country (usually end of May to November). It is in the midst of the Southern Alps, approximately 65km from the sea and 118km from Christchurch. Unfortunately, chains are often required on the road to the field. The ski slopes are in a south facing basin between 1600m and 2075m and receive regular top-ups of dry powder during the season. The closest town is Methven, 26km away. The skiable area is 365ha.

Lifts
1 quad chair, 1 triple chair, 3 T-bars, 2 platters, 3 grip tows - vertical lift is 655m.

Trails
25% beginner, 50% intermediate, 25% advanced.

Facilities
These include cafe/restaurant, a mobile food shop which moves around the mountain dispensing drinks and snacks, ski rental, retail shop, helipad, snow groomers, ski school, heliskiing. Snowphone 090 099 766, Information ph (03) 308 5074. Contact: Box 14, Methven.

Prices
Lifts - full day $52 adult, $26 child;
half day $39 adult, $20 child;
novice $33 adult, $18 child; season pass $1349 adult, $622 child.

Rental - full ski $26 adult, $18 child; perform ski $40 adult; full board $40 adult, $30 child.
Lessons - Ski school: group lesson $33 adult, $20 child; private lesson $65 adult, $50 child; starter pack $66 adult, $42 child. Boarding school: group lesson %33 adult, $20 child; private lesson $65 adult, $50 child; learner pack $85 adult, $60 child.

Accommodation
Methven is the closest town - see Erewhon Field.

Erewhon
Erewhon field is off SH 72, 55km south-west of Methven and 30km north of Geraldine. The season usually lasts from June to the end of September. This is a small commercial field, and the locals will tell you that the name is 'nowhere' spelt backwards (perhaps they can't spell!). The access road is 8km unsealed and 4WD is recommended.

Lifts
4 rope tows - vertical lift is 530m.

Trails
20% beginner, 50% intermediate, 30% advanced.

Facilities
Lodge restaurant, ski hire, snowboard hire, powder and gunbarrel areas. Snowphone (03) 303 9883, Information ph (03) 303 9883. Contact: c/- Mt Somers Station, Mount Somers.

Accommodation
Methven or Geraldine are the closest. Here is a selection of accommodation, with prices for a double room per night, which should be used as a guide only.
The telephone area code is 03.
Methven
Centrepoint Resort Hotel, Ashburton-Rakaia Gorge Road, ph 302 8724, fax 302 8870 - 44 rooms, licensed restaurant, bars, hot pools, sauna, spa - $105-155 (winter), $90-135 (summer).
The Homestead Mt Hutt Station Resort, Junction SH 72 and SH 77, ph 302 8130, fax 302 8102 - 9 units, licensed restaurant, bar, airstrip, deer farm - $115+.
Aorangi Lodge, 38 Spaxton Street, ph/fax 302 8482 - 11 rooms,

licensed restaurant, bar, spa - B&B $25-45 (winter), $25 (summer).

Mount Hutt Motel, 205 Ashburton-Rakaia Gorge Road, SH 77, ph/fax 302 8382 - 10 units, spa - $80-92 (winter), $70 (summer).

Kohuia Lodge of Pudding Hill, SH 72, ph 302 8416, fax 302 9255 - licensed restaurant, spa - apartments $60-90; ski lodge $40-66; backpackers $15-20; tent sites $6-7; powered sites $7-9.

Geraldine

The Crossing, Woodbury Road, ph 693 9689, fax 693 9789 - 4 rooms (private facilities), licensed restaurant - $90-134.

Crown Hotel, 31 Talbot Street, ph 693 8458, fax 693 9565 - 10 rooms (some with private facilities), restaurant - $55-65 (backpacker accommodation $20) includes continental breakfast.

Andorra Motel, 16 McKenzie Street, ph 693 8622, fax 693 9731 - 10 units, swimming pool, spa - $65-75.

Geraldine Motel, 97 Talbot St, ph/fax 693 8501 - 6 units - $60-64.

Geraldine Motor Camp, Hislop Street, ph/fax 693 8147 - sites $8 per person; cabins (sleep 2-5) $15 per person.

Mount Cook Area

There is no beginner's skiing at Mount Cook, only heliskiing or Tasman Glacier skiing.

Glacier skiing offers an 8-10km descent, 2km wide in places, to small groups of intermediate to advanced skiers over the age of 12, who are led by an Alpine Guide. Skiers must be reasonably fit and have at least one season's skiing experience. Standard downhill skis (well waxed) are used. Good gloves, sunglasses and windproof ski clothes are necessary. Alpine Guides offer ski rental, including soft-flex Atomic skis, Salomon boots, as well as all clothing and accessories. Contact Alpine Guides at Mount Cook, ph (03) 435 1834 (PO Box 20, Mount Cook Village).

Heliskiing on Fox Glacier offers a six hour cruise down 3000 vertical feet through incredible scenery. The day will cost you around $600, and there is also an accommodation package available. Contact Alpine Guides Weekend, PO Box 38, Fox Glacier, ph (03) 751 0825.

Ohau Ski Field

The field overlooks the lake of the same name. It is 42km from Twizel (approximately 30 minutes' drive) and 50km (approximately 90 minutes drive) south of Mount Cook. The turn-off is on SH 8, 21km south of Twizel and is well marked. It is 24km from the turn-off to the field and it is sealed for more than half of the way. The field is in a large east-facing basin within the north-facing slopes of Mount Sutton. In good seasons there is a lot of powder here. There is only a small area suitable for beginners, but experienced skiers will find plenty of challenges here. It is usually open from July to October. The skiable area is 125ha.

Lifts

1 T-bar, 1 platter, 1 learners tow - vertical lift is 400m. The T-bar is 1033m, the longest in New Zealand.

Trails

20% beginner, 50% intermediate, 30% advanced.

Facilities

Day lodge with cafeteria, ski school, ski patrol, snow grooming, snowboard events, shuttle service to/from Christchurch. Snowphone 090 034 444, Information (03) 438 9885. Contact: Box 51, Twizel.

Prices

Lifts - full day $39 adult, $13 child; half day $28 adult, $10 child; learners $20 adult, $10 child.

Accommodation

Lake Ohau Lodge, 15 minutes from the slopes, ph (03) 438 9885, has a dinner, bed and breakfast package for $65 per adult, twin share. Other accommodation can be found in **Twizel** and **Omarama.**

Mount Dobson

Mount Dobson is 26km from Fairlie, just off SH 8. Dobson has some great learner packages, and the longest platter lift in New Zealand. There are also large areas for intermediate skiers, as well as challenging terrain for experts. The skiable area is 243ha, and the field is usually open June to October.

Apart from Fairlie, some use Tekapo and Burkes Pass as bases. For transport to the field contact Mt Dobson Ski Area Transport, ph (03) 693 9656.

Lifts
1 T-bar, 2 platters, 1 learners tow - vertical lift is 415m.

Trails
30% beginner, 50% intermediate, 20% advanced.

Facilities
Canteen, ski hire, ski school, ski patrol, snow grooming, snowboard hire.
Snowphone 090 039 888, Information ph (03) 685 8039. Contact: Alloway Road, Fairlie.

Prices
Lifts - full day $37 adult, $30 child; half day $30 adult, $25 child; learners $28 adult, $24 child; season pass $625 per person. Road toll $5.

Fox Peak

Fox Peak is a club field 198km from Christchurch and 29km from Fairlie. It offers long runs with a good variety of terrain. The skiable area is 385ha.

Lifts
5 rope tows - vertical lift is 680m. The learner tow is free.

Trails
15% beginner, 60% intermediate, 25% advanced.

Facilities
Canteen on field, day shelter plus accommodation, ski patrol, ski school, but no ski hire.

Wanaka Area

There are two international standard ski fields less than an hour's drive from Wanaka - Cardrona and Treble Cone. Both these fields offer long months of spring skiing. Cardrona in particular has wonderful powder snow. There is also heliskiing on the Harris and Richardson Mountains.

Cardrona

Cardrona is in the Crown Range, 57km from Queenstown and 26km from Wanaka. The road is steeper than those to Coronet Peak or The Remarkables, but it is still reasonable. The road from Wanaka is mostly metal and the toll gate is at the bottom of the mountain just past the Cardrona Hotel, which is a popular 'watering hole' on the return journey. The road up the mountain is wide, but it can sometimes be slippery on the way down. There are two carparks. The larger one is at the top and is generally full by 10.30am, but don't worry if you have to park in the bottom one as there is a tractor-pulled trailer which takes skiers and their gear up to the ticket office. From the top of the ridge it is possible to see the back of Coronet Peak. The field faces south and can be bitterly cold on a bad day, but the snow is better here and stays longer. Cardrona is noted for its dry powder snow. You can't have it both ways. There are three basins and the field overlooks the Pisa Range. The skiable area is 350ha and the season usually lasts from June to mid-October.

Lifts
2 quad chairs, 1 double chair, 1 rope tow, 1 grip tow - vertical lift is 340m.

Trails
20% beginner, 55% intermediate, 25% advanced.

Facilities
Restaurant, cafe, ski school, ski hire, snowboard school, snowboard hire, ski patrol, heliskiing. Snowphone 090 034 444, Information ph (03) 443 7411. Contact: Box 117 Wanaka.

Prices

Lifts - full day $56 adult, $27 child; half day $40 adult, $21 child; learners $26 per person; season pass $825 adult, $360 child.

Rental - full ski $28 adult, $21 child; carving skis $35 adult, $26 child; full board $43 adult, $32 child; board half day $30 adult, $24 child.

Treble Cone

This field is 19km from Wanaka and 89km from Queenstown. The road is sealed to the toll gate and then it rises steeply to the field. It can be rather slippery on the way down and care is needed at all times. A bus runs between the toll gate and field if you would rather not drive. Treble Cone is one of the most scenic ski fields in the world. The view down to Lake Wanaka is magnificent. It is not quite as commercialised as the other fields in the area. It is a friendly place as well as being one of the highest ski fields in the South Island. Runs to 2073m provide challenges for experienced skiers, but now it also has good beginner and intermediate terrain. It is usually open from late June to October. The skiable area is 500ha.

Lifts

1 double chair, 2 T-bars, 1 platter, 1 six seater, 1 learners tow - the vertical lift is 660m.

Trails

15% beginner, 45% intermediate, 40% advanced.

Facilities

Full hire facilities, ski tuition, cafeteria, snow grooming, snow making. Snowphone 090 034 444, Information ph (03) 443 7443. Contact: Box 206 Wanaka.

Prices

Lifts - full day $55 adult, $27 child; half day $42 adult, $19 child; learners $25 adult, $15 child; season pass $1080 adult, $550 child.

Rental - full ski $22 adult, $17 child; skis only $18 adult, $15 child; full board $40 adult $33 child.

Lessons - Ski school: group lesson $32 adult, $22 child; private lesson $60 per person; learners pack $40 adult, $30 child. Boarding school: group lesson $32 adult, $22 child; private lesson $60 per person; learners pack $50 adult, $40 child.

Accommodation
Wanaka has a good selection of accommodation. See Otago chapter.

Queenstown Area

Coronet Peak
This is the best known and longest established ski field in the South Island. It is 18km from Queenstown on a sealed, all weather road, and there is no road toll. The main chairlift operates all year round to take visitors to the summit (1650m), and there is also a mountain slide operating in summer. It faces the south-west and doesn't get heavy falls of snow, but regular sprinklings all through the season, usually at night. It is not as high as most of the other fields and the snow cover varies considerably from week to week. The skiable area is 280ha, and the field offers good intermediate skiing. The season lasts from mid-July to late September. The lower slopes are floodlit each Fri and Sat between 4pm and 10pm (July to mid September).

Lifts
1 quad chair, 1 triple chair, 1 double chair, 1 T-bar, 1 platter, 1 rope tow - vertical lift is 434m.

Trails
15% beginner, 45% intermediate, 40% advanced.

Facilities
Coronet Peak has some of the best on-field facilities in New Zealand - day room, restaurant, snack bar, ski hire, ski storage, souvenir shop, ski patrol, ski school, ski kindergarten, creche, and shuttle bus from Queenstown. Snowphone 909 099 766, Information (03) 442 4620, PO Box 359, Queenstown.

Prices
Lifts - full day $58 adult, $29 child; half day $43 adult, $23

child; novice $35 adult, $20 child; night $30 adult, $20 child; season pass $1499 adult, $799 child.

Rental - full ski $29 adult, $20 child; perform ski $45 per person; full board $45 adult, $35 child.

Lessons - Ski School: group lesson $37 adult, $25 child; private lesson $80 adult, $65 child; starter pack $66 adult, $42 child. Boarding school: group lesson $37 adult, $25 child; private lesson $80 adult, $65 child; learner pack $85 adult, $60 child.

Accommodation
See Queenstown.

The Remarkables

The Remarkables field was only opened in 1986 after years of planning. It is 24km from Queenstown via the Kingston Road. Queenstown to the toll gate is 10km, and it is 14km from the toll gate to the base on a two lane gravel road with a maximum grade of 1:8. There is parking for 500 cars. The field is on the other side of the lake, and the complex is 1600m above sea-level. There are three separate and distinct basins facing north, east and west, each of which is serviced by a chairlift rising to a maximum height of 1957m. They are in a huge sunny valley which has potential for expansion. It has plenty of beginner and low intermediate runs. It is ideally suited for families as the lower slopes are gently rounded, while the upper slopes are more challenging and offer magnificent views of Lake Wakatipu and Queenstown. The area lends itself to both telemark and cross-country skiing, and instruction and equipment are available for both of these modes of nordic skiing. There is a cross-country track which goes around Lake Alta at the foot of the Double Cone, the highest point in the Remarkables Range. The season usually lasts from early July to early October.

Lifts
2 quad chairs, 1 double chair, 2 learner tows - the vertical lift is 321m.

Trails
30% beginner, 40% intermediate, 30% advanced.

Facilities
These include an upmarket common room, sun decks, souvenir shops, first aid, ski hire and repair shop, storage room, information office, large ski school, restaurant and fast food service, as well as a creche for 4-6 year olds. Concession packages are available. Bus to the field from Queenstown. Snowphone 090 099 766, Information (03) 442 4615, PO Box 359, Queenstown.

Prices
Lifts - full day $55 adult, $27 child; half day $41 adult, $22 child; novice $35 adult, $20 child; season pass $1499 adult, $679 child.

Rental - full ski $29 adult, $20 child; perform ski $45 per person; full board $45 adult, $35 child.

Lessons - Ski School: group lesson $37 adult, $25 child; private lesson $80 adult, $65 child; starter pack $66 adult, $42 child. Boarding school: group lesson $37 adult, $25 child; private lesson $80 adult, $65 child; starter pack $85 adult, $60 child.

Accommodation
See Queenstown.

Harris Mountains Heli-Ski

This is the largest heliskiing operation in New Zealand, and it has flights out of Wanaka and Queenstown. There are one day packages of 3 runs, 5 runs or 8 runs (for the very fit) and multi-day packages of up to 12 days. For more information and prices contact PO Box 345, Wanaka, ph (03) 443 7930, fax 443 8876.

The Tracks

There are two ways you can walk the tracks - either as an independent walker, or with an organised tour. The second alternative is the best way if you are an inexperienced walker, but independent walkers have more flexibility. If you are staying at Youth Hostels, though, you may meet up with experienced walkers who are willing for you to 'tag along'.

As an independent walker you carry your food, sleeping bag, clothes, etc, and stay in huts belonging to the Department of Conservation (DOC), which cost from $4 to $20 per person per night. And you do your own cooking. The huts can be very crowded in summer and you may have to sleep on the floor.

On an organised walk you will be guided by someone who is responsible for your safety, and you will only be required to carry your clothes and personal items, as sleeping bags and food are provided in first-class huts, and you will be sure of a bed. Obviously these walks are much more expensive, and bookings must be made well in advance.

In New Zealand there are three different terms for walkways:

A walk is a pathway that has been benched, graded and well-signposted, and provides safe, easy walking for all people year round. Walks are often quite short and are usually based around some feature of natural or historical interest.

A track is a well-marked pathway which, while providing relatively straightforward walking for much of the time, has not been constructed to the same standard as a walk. A reasonable standard of fitness is required.

A route is a footway with minimal marking and no construction, often crossing difficult terrain, for use by well-equipped and experienced trampers.

Equipment

It is best to invest in a pair of boots as the ground is usually rough or muddy, or both, and joggers don't stand up to that country very well. Boots can sometimes be hired from hotels in the national parks. Always take good waterproof clothing and a woollen jersey or jumper, gloves and headgear even in summer, as the weather can change rapidly in the mountains. It can be brilliant blue sky one minute, and then you won't be able to see the next marker pole as the clouds roll in and the temperature drops.

Fiordland

Transport to the Tracks for independent walkers in the Queenstown Area

Glenorchy Holiday Park, 2 Oban Street, Glenorchy (PO Box 4), ph (03) 442 9939, has a Backpacker Express bus service to and from the camp to all tracks and Queenstown daily (summer only). Accommodation is available in the hostel, cabins and cottages; or there are tent sites.

InterCity have a bus service to the southern end of the Routeburn and Hollyford Tracks. If there are four people, it may be not much more expensive to hire a taxi. It's worth checking out anyway.

The *Magic Bus* will also take you to the tracks and it can be booked through the Youth Hostels in Queenstown or Te Anau.

Hut Fees

Hut tickets can be obtained from all Department of Conservation offices and Visitor Centres. The number of tickets needed depends on the category of the hut.

Category I - Fully serviced - gas cooking/lighting, coal fire, drying room, flush toilet, and a custodian during the season.

Category II - Intermediate - mattresses, coal (no gas).

Category III - Basic - no cooker or fuel supplied.

For further information on the Fiordland National Park, contact Department of Conservation, PO Box 29, Te Anau, ph (03) 249 7921.

The Routeburn Track

This track is 40km long and can be walked from the Divide on the Milford/Te Anau Highway or from the road end above Glenorchy. From the Divide the track climbs to the key summit turn-off, descends to Lake Howden, then climbs to the bush-line before descending into the Mackenzie basin. A steep climb is followed by a sidle through the alpine zone before the track crosses the Harris saddle and descends into the Routeburn Valley.

It usually takes 3 days and there is a booking system, with pre-booked tickets essential from October 30 to April 19. Huts (Category I) are available and costs range from $17.50 to $25 depending on the season. Camping is only permitted at the Routeburn Flats, Lake MacKenzie and twenty minutes down the Greenstone from Lake Howden. Public transport is available at either end of the track. Contact the Department of Conservation for further information - Queenstown, PO Box 811, ph (03) 442 7933; Glenorchy, cnr Mull & Oban Streets, ph (03) 442 9937; Te Anau, PO Box 29, ph (03) 249 7921.

The Kepler Track

The start/finish of the Kepler Track is within one hour's walk of Te Anau, and the round trip takes 3-4 days.

The track climbs steadily from the lakeshore to Luxmore Hut (1085m), then crosses exposed alpine ridge tops and descends to the Iris Burn Hut. It then follows the Iris Burn, a glacial carved valley to Moturau Hut on the shore of the Waiau River before returning to the starting point.

An alternative is to finish at Rainbow Reach swing bridge, where there is road access and daily public transport to Te Anau during the summer season. The 40-bunk huts are Category I, and camping is only permitted near the lake shore at Dock Bay, Brod Bay and Shallow Bay.

The Greenstone/Caples Track

The 35km Greenstone Track follows an ancient Maori trail through alpine valleys and over saddles, and is rated an easy medium. It is less crowded than the Routeburn and takes 3-4 days from Glenorchy or the Main Divide. Alternatively a circular walk encompassing the Greenstone and Caples Valleys takes 5-6 days.

This track branches off the Routeburn Track at Lake Howden, then it turns south into the Greenstone Valley. From Lake McKellar, you can either follow the Greenstone Valley to its outlet into Lake Wakatipu, or you can take the steep climb to

McKellar saddle and the Upper Caples Valley. The Greenstone and Caples River systems then run parallel with each other before joining and flowing into Lake Wakatipu.

There are huts in each valley and camping is permitted. Bus and boat transport is available from the Greenstone carpark/wharf to Glenorchy, and public transport is available to the Divide daily.

The Rees-Dart Track

Beginning 29km past Glenorchy, this walk can be easily achieved in 2 days. The huts in the valley have beds and heating, but all firewood has to be restocked after use. The walk covers varied ground from glacial formed valleys to gravel flats.

Milford Track

This is the other track in Fiordland that has to be booked in advance by writing to the Department of Conservation, PO Box 29, Te Anau, ph (03) 249 7921.

It begins at the head of Lake Te Anau, then it follows the Clinton River to its source, crosses an alpine pass and continues down the Arthur Valley to Milford Sound. It is possible to make a side trip to Sutherland Falls.

Boat transport is available at either end, and bus connections to and from Te Anau, but only during the track season (November to mid-April). The 53km tramp takes four days and huts are provided, but camping is not permitted. It is necessary to make early bookings for the peak period of December-February.

Guided Walks

Milford Track

Arranged by the SPHC Group in association with transport operators, this is a six day guided walk that ends with a Red Boats cruise on Milford Sound. There is a range of costs and options, and two seasons. Low season is from November 1 until November 30, and from March 14 until the end of April; high season is from December 1 until March 13.

The *Te Anau/Queenstown* option involves flying direct to

Queenstown following the Milford Sound cruise.

The *Partners Package* is designed for one walking and one non-walking partner.

Children under 10 years are not permitted on these walks, and all participants are expected to have a reasonable degree of fitness.

Prices, in NZ$, are:

Te Anau/Te Anau

- Low Season - Adult $1324 + GST, Child $750 + GST

- High Season - Adult $1410 + GST, Child $750 + GST

Te Anau/Queenstown

- Low Season - Adult $1418 + GST, Child $840 + GST

- High Season - Adult $1520 + GST, Child $840 + GST

Partners Package - Tea Anau/Tea AnauD

- Low Season - Adult $ 925 + GST

- High Season - Adult $1000 + GST

Partners Package - Te Anau/Queenstown

- Low Season - Adult $1020 + GST

- High Season - Adult $1110 + GST

For bookings and more information contact Milford Track Guided Walk, PO Box 185, Te Anau, ph (03) 249 7411, fax (03) 249 7590.

The Greenstone/Routeburn Walks

These can be walked separately or can be combined. The combined walk takes six days, individually they each take three days. Children under 10 years are not permitted on these walks, and a reasonable degree of fitness is expected of all walkers.

Prices, in NZ$ inclusive of GST, are:

Routeburn Walk   - Adult $ 950, Child $ 850

Greenstone Valley - Adult $ 950, Child $ 850

Grand Traverse   - Adult $1250, Child $1150

For further information contact Routeburn Walk Ltd, PO Box 568, Queenstown, ph (03) 442 8200, fax (03) 442 8200; for bookings contact Routeburn Reservations, PO Box 185, Te Anau, ph (03) 249 7411, fax (03) 249 7590.

Hollyford Valley Walk

There are three options for this walk: the five day walk in/walk out tour; the four day fly out tour; or the three day fly out tour.

All tours involve walking the track on the first day plus a jet boat ride to Pyke Lodge. The next day it's a jet boat to Martins Bay with sightseeing of the seal and penguin colonies and beach areas over one and two days. The optional scenic flight out over Milford Sound arrives in time for an optional launch trip and afternoon coach and aircraft connections to Te Anau and Queenstown.

Prices for the 3 day tour are $935 adult, $725 child incl GST.

The track is usually easy walking, but can be challenging if wet and muddy. Bookings can be made through Hollyford Valley Walk Ltd., PO Box 205 Wakatipu, Central Otago, ph (03) 442 3760, fax (03) 442 3761.

Arthurs Pass National Park

Arthurs Pass National Park is the fourth largest park in New Zealand. The park is a rugged, mountainous area, with deep valleys and swift rivers. Most walks are either half or full day, but there are some that can take two or three days. Details can be obtained from park headquarters or write to Arthurs Pass National Park, PO Box 8, Arthurs Pass, NZ.

There are no camping facilities in the park, but there are areas with day shelters, public toilets and fresh water. Anyone intending to tramp or camp must leave details of their intentions and time of return with the Visitors Centre. Huts around the park are in radio contact with the park headquarters, and most have a solid fuel heating unit, but visitors are encouraged to have their own primus stoves for cooking.

Abel Tasman National Park

This is the smallest national park in the country, though one of the most scenic, and it has two main track systems - a coastal and an inland. The coastal track is the most popular and needs little previous tramping experience. It covers nearly 35km and takes three to five days to walk. There are five huts along the track, each with 24 bunks, but during the summer season (November-March) it is advisable to carry a tent.

For more information contact the Department of Conservation Waimea District, cnr King Edward & High Streets (PO Box 97), Motueka, NZ, ph (03) 528 9117.

A 3-day guided walk is available from Abel Tasman

National Park Enterprises, 234 High Street, Motueka RD3, Nelson, New Zealand, ph (03) 528 7801, fax (03) 528 6087. Costs are NZ$625 adult (the 5-day walk costs NZ$895.

North-West Nelson Forest Park

There are 650km of marked walking tracks in this forest, ranging from easy walks for family groups to routes only for experienced and fit trampers.

The huts in the park all have bunks, stoves, cooking utensils, shovels, axes, rainwater tanks and toilets, but because of the popularity of the tracks, it is still advisable to carry a tent. Camping is only allowed around the hut sites.

More information on both of the following tracks can be obtained from the Visitor Information Office in Nelson, or by contacting Department of Conservation Golden Bay District, PO Box 53, Takaka, NZ, ph (03) 525 8026.

Heaphy Track

The 77km Heaphy Track is best walked east to west (from Collingwood to near Karamea) as most of the climbing is done the first day. The track is rated mild to medium, but has fairly steep climbs. The trip along the track usually takes four to five days, and there are six huts along the way. It is not as often walked as the Abel Tasman Track, and is recommended only for experienced hikers to undertake without a guide. There are telephones at both ends of the track from where transport can be arranged. Abel Tasman National Park Enterprises, ph (03) 548 0285, and Bickley Motors, Nelson, ph (03) 525 8352, offer transport from Nelson to the Collingwood end of the Heaphy Track as do Northwest Nelson Trampers Service, ph (03) 528 6332, from Motueka. Westport Cunningham Bus Services, ph (03) 789 7177, runs a five day service from Karamea to Westport, and Karaka Tours offer an on-demand service for the same route, ph (03) 789 5080.

The Wangapeka Track

The 65km Wangapeka Track is rated strenuous and not for the 'new chum'. There are five huts along the track, it usually takes 5 days to walk, and is also best walked east to west.

Index

Index of Maps